MANY SHADES OF BLACK

MANY SHADES

OF BLACK

Edited by Stanton L. Wormley

and Lewis H. Fenderson

1969 ▦ NEW YORK

WILLIAM MORROW AND COMPANY, INC.

Published simultaneously in Canada by
George J. McLeod Limited, Toronto.

Printed in the United States of America by
The Cornwall Press, Inc., Cornwall, New York.

Library of Congress Catalog Card Number 69-14234

To our wives

Freida and Lettie

for their patience and encouragement throughout the long months of our involvement with this book

we are deeply grateful

CONTENTS

INTRODUCTION

AS a result of the growing demand for material about the Negro
—or black American—there have appeared a number of books,
pamphlets, and articles concerning various aspects of this nation's
largest minority group. To augment the valuable and much-needed
information of historical and social import furnished by these publications, this book was conceived as a vehicle through which the
convictions, judgments, and personal views of a broad range of outstanding individuals might be expressed—what these individuals
think and feel about themselves, the problems of this nation, and
life in general.

We have made no effort to include all who have achieved eminence, but we have attempted to present notable figures from various walks of life. We realize, of course, that there are many others
equally prominent whose names do not appear here. It would be
impossible to present in a single volume all of those who have made
valuable contributions to their race and country.

Each person represented in the collection has made a substantial
contribution to society in his own right. Each was asked to write a
personal essay, unrestricted as to form or style, and to comment,
if he wished, on such topics as the factors involved in his success,
obstacles or difficulties encountered in the pursuit of his goals, present and future opportunities in his field, Civil Rights, human
relations, religion, and his basic philosophy of life. Whether he
considered any, all, or none of the topics suggested was left to his
discretion. We hoped that this latitude would provide for diversified views on a number of subjects.

With the exception of those in the section entitled "Thrust for
Identity," the essays were assigned to categories on the basis of

each writer's major emphasis and interests. That the classifications in some instances may be arguable is a point that we fully recognize. Only for the "Thrust for Identity" section were the contributors asked to discuss a specific topic: some aspect of "black consciousness." Regardless of the categories of their essays, all the writers are concerned with the racial problems of our times. Each, in his own manner, has something significant to say.

The essays range in style from the formal type to the informal "chat on paper," and the book contains such variations as the interview, the vignette, and the extemporaneous soliloquy. The ideas expressed in the collection are highly personal, and the editors neither accept responsibility for any statements made nor subscribe necessarily to the views presented.

The authors have been most cooperative, and we sincerely hope that this book, to which they have so generously contributed, will be not only a valuable compendium of individual philosophies heretofore unavailable, but also a significant source of enlightenment and inspiration. As individuals who have struggled against the odds of prejudice, discrimination, and frustration and have risen above these handicaps, the essayists, we believe, are models that others—particularly the youth of today—might well emulate.

"Black" is to many in this land more than a word. It is a concept, a philosophy, a way of life; and, as these essays reveal, "black comes in many shades."

Stanton L. Wormley
Lewis H. Fenderson

Civil Rights and

Social Action

JOHN CONYERS, JR.

Congressman John Conyers, Jr., Democrat from the First District of Michigan, is currently serving his second term in the U.S. House of Representatives, having been elected by eighty-four percent of the vote. Born in Detroit, Michigan, on May 16, 1929, he received his B.A. and LL.B. degrees from Wayne State University.

Before becoming a member of Congress, he served as senior partner in the firm of Conyers, Bell, and Townsend (1958–61) and as Referee for the Michigan Workmen's Compensation Department (1961–64). Prior to his first campaign for Congress, he was invited by President John F. Kennedy to join in founding the Lawyers Committee for Civil Rights Under Law.

Among the other positions he has held are the following: Field Assistant to Congressman John Dingell, Jr. of Michigan; Director of Education, Local 900, United Auto Workers; Executive Board Member, Detroit Branch of the NAACP; Advisory Council Member, Michigan Civil Liberties Union; General Counsel for the Detroit Trade Union Leadership Council; and Executive Board Member of the Wolverine Bar Association.

Congressman Conyers' election to the House Judiciary Committee in 1965 made him the first and only Negro member of the committee which handles all Civil Rights legislation. As a member of this committee, he was an active supporter of the Mississippi Challenge in 1965, the Voting Rights Act of 1965, and the Civil Rights Act of 1966.

In the 89th Congress he joined in sponsoring the following bills which were passed into law: Voting Rights Act, Medicare, Immigration Reform, Cold-War G.I. Bill of Rights, National Arts and Humanities Foundation, and Truth-in-Packaging. He also sponsored the only amendment passed by the House of Representatives which strengthened the Fair Housing Section of the 1966 Civil Rights Bill, and he organized two fact-finding investigations by congress-

3

men on the protection of Civil Rights (Alabama in 1965 and Mississippi in 1966).

John Conyers, Jr. has also sponsored bills relating to such matters as the following: home rule for the District of Columbia, Federal standards for nondiscriminatory jury selection, effective Federal criminal penalties for racial violence against Negro Americans and Civil Rights workers, elimination of housing and de facto school segregation, truth-in-lending, and abolition of the House Un-American Activities Committee.

TO CHANGE THE COURSE

OF HISTORY

by John Conyers, Jr.

SOMEONE once said that for six days of the week we perform like a weaver behind his loom, busily fingering the threads of some intricate pattern, and on the seventh day the church of worship is supposed to bring us around in front of the loom to look at the pattern on which we have been working. Whether we undergo this self-examination regularly or infrequently, those of us who do, and who are entirely honest with ourselves, will readily admit that almost always we need to cut a few threads, pull others together more tightly, and, most important of all, review our concept of the whole plan.

Today, our entire nation is in dire need of self-examination, for America is in her darkest hour, and nothing but a daring new plan will achieve for us a true and workable democracy.

As I watched television recently, a newscaster commenting upon the disorders that have torn asunder one city after another in our nation was interrupted by the network's swing into a commercial urging all of us listening to fly Pan American because, among other things, meals on board Pan American flights are served by Maxim's of Paris. Another advertisement cut in later reminding listeners of the vacation facilities that are at their disposal in the Caribbean and of the possibility of flying now and paying later. Of course it occurred to me and it must have occurred time and time again to every reader of this essay that there exists an undeniable relationship between those fine inducements to the good life—the life of the credit card and the expense account—and the disorders that have ripped apart the fabric of our society.

There are no ghetto TV stations and no separate desires on the

5

part of ghetto TV viewers. The poor and the disenfranchised in America see and have the same desires built up in them and the same wants created for them as those of any family in America's white suburbs. And, like the whites, those in black America, especially the young, want to live the good life that TV says everybody should live, notwithstanding that they are cut off from the mainstream of society. Our youngsters on street corners in Detroit or Roxbury, or wherever they are, have been influenced by society mores that make them wish, if they do in fact stand on corners, to do so in twenty-five-dollar Florsheim shoes and cashmere sweaters. They did not come into this world with this kind of aspiration; they are the products of a society that tells them they do not count even among their own peers unless they come to the corner appropriately attired.

How did they get this way? How can we reach them and repair their values? What can our leadership—especially our black leadership—in America say to these growing numbers of young people who have decided to quit the slow pace at which we are moving toward our goal in America? This indeed is the American dilemma—how this wealthiest country in the world, the one most addicted to the pursuit of luxury, seems unable to improve conditions for so many of the desperately poor who are beginning what can be termed a social revolution.

Perhaps some of us who have resisted social evolution have unwittingly invited and hastened a social revolution. For without evolution in our drastically changing world there will undoubtedly result some form of revolution. Man cannot hold back the tide of change; we cannot experience the drastic transformations that have taken place in our physical world which are affecting our means of communication and transportation and still maintain an absolute status quo in our society. The unfortunate thing is that man exalts change in almost everything but himself. We have moved centuries ahead in inventing a new world in which to live, but we know little or nothing about our own role in this changing world, how to adjust morally and spiritually, how to accommodate. And so there is a strong effort on the part of many in this country to maintain obsolete customs and mores, traditions of an outmoded society in this new world in which we find ourselves—trying, as someone once said, to continue putting new wine in old bottles and new patches on old garments.

Our nation is in crisis. We are engaged in a war 10,000 miles away and face despair and disruption in every city at home. The deprived, both in Vietnam and in our own ghettos, cry out for justice and independence, but their cries go unheard. The violent rebellions are attributed to causes that do not really exist, such as external conspirators or agitators named as scapegoats for this ripping of the social fabric. Even in the midst of desperate violence the oppressed are, in effect, ignored. I feel that America is threatened not only by its overwhelming problems, but also—which is worse— by the dangerous consequences of its response: a combination of fear and repression in domestic and foreign policy considerations alike that ultimately may rend the very soul of this nation.

Our salvation lies in a national movement for social reconstruction to help reverse the dangerous drift to reaction that currently threatens all sectors of our public and private life. We must acknowledge the great crisis of our ghettos and admit once and for all that it is more urgent and critical than the war in Vietnam. Somehow or other, if we are to bring real and lasting peace to our cities, we must bring about an end to this war in Asia. America must turn from its present course of escalation and, instead, offer a compromise of peace which accepts a coalition government of that tiny nation no larger than the state of Missouri, and eventually look toward the honorable withdrawal of our men and women stationed there as troops.

Next, we must begin, in effect, a Marshall Plan for our cities. A redistribution of America's affluence must be made, and a new plan drawn for the full participation of the nation's deprived in reconstructing every ghetto in every city of our country. We cannot continue the piecemeal, inadequate modifications that are being attempted in terms of urban renewal, which so frequently is not renewal at all but merely Negro removal. The planners of these changes give no thought to the needs of relocating human beings and families but think only in terms of cold statistics and impersonal blueprints. We must recognize the need both to stretch our public resources to their limit and to take from our military programs funds that are necessary to make this evolutionary change in our society. We must also call upon the comfortable and the affluent of the nation for personal commitments and material sacrifices in this momentous undertaking.

And so this country must turn about in its course; it must alter its priorities and limit its fruitless preoccupation with other continents and face, in its greatest Christian moment, itself. To complete this task, which is a necessity now and no longer a choice, we must enlist the full force of the black community, including the black church, its leadership and its followers. America's worth to the world clearly will not be measured by its ability to force its will upon other helpless nations but by the degree to which it successfully achieves a resolution of its own internal problems that have gone unsolved for so long: the right of all citizens to vote, to eat a hamburger wherever they wish to do so, to have a desirable job, to live in a house fit for human habitation. No longer should these rights have to be litigated or negotiated, and it is a national shame that we have had to resort to Civil Rights marches, sit-ins, lie-ins, pray-ins, wade-ins, and other demonstrations to achieve just a small measure of these rights.

It is ironic to have the rest of the nation, as it were, turn around to us and ask what are you still complaining about, what more do you want, what's wrong over there? Remarks like this remind me of Dick Gregory's story about telling a person in a hopeless traffic jam that he should not be too upset that he has to spend the night in his car, because, after all, he is half-way home.

I feel strongly that we must reaffirm our belief that one advantage of the American system is the fact that the minority has the unique power to transform or at least influence the will of the majority. In essence, that is how the Christian church was developed. A few devout people gathered together a long time ago and gradually transformed through their dedication, through their will, and through their belief, the thinking of millions of people throughout the world. That is what must happen in this country: a few must influence the majority to do something about the despair and the tragedy engulfing America. I have studied all the great statements about the divisions in America: the alienated angry young black people; the middle-class citizens who do not care what happens, now that they have been able to escape from the teeming cities; the white polarized groups that refuse to hear the cries of desperate black people throughout the community but concern themselves only with what they describe as our President's insane policy of never-ending escalation. How can we solve all of these problems at once? There are those who answer by saying that it can't be done; that there is going to be a revolution in this country, black against white. They say that it will result in the greatest tactics of repression employed since those of Nazi Germany. There will be blood in the streets of America. There is nothing left for us to do but prepare as best we can for an armed confrontation of race against race. Many of us have heard this kind of statement, and we've seen the beginning of activity in this direction. But we must remember that our Christian heritage, combined with the historical spirit of this country, will sustain those few of us who desire to change the course of our nation.

Let us consider some examples from our history that illustrate the general satisfaction of the majority in maintaining the status quo and the effectiveness of a determined minority in bringing about needed change. If we had sought a consensus in 1776, we would never have had the Revolutionary War. If there had been a poll taker instead of a Paul Revere, we would have found that a great body of people at that time did not care one way or the other about a revolution. There was another substantial group of persons opposed to a revolution; they liked their relationship with the mother country, England, and were profiting by it. And then there was a group determined to separate from a nation that believed in taxation without representation. Thus, if Jefferson and Washington and Patrick Henry and Madison and Adams and Franklin had stopped to take a poll, to examine a cross-section, to seek a consensus, there would have been a great body arguing as we are doing among ourselves today.

Again, in pre-Civil War America, had a consensus been sought, it would have revealed that the great body of Americans did not care one way or the other what happened to the question of black people in a supposedly democratic society. The striking of the chains from the arms and legs of Negroes was brought about by a few people in this country, among whom were militant abolitionists, a few ministers, and a group of white citizens, who did not share the prevailing view. This small but determined group persisted and slowly built the question of slavery up to such a level that it became a focal point of the Civil War.

Today, there are individuals who say also that America's problems are so acute that no solutions are possible. This is a common view. But the lessons of history show that such problems can be solved.

We must look at our Constitution's preamble again. It says: "In order to form a more perfect union, establish justice, insure domestic tranquility, provide for the common defense, promote the general welfare, and secure the blessings of liberty to ourselves and our posterity . . . " That's what the struggle of black America is all about—trying to make a reality of the constitutional provisions that date back to 1789.

There are other historical words that speak of self-evident truths: that all men are created equal and are endowed by their Creator with unalienable rights such as liberty and the pursuit of happiness—these, too, are what the struggle of black America is all about. To secure these rights, governments are instituted among men which receive their power from the consent of the governed; but whenever any form of government becomes destructive of these ends, it is the right of the people to alter or abolish it and to institute a new government. All of these considerations are what the struggle of black America is all about, and we must try to understand the angry young black Americans who, unable to get jobs, articulate in their own way the failures of our society. They are the victims of lies and hypocrisy, of neglect and rejection. These young people have themselves rejected a society which they consider hostile to them, and they voice their objections bitterly. A few of us who hear them say wait a minute, let us lead you, let us give you some legitimacy, let us give you a voice, let us join with you and stand with you in the front ranks because we see the grain of a Christian ethic in even the illegal activity in which you are engaged. We see the legitimacy of the people's voice even as you break laws passed by lawmakers. We understand this plea that has been voiced by millions of people in various civilizations who wanted their fair share of whatever their civilization had to offer. And so we say that conscience is the perfect interpreter of life. Thomas Wolfe once said, "So then to every man his chance, to every man, regardless of his birth, his golden shining opportunity, to every man his right to live, to work, to be himself, become whatever thing that his manhood and his courage will combine to make him." This is what is being said today in the slums of America. This is the promise of America. This is what some who cannot read or write, who've never had a steady job, are trying to make real. We should all pray for the will and the capacity to grow, the sensitivity and the receptivity to see a new way, and for understanding and brotherhood. We should all recognize how little we have grown, how little we have seen, and how much more we must do to make our religion and our ethics a reality in our lifetime.

LEON HOWARD SULLIVAN

The Reverend Leon Howard Sullivan is the Pastor of Zion Baptist Church in Philadelphia. He is also founder and Chairman of the Board of Directors of the Opportunities Industrialization Center, a program in Philadelphia sponsoring training and retraining on a massive scale. It is the first program of its kind in the United States, and is being successfully imitated in several other cities.

Born on October 16, 1922, in Charleston, West Virginia, the Reverend Mr. Sullivan was educated at West Virginia State College, Union Theological Seminary, and Columbia University. He holds the earned degrees of Bachelor of Arts and Master of Arts and the honorary degrees of Doctor of Divinity, Doctor of Humanities, Doctor of Social Sciences, and Doctor of Laws.

At the age of twenty he was named Assistant Pastor of the Abyssinia Baptist Church in New York City, which has the largest Negro congregation in America. He came to Philadelphia and the Zion Baptist Church in 1950. Since then, the membership of the Church has grown from six hundred to four thousand. In his efforts to serve as many persons as possible, he learned sign language in order to carry his ministry to the deaf. The activities of the Zion Baptist Church include a Day Care Center, a Federal Credit Union, a Community Center Program for Youth and Adult Activities, an Employment Agency, Adult Education Classes, an Educational Counseling Program, Scout Programs, Remedial Reading Classes, Athletic Activities, Choral Groups, and a Family Counseling Service. Other organizations of the Church founded by him are the Zion Non-Profit Corporation (ZNC) and the Zion Investment Corporation (ZIC), described by the Reverend Mr. Sullivan as defining "Black Power" as it should be applied. ZNC has built a million-dollar, 96-unit garden apartment complex called Zion Gardens. Zion Investment Associates (ZIA), a profit-making organization, is presently building a 1.5 million-dollar modern shopping center called "Progress Plaza."

He has received some highly coveted award almost every year since 1955, when he was chosen the Outstanding Young Man in the City of Philadelphia and one of the Ten Outstanding Young Men in America by the National Junior Chamber of Commerce. Other honors accorded him include: the City of Philadelphia Good Citizenship Award, the Afro-American Achievement Award, the Silver Beaver Award by the Boy Scouts of America, the Outstanding Alumnus Award by West Virginia State College, the Freedom Foundation Award, the Russwurm Award (given annually to ten outstanding Negroes of the year) by the National Publishers Association, the Army's Outstanding Civilian Service Award, the Philadelphia Fellowship Commission Award, the Bok Award (an award of $10,000 given annually to an outstanding Philadelphia citizen), and the William Penn Award by the Philadelphia Chamber of Commerce.

HELPING OTHERS TO

HELP THEMSELVES

by Leon H. Sullivan

THERE is an old expression that goes something like this: you can do anything you want to do, if your "want to" is strong enough. I have great respect for old sayings, and as a minister in our modern age I've invented some new sayings myself. In fact, one of my favorites relevant to the American Negro is that he must "prepare and produce." But I really don't think a man's "want to" can always be held responsible if he doesn't make progress toward the goals he has in mind. There are very few of us who have had success who don't owe at least part of that success to others; I would never have come North and probably never have become a minister in Philadelphia if I hadn't been befriended during my early years on many occasions. And I owe much to the inspiration I received from my parents, who struggled along on meager wages but who were always willing to give others a helping hand when they could.

So just wanting to do something is not enough, although the strength of your ambition, your "want to," is usually what puts you in the right frame of mind to accept the help you need; sometimes it puts you in the right place at the right time too.

Man is not only a thinking animal, he's a cooperative animal; men have always known that they have to work together, that as a group they can achieve more than they can as individuals. Sometimes there are frictions that keep them from cooperating; sometimes they just aren't sure what they should try to do first to achieve their final objectives. In periods of great change, such as the one we are living in now, there may be so many choices of action open to a man that he just doesn't know where to begin, and he doesn't know where to turn for the kind of help he needs. He may not even realize that he can be helped. All he can see is that whatever it is he's doing, it isn't changing anything important in his life. Perhaps all he feels is that something has gone wrong, and a man who feels that way long enough is very apt to do wrong. This man doesn't need a panel of experts or a million dollars: he needs to know he's not alone, and he needs to know that other men—men better able than he is to analyze his problems—care enough about him to help him out. *Help* is one of the few things in this world that multiplies the more you use it; you just can't give it away, because it always comes back when you're the one who needs it most.

In 1961 a group of Negro ministers in Philadelphia cooperated so successfully, leading their congregations in a massive boycott which they called "Selective Patronage," that within three years thousands of job opportunities were opened to Philadelphia Negroes. These men were not economic experts, but they were intelligent enough to have observed that although businesses in Philadelphia advertised their wares in the Negro community and through radio stations aimed at Negro listeners, and that although these businesses didn't seem to care about a man's color as long as his money was green, they did seem to care about a man's color when he applied for a job. A few of them got together and discussed among themselves what could be done, and the word spread. Finally there were 400 ministers, and they had one plan: they said to their congregations that they could no longer remain silent while members of their congregations patronized companies that discriminated in employment. Their program of "selective patronage" originated as an act of conscience, but it would have been ineffective if it had not turned into an act of cooperation. Philadelphia's efforts have been duplicated in cities all over the nation, and the results have been the same: vast new opportunities have opened up in employment for the disadvantaged.

At this point, however, the leaders of these efforts faced a new problem: the members of the community who most needed such employment were the very ones whose preparation for work was most inadequate. We came to realize that "integration without preparation is frustration"—that the necessary preparation was education.

It was out of this realization that our Opportunities Industrialization Center was born in 1964, in an old jailhouse given to us by the city. In another cooperative effort, we canvassed door to door through the slums and the downtown "pocket communities"; and from householders and small businessmen we managed to raise over $100,000. Local corporations donated $250,000 in cash and equipment; the United States Department of Labor gave us a grant; the Ford Foundation gave $200,000. I like to say that when we started out we didn't even have a screwdriver—the basement was flooded, the ceilings were coming down—and now we have a shipshape business going. *That* is what you can do with cooperation.

In the beginning we decided to concentrate on job preparation: get the man ready to work as soon as possible and get him to the job. You get results faster when you concentrate on one objective at a time. This we had discovered during our boycott movement, when we concentrated on one business at a time. We soon found, however, that many of our applicants had to be prepared *before* they could start the technological training they needed for the jobs they wanted to get. Our Feeder School was created to fill that need: it is probably the first prevocational school of its kind in the history of the world.

In our Feeder School, trainees are taught the basic elements of reading, writing, and arithmetic—only we never call it reading, writing, and arithmetic. People are reluctant to have others know that they want to learn—and need to learn—at such an elementary level; and so we label our courses "Communication Skills" and "Computational Arts."

We also teach minority history—we teach a man that he has roots. A man is like a tree: if he has no roots, the smallest wind can blow him down; but if his roots go deep, he can withstand a hurricane. We teach him how to appreciate his fellow-man: we teach him about the contributions to American life made by Asian-Americans, Italo-Americans, Irish-Americans, and others.

We teach him how to groom himself, how to know the value of the dollar, how to tell a fresh loaf of bread from a stale loaf by the markings on the wrapper. We teach him the meaning of food values. We teach him how to sit, how to walk, how to talk. But most of all, we teach him how to put his head up and his shoulders back, for we have found that the most important aspect of motivation is self-respect. If a man respects himself, he'll get up and make life for himself better—for himself and for his family.

Essentially, our Feeder School is designed to "unwash the brain-washed minds" of those who, for 100 years, have been brainwashed into inferiority. We teach that "Genius is color-blind, and that, like a balloon, a man will rise not because of his color but because of what's inside him." We teach him that he is an investment; that he has a responsibility to the company for which he works; that he must produce in order to insure his employment.

After spending from two weeks to three months in the Feeder Program, depending upon where he is when we get him, the enrollee is assigned to an OIC Technical Training Center where he learns the skill which will make him employable. He leaves the Feeder Center motivated to make something of himself, to produce and to take advantage of his newly found opportunities. He is paid nothing for his training: his motivation to stay comes from self-respect and the realization that if he stays with the program there will be a job at the end. That motivation is his "want to."

To date, an additional 4,000 students have been enrolled in training courses in OIC Feeder Schools and in our OIC Technical Training Centers in Philadelphia. Of that number, more than 3,000 will unquestionably be placed in productive employment, bringing our total to more than 6,000 people trained and employed. More than 35 percent of our trainees come to us from the relief rolls, and no less than 97 percent of them fall in the poverty category. We hope that within the next three or four months an additional 7,000 persons will be reached by Special Adult Armchair Education Programs meeting in 150 neighborhood homes, thus further decentralizing the OIC concept and extending our philosophy of self-help deeper into the hard core of the community. This "Feeder Feeder" plan involves triple the number of trainees enrolled in present schools.

We have discovered that lack of preparation is not related to race alone. Although our program was begun by colored people in the colored community, scores of white men and women are now enrolled in the OIC and hundreds are on the waiting list, which now totals more than 6,000 people. Both our student body and our staff are integrated. We expect this trend will continue, because the need for opportunity in America is not a color problem: it is an American problem. Lack of preparation knows no color bounds.

It is this dynamic, grass-roots nature of the program that distinguishes it from any other in the training field anywhere. Other programs have been handed to the people from the top down, but OIC is handed by the people themselves from the bottom up. As in the case of many other kinds of vocational training programs, there has been a tendency to screen people out. In OIC, "everybody is screened in." The door is open to all.

The OIC concept is spreading. It is taking on the proportions of a movement led by religious, civil rights, business, and neighborhood leaders. It is the one program that is pulling us all together again: white and black, rich and poor, Jew and Gentile, Catholic and Protestant—for the common good of all. Essentially, OIC is in the business of reaching the unreached and uniting us all. If the war against poverty is to be won, it can be won only in this manner.

OIC is a program in a hurry. It is spreading rapidly among the people. There are now OIC units in more than sixty cities across America in some degree of development. The idea has spread to Puerto Rico. And it has to spread even farther. For every day new poverty children are born in poverty homes, and every day impoverished older men and women are living longer as a result of the accomplishments of medicine and science. And every day automation is taking away more and more jobs from the poverty-stricken in our communities. So OIC has to be a program in a hurry. We can't wait to be perfect before we move, or we'll never make a start.

OIC comes to give poor people hope—hope to people who have become conditioned to despair. It brings new expectations to our free-enterprise system and our democratic way of life. *This is a new kind of revolution.* It is a revolution in a new direction. It is a revolution of massive opportunity in which all of us can play a part, from the most conservative to the most militant. All of us then must join hands with the impoverished citizens of our communities who may some day come to us for support and counsel in the development of an OIC. OIC and industry must perform this great task. Either they will do it together or it will not be done at all. OIC has the manpower, and industry has the jobs. And it must be done in the local community. Businessmen must not help OIC for paternalistic reasons or just for good will. Business must support OIC as a commitment.

We cannot reach our goals without this support of industry. All of our curriculum is checked and rechecked by industry, and most of our equipment is given by industry. Industry keeps OIC up-to-date, because we realize that we cannot prepare men for today's jobs using yesterday's tools. Industry is constantly making available new job opportunities for our trainees. For example, OIC is currently working very closely with Rentex Corporation, which is a part of the Linen Supply Association of America. We are jointly preparing an in-service training program for the present employees of this organization as well as recruiting people for the industrial laundry business. This will be the first time that this kind of cooperative arrangement of on-site business training will have been undertaken by our organization, and we would like it to be a pilot program for many others to follow.

Philanthropy has supported us also. There are philanthropic sources available in every community of any size to assist programs of self-improvement initiated by the people themselves. Say what you will, I've found that America is not selfish, and that just as God helps those who help themselves, Americans will join those who strive on their own behalf.

Government, we are glad to say, has now joined with industry and philanthropy in partnership with us. Within the past year, more than seven million dollars has been put into OIC by the Federal Government through the Office of Economic Opportunity and the Department of Labor. OIC has become not only a cooperative part but an integral part of poverty programming in Philadelphia.

No industry can wisely come into a community unless there is a productive labor force sufficient to make its coming feasible, productive, and profitable. The smart businessman knows that the most reliable gauge of his company's ability to compete, to produce for tomorrow as well as today, is the same gauge by which one measures community prosperity: the fullest possible employment of manpower in that community. This is not philanthropy, it is just good business; and this is the economics of cooperation. If we can learn how best to put each other to work, we will be solving our problems in such a way that we can share the benefits and—not least important—share mutual pride in our endeavor.

Some people have said—or thought—that what I'm doing in

Philadelphia represents "Black Power." I say that Black Power without green power and brainpower is no power; but when Black Power is linked with white power it becomes American power, becomes creating power: when you work for America, you work for yourself.

I persuaded 200 members of my church to put aside ten dollars every month for thirty-six months. With that money we built a million-dollar complex. That was green power: colored people putting their money together to "build, brother, build." For the first time I see colored people becoming a part of the economic development of this country—building for America. This has been my dream and ambition.

If I can contribute in any way to helping others help themselves, then I will have made my ministry relevant to my day, because I see my ministry not as helping people get into Heaven, but helping Heaven get into people; not as giving them milk and honey in Heaven, but giving them ham and eggs on earth.

PERCIVAL L. PRATTIS

Before assuming the position of Director of the Youth Education Project of Frontiers International in 1965, Percival L. Prattis, who was born in Philadelphia, Pennsylvania, on April 27, 1895, had completed a career as journalist which lasted for nearly half a century.

Educated at Christiansburg Industrial Institute, Hampton Institute, and Ferris Institute, he began his journalistic career as Editor of the *Michigan State News* in 1919. Uninterruptedly thereafter, he held a series of editorial and administrative posts with various journalistic enterprises: City Editor, *Chicago Defender* (1921–22); News Editor, Associated Negro Press (1923–35); and City Editor, *Amsterdam News* (1935). From 1936 to 1965 he was associated with the *Pittsburgh Courier* in the following capacities: City Editor, Executive Editor, and Associate Publisher and Assistant Treasurer.

His more important journalistic assignments include coverage of the Moton Commission on Education in Haiti, the United Nations San Francisco Conference, The World Trade Union Conference in Paris, and special surveys in Europe and the Near East. He has interviewed many of the world's leaders, including Emperor Haile Selassie, King Edward VII, and Prime Minister Nehru.

Mr. Prattis has been active in civic affairs at both the national and local levels. He has served on the Board of Directors of such organizations as the American Council on Race Relations, the Commission on Mass Communication, and the National Federation of Settlements and Neighborhood Centers. At the local level he has been associated with boards and committees of the Y.M.C.A., the Health and Welfare Association, the Council on Intercultural Education, the Planned Parenthood Clinic, the Urban League, the NAACP, the Selective Service, Frontiers of America, and the Foreign Policy Association. He has also served as a member of the Board of Trustees of the Pennsylvania State Training School.

Among the many honors Percival L. Prattis has received are the Outstanding Alumnus Award of Hampton Institute, the honorary degree of Doctor of Laws from Wiley College, and the National Order of Honor and Merit from the Republic of Haiti.

COMPLACENCY, CONCERN,

FRUSTRATION, OPPORTUNITY

by P. L. Prattis

THERE is nothing auspicious about being born in the same year that Frederick Douglass died, the same year that Booker T. Washington delivered his famous "Drop Down Your Buckets Where You Are" oration in Atlanta, and thirty years, almost to the exact date, after General Robert E. Lee surrendered. It might be noteworthy, however, to point out that before 1895, most American Negroes had been debased and degraded by 244 years of slavery, thirteen years of freedom that didn't jell, and nineteen years of degenerating peonage that continues until this very day.

In 1895 Booker T. Washington was urging Negroes to till the land; W. E. Burghardt Du Bois was exhorting the so-called Talented Tenth to learn more Greek and Latin; and the white folk down South who "knew Negroes best" were systematically burning and hanging scores of Negro men, women, and children and robbing others of their right to vote.

Although the year 1895 is neither auspicious nor really significant, it is a good point in history for raising one's binoculars and obtaining a Janus-faced view of the past and future of the disconcerted and confused American Negro. My memory is fresh as far back as the assassination of President McKinley. However, I was not aware then of how some Southerners were slow-burning women and children to death in Mississippi and Georgia.

There were problems, but they did not seem to exist for me at that time. Bread was only five cents a loaf. Steak was fifteen cents a pound. Neckbones (at three cents a pound) and navy beans were almost as sweet as ambrosia. Board and lodging could be had for $4.50 a week. There wasn't much money then, and you didn't need much. Peace prevailed in the land, believe it or not, and nobody ever thought of America as being in a war in those days. War belonged to history, not to the present. All we wanted to do, all we thought of doing, was working, staying out of the poorhouse, and going to heaven.

In 1917 we said good-bye to the peace we had known for fifty-two years. The First World War ended an era, increased tempos and tensions, and exposed social and economic blotches. Even the rate of lynching Negroes went up, and Dr. Du Bois became the first nonviolent demonstrator on the broad avenues of New York City. Negroes didn't welcome the war, but neither did they resist it. They were hopeful. They sensed a new era marked by concern, not complacency. They thought that if they went to France and made a good showing, the "way of life" in the United States would change, and the "cotton-pickin' deducts" on the plantations would vanish.

Negro youngsters from the plantations and the streets of our big cities went to France, and they made their good showing. The French pinned so many bravery badges on them that you would have thought they were black Russian field marshals. But that didn't matter back home. In 1919, after the war was over, more Negroes were lynched than in any year before or since.

Ironically, the period sparked by the National Association for the Advancement of Colored People, the National Urban League, and Marcus Garvey's Universal Negro Improvement Association—this period of concern which manifested itself during the First World War and lasted until Hoover's election—was also marked by euphoria. Thousands of Negroes thought that they had come out of the wilderness and were on their way to the Promised Land. Using his *Chicago Defender* as a trumpet to awaken Negro victims of peonage-slavery in the South, Robert S. Abbott beckoned Negroes to come North. They came by the thousands—to Chicago, to New York, to Cleveland, to Philadelphia, to Detroit, to St. Louis, to Cincinnati, and to Pittsburgh. The sharecroppers did not flee alone; they were followed by Negro business and professional men of the South. These latter were a competent lot. At that time one heard little about ghettos or slums. Negroes grew proud of "communities within communities."

Those were the years of the New Negro. Those were the years which first knew Countee Cullen, Langston Hughes, Wallace

Thurman, Jessie Fauset, Alain Locke, E. Franklin Frazier, Charles S. Johnson, and many other distinguished writers. Those were the years during which Negro singers, dancers, the big bands, and the big shows flashed across the horizon; and thousands of whites sought places like Harlem because they suspected that genius was harbored there. Negroes in Chicago won great political power and sent the first member of their race in the twentieth century to Congress. Political patronage strengthened the economy, and Negro businesses prospered.

As the decade of the twenties drew to an end, Negroes, generally, little suspected what lay ahead. They didn't know what a stock market crash or what overstocked warehouses with huge inventories could do to them. Although there were dark clouds in the skies, Negroes could not foresee that they were passing from an era of euphoria into an era of great concern, depression, and acute, hope-killing frustration—an era which was to span three generations. The job market dwindled to almost nothing. Dirty, hot jobs which had been more or less allocated to Negroes ever since the prevalence of Black Codes in the South were now seized by whites—and Negroes were thrust inevitably on relief. It could not be foreseen that this dependence on public charity would spell doom for thousands of Negro families and would deprive innumerable Negro youths of a future.

Economically, the masses of Negroes stagnated, and thousands of them were pauperized as they unwittingly became victims of the Depression. The marks of the Depression remain today in thousands of homes where men were deprived of jobs in the early thirties. The problems which took root then remain with us and would be much worse today had not the Wagner Labor Relations Act of 1934 facilitated the birth of industrial unions. These unions accepted Negroes as members but did not eliminate on-the-job discrimination. The median income of the Negro family today is still less than half that of the white family. And Negroes, no matter what the level of their education and training, earn substantially less than whites with the same level of learning and training.

As the second half of the twentieth century began, Negroes could see little basic change in their economic, social, and political positions. They were the low group on the totem pole. This was true despite notable court victories won by the NAACP in behalf of Negroes. One such victory, however, was to set the stage for the so-called Negro revolution which has pursued a troubled course from "nonviolence" to "black power." The great victory was the decision of the United States Supreme Court in 1954 against racial segregation in public schools. The mood created by this decision led to the death of gradualism and of "half-a-loafism," to the bus boycott in Montgomery, and to the subsequent sit-ins, wade-ins, kneel-ins, and other diverse "ins" and "outs."

Historians must accord to the late Rev. Dr. Martin Luther King, Jr. much of the credit for the forward steps made by Negroes since the Supreme Court decision. Not to be discounted, too, are the gains achieved over the years by the NAACP in numerous Supreme Court decisions won by Thurgood Marshall, who later became United States Solicitor General and Supreme Court Justice. King, in raising the banner of nonviolence, did not offer a cure-all. He did, however, unfurl a flag behind which millions of Americans of all colors and religious persuasions were proud to march. His, truly, was the Grand Army of the Republic which evolved into the magnificent and historic March on Washington. This tremendous demonstration of a quarter of a million whites and Negroes created the mood in the nation for the enactment of the Kennedy-Johnson Civil Rights legislation. King's eloquence and his "safe" position united Negro and white leadership behind the Great Cause.

As of today, the leadership has been stymied. The army which marched to Washington is in a shambles and suffers from massive defections. It is ironic to observe that the same stratagem (even ruse, if you wish) which brought the army together behind King, Randolph, Wilkins, Young, Farmer, and Lewis, is the one which has led to the dissipation of the army. Nonviolence didn't and couldn't have meant to Negroes in the United States what it meant to Indians in India. It could not have been the same kind of tool, or as useful a tool. There were two or three hundred Indians to every Briton in India. The Indians, by virtue of mere numbers, were able to make nonviolence and boycotts effective. In the United States, there were ten whites to every Negro; and whites had practically all the money and power. However, semantically, there was power in the term "nonviolence." Thousands flocked to enlist in a "nonviolent" army. The recruits, white and black, remained in the army, despite rioting and looting all over the land. Then came the semantically stupid term "black power" from Stokely Carmichael, who succeeded John Lewis as the leader of the Student Nonviolent Coordinating Committee. There is indeed nothing wrong with what Carmichael sought and seeks. Negroes do need power—economic power, political power, educational power, spiritual power. The bell has rung for them to help themselves, to use their own strengths to solve their own problems. But any fool should have known that our enemies would be quick to use the term "black power" to frighten our friends and muddy the water.

There is nothing cowardly about resorting to semantics. In the First World War, we boasted that we were fighting to make the world "safe for democracy" although everybody knew that we would not have been in the war at all if the Germans had not started sinking our ships. And certainly, Negroes in the United States knew that we were not fighting to make the United States "safe for democracy." But making the world "safe for democracy" sounded good to our allies—and to some Americans. Also, we honed the blades of our soldiers' bayonets by dubbing the Germans "Huns" and "krauts." And almost without any American's knowing what was going on after World War II, we threw the term "War Department" out the window and substituted "Defense Department." *Defense* must always be *right*. If the momentum of the Civil Rights movement is to be regained, a substitute for the term "black power," meaning the same thing, must be found.

The Negro revolution was on a winning course until Stokely Carmichael unwittingly violated the laws of semantics. Fortunately, Brother Carmichael did not frighten all whites. There are thousand of whites who can still remember the murders of blacks and whites along the road from Selma to Montgomery. They can still recall the savage outbreaks in Little Rock, Arkansas, and in Oxford, Mississippi. They can still see Meredith squirming from buckshot in his back on a Mississippi highway. They know what Stokely is after, and they know he is right. They deplore his indifference to semantics.

If the goals of the Negro revolution are to be attained, there are some essential steps which must be taken:

First, Negro leadership must find a common front and unite upon it.

Second, Negroes must realize that there is nothing which twenty million Negroes can take from 180 million whites by force.

Third, Negroes must learn how to propagandize in order to win defectors, or friends, from the white side. Negroes must cherish their white friends and use the strength of their support to destroy the influence of their white enemies like Lester Maddox, ex-Sheriff Bill Clark of Selma, "Bull" Connor of Birmingham, and of hate-mongering groups like the Ku Klux Klan and the White Citizens Councils.

Fourth, Negroes must shrewdly seek to restore the white mood as it existed B. C. (Before Carmichael).

Fifth, Negroes must look themselves straight in the face. They should study their own weaknesses and faults. They should recognize the strength of "payroll power." The Southern Christian Leadership Conference could well postpone or cancel demonstrations in Northern cities and use its influence and skill to help build up Negro business with "payroll power."

Sixth, Negroes must refrain from inciting others to violence and from engaging in violence themselves. Almost every riot in the last two or three years has been sparked by bad judgment and killing on the part of the police. But even that does not justify looting, arson, and harm to innocent people.

Seventh, all Negroes who are physically able to do so should reject relief from either the state or federal government. Public assistance has pauperized three generations of Americans. Negroes should resist the trend toward permanent pauperism. The National Urban League and its branches should try to develop plans and guidelines for a "war on poverty" throughout the country using private brains and private funds. There is no reason why poverty in Pittsburgh, Philadelphia, New York, Detroit, Birmingham, Los Angeles, or anywhere else should not be a primary concern of the businesses and corporations and unions in the community involved. The private sector has the brains and the means to reduce poverty to a minimum in any community. All it lacks is the will to try and the sense of responsibility.

Eighth, Negroes must seek the cooperation of schools, churches, and all other organizations with influence in the community to reach Negro youths and prove to them that this is not the world of their parents and grandparents. It must be demonstrated that the doors which were closed to their parents and grandparents are not closed to them. There are myriad examples to convince Negro youth that there is a place at the top for them if they will develop character and prepare through education. To raise the sights of Negro youth is a responsibility not only of churches, schools, other organizations, and parents, but also of every responsible person in every community.

It is up to us all to make our age the period of opportunities unbounded.

PATRICIA ROBERTS HARRIS

Before she recently returned to the teaching of law, Patricia R. Harris was U.S. Ambassador to Luxembourg, an appointment made by President Lyndon B. Johnson.

Born in Mattoon, Illinois, she received her public school training in that city and in Chicago. After earning an A.B. degree at Howard University, she did postgraduate work at the University of Chicago and at American University. Subsequently, she entered the George Washington University School of Law, from which she received the J.D. degree.

Prior to her appointment as U.S. Ambassador, she had served as Program Director of the Y.W.C.A. in Chicago, Assistant Director of the American Council on Human Rights, Executive Director of Delta Sigma Theta Sorority, and Trial Attorney of the U.S. Department of Justice. Since 1961 she has been connected with Howard University first as Associate Dean of Students and later as a member of the faculty of the School of Law. It was from this latter post that she took leave of absence from 1965 to 1967 to accept the Luxembourg ambassadorship.

Patricia Roberts Harris has been extremely active in professional and civic affairs and has been accorded honors by many organizations. Among the educational institutions which have recognized her achievements are Lindenwood College and Morgan State College, which have conferred upon her the honorary degree of Doctor of Laws, Miami University, which has awarded her the honorary degree of Doctor of Humane Letters, and Beaver College, which awarded her the degree of Doctor of Civil Law. In other Presidential appointments she was named Co-Chairman of the National Women's Committee on Civil Rights by President John F. Kennedy, and Member of the U.S. Commission on the Status of Puerto Rico and the National Commission on the Causes and Prevention of Violence by President Lyndon B. Johnson.

33

TO FILL THE GAP

by Patricia Roberts Harris

AMERICANS of Negro descent with significant positions in non-segregated institutions should be concerned by the fact that they are often unique among those with whom they serve. "Successful Negroes" must wonder, when they find themselves the "first Negro," whether they will also be the only Negro at high levels. Since beginning at the top is unusual, it is natural to look below to see whether the upper reaches will be attained in due course by others who are also of Negro descent. Often the prognosis is discouraging, because the middle ranks, the preparatory field for those who will ultimately move to the top, are often as devoid of Negroes as the top once was. Those who have been fortunate enough to enter the top ranks of either the private or public sector are forced to give attention to finding ways of insuring the presence of Negroes at the top in the future, and at other levels now. In order to achieve this, a program must be designed to compensate for the years of exclusion of Negroes, a program which will make it possible to eliminate quickly the inequalities that exist in the distribution of Negroes in all sectors.

For many years the goal of those who fought for the elimination of racial segregation and discrimination was the achievement of a condition under which individuals would be judged, selected, or rejected "without regard to race, creed or color." This condition of color blindness and religious neutralism seemed the only possible aim for adherents of a Constitution characterized as "color-blind" and of a society established with the ringing words that "all men are created equal." For if every man whose skin was black or whose ancestor was a slave could have these facts erased from the consciousness of his fellow-man, he could clearly rise upon the basis of his proven ability. This was in fact the liberal catechism, and it was adopted by the Negro community.

In recent years it has become clear that this is an ultimate goal which cannot be realized quickly. Two events, separated by many years and different degrees of personal involvement, demonstrate that there is a fundamental error in the premature elimination of awareness of race.

In the early fifties, shortly after the institution of a new non-discrimination policy, a government agency that had been accused of discrimination in the employment and promotion of Negroes was asked by a Civil Rights agency to supply figures on its Negro employees and their grades and length of time in grade. The responsible administrator replied that such data were unavailable because in implementing the nondiscrimination policy "no statistics on race or color are kept."

The second event involved a brilliant man who was the sole Negro at the time in a high-ranking political position. Despite an incumbency characterized as outstanding, he was summarily displaced, against his wishes and those of the Negro community, by the undistinguished scion of an old, rich, and powerful political dynasty.

Both events made it clear that the Negro's problem of recognition and acceptance was too deep to be solved by the espousal of slogans of equality. In the instance of statisticless noninformation, it was patent that the ingrained habit of exclusion of Negroes was enhanced by the elimination of a practice which, despite its negative potential, served to alert the community to the existence of racial discrimination.

In the case of the dismissed official, the existence of outstanding qualifications for office was not adequate to protect the interests of the Negro community by the presence of at least one Negro in a top position in the federal government.

Many were quick to point out that the officeholder would have been treated in the same manner had he been white, and that there was good reason to believe that the statisticless federal agency was in fact recruiting without regard to race, even though this resulted in the failure to find "qualified Negroes."

For persons who are Negro, such "equality" is neither relevant nor reassuring. After three hundred years of enforced inequality, of exclusion and separation from the mainstream of American society, the institution of a policy of nondiscrimination and the instant implementation of rigid equality often result in perpetuating the inequality which racial discrimination has imposed upon the Negro. Until the effects of past racial discrimination are erased, it is essential to ask whether there are Negroes present, and to insist that Negroes be represented at all levels. Thus, some racial count is necessary; and it is legitimate to require that if a Negro is displaced, the displacement does not mean the end of the Negro presence. Such positively oriented racial consciousness will hasten the day when the experience of the Negro community will approximate that of the white community, and eliminate those disadvantages which are the outgrowth of invidious racial distinctions.

However, all Negroes in today's society once faced a reality in which race was a bar to achievement. There can be no question that past discrimination has placed most American Negroes far behind white citizens in the race to achieve the good life. Even those privileged Negroes who have excellent educational credentials often find that as a result of discrimination they have been denied certain preparatory experiences essential to progressive movement to the top of their professions. It is not far-fetched to suggest that those who start behind are likely to stay behind, unless the handicap of the past is recognized and dealt with in official policy. If the practice of excluding Negroes from significant parts of American life is to be eliminated, it will be eliminated consciously, and not by random chance.

This seems so eminently fair that it is surprising to find that the white community, liberal and conservative alike, fears the notion. Those who have suggested that an employment policy be adopted which compensates as much as possible for deficiencies resulting from past racial discrimination are accused of reverse racism and discrimination against non-Negroes. The position taken is that racial discrimination qua racial discrimination is a thing of the past, and that we must all now look to the future in which each man, black and white, will be judged on his ability to compete with others. Therefore, if the Negro is more qualified for a job, he will receive it. But if a white man is better, the Negro should not complain, because he has had equality of opportunity to compete and has been found wanting not, as of yore, because of his race, but because of his individual inability to prove himself superior.

Concerned persons must reject this approach and adopt in its stead a demand for programs consciously designed to compensate for the fact of past racial discrimination and the social disadvantage that flowed therefrom. This demand must be made without apology and without any sense of guilt. The Negro received for three hundred years a special negative treatment. Failure to admit the need to take steps to compensate for three centuries of exclusion of Negroes from the effective life of American society will result in freezing the Negro in his position at the base of the society. This clearly identifiable ten percent of the society, resting always at the bottom, will serve to reinforce the still not discredited notion that the Negro is at the bottom because inherently he is not capable of rising to the top. In order to change the position of the Negro, conscious effort is required.

Such effort has been made in many places with remarkable success. Those who remember when one never found Negroes in sales positions in retail stores, as tellers in banks, or as executives in private industry and government, see clearly the beneficial results of a conscious policy of including Negroes in places from which they had been absent. However, it is important that such conscious inclusion of Negroes not be limited to a few visible or token positions, but that the effort be extended to insure that Negroes are found in representative proportions in all sectors.

Problems arise because the potential new employer of Negroes, or those who are asked to upgrade Negro employment, wish to avoid the possibility of their employees' failure. This concern is, of course, not unique to the consideration of potential minority group employees, but it is perhaps more acute when Negroes are involved. One must agree that no matter how great one's concern for providing new opportunities for Negroes, it would not be reasonable to tell an employer that he must hire an individual who, if hired, might materially cripple the operation in which the employer is engaged.

But it is reasonable to ask an employer to be concerned with the question of the opportunities available to minority group members, and to require him to make certain decisions about the employment of such persons which are not identical with the decisions he might make were those potential employees non-Negro.

The basic question to be determined in dealing with Negro candidates for any level is whether the individual considered can perform satisfactorily the job for which he is being evaluated. If the answer is "Yes," the second question is whether the Negro is the best of all the applicants for the position. If the answer is "Yes," most admit the Negro should be employed. However, for the doctrinaire egalitarians, a negative answer would require acceptance of the best candidate, and rejection of the individual who is not so competent.

It is at this point that those concerned with remedying the conditions resulting from three hundred years of inequality part company with the egalitarians.

The fact that rigid egalitarianism fails to note that the Negro may not be the best because in the past he did not have the opportunity to sharpen his skills, either because he was denied the experience required for skill development or because discrimination limited his aspiration, is ignored in the enthusiasm for equality. Rigid egalitarianism fails to recognize that there is no standard for weighting the true competence of those newly arrived to competition as opposed to those for whom opportunity has always been available.

Special attention must be given to the placement of the Negro because he is a newcomer. There is sufficient experience now available to demonstrate that no sector has suffered from a policy of employing Negroes because, given adequate opportunity, Negroes function as well as the average of their white peers.

Where there are no Negroes, or only limited numbers of them, special steps must be taken to increase this minority group's presence. In such cases the decision to employ should be made on the grounds that the Negro applicant is capable of doing the job, even though there may be other non-Negro candidates who appear to be better. To compensate for past discrimination, the purpose is to give the Negro today the opportunity he undoubtedly would have had, in the absence of past racial discrimination, to function at the level he would be likely to be found had he not been the victim of racial prejudice.

Such consideration will not be unique. Veterans, persons with physical handicaps, and others are given special preferences, not because they are better qualified to do a particular job, but because there is a social policy which says that such persons deserve extra help in adapting themselves to societal demands. Certainly the real and psychic handicaps accruing to Negroes are no less important than those suffered by the veteran or the physically handicapped. It will be useful to remind those who object that it will take a great many instances of discrimination *in favor* of Negroes to equal the past acts of discrimination *against* Negroes.

There are many Negroes who will reject notions of compensatory consideration, because these Negroes are aware of the fact that in any fair and open competition, free of prejudice and condescension, they will stand out as exceptional human beings. These are the men and women who have overcome obstacles of great magnitude and who have justifiable confidence in their ability to measure up to any standard which might be applied, regardless of how rigorous it might be. For these men and women, no policy of compensatory hiring is wanted or needed.

But wherever the Negro is competitively disadvantaged because he has been denied access to that which might have prepared him to compete at the highest level, he must be given a special chance to demonstrate whether he can do the job, a special chance which might not be given one who suffered no past disadvantage.

Of course, many supportive elements are required to make such a program of compensatory employment selection work, the most important being a full employment economy. A high level of unemployment is fraught with the possibility of sharply increasing racial antagonism. This would presumably be true when nonminority group members perceived a selectivity process which deprived them of a long-accepted preference vis-à-vis the Negro, reversing the usual pattern.

Another essential supportive element is a steadily improving educational system that will eliminate differences between whites and Negroes and thus make it possible for Negroes to begin their working careers on a basis of real equality with their white peers, progressively eliminating the need for compensatory selection.

What must be prevented at all costs is a situation similar to one described a few years ago by the Negro head of a municipal agency. There were, he reported, only two Negroes in his agency: he, as Director, and his Negro chauffeur. It is to fill the all-too-symbolic gap between two such employees that a compensatory employment policy must be designed.

STERLING TUCKER

Sterling Tucker is Executive Director of the Washington, D.C., Urban League and also serves as a member of the Senior Staff and as Consultant to the National Urban League.

Born in Akron, Ohio, on December 21, 1923, Mr. Tucker attended public schools there and was graduated from the University of Akron with the B.A. degree in 1946 and the M.A. degree in social psychology in 1950. He is a member of the Academy of Certified Social Workers, the National Association of Social Workers, and other professional organizations in his field.

Mr. Tucker has traveled widely in connection with his work. In 1952, on special assignment as Industrial Relations Specialist to the League's National Office, he traveled, under a grant from the Field Foundation, throughout the United States gathering information on the situation of Negroes in the country's major industries with a view to finding ways to consolidate gains made during the period of high employment at the time of the Korean War. His most recent trip, undertaken at the request of the State Department, has involved travel to the Far East as an American Specialist in community development and urban planning.

Mr. Tucker has assumed numerous responsibilities in both national and local affairs. He served as Vice Chairman and organizer of the 1963 March on Washington. In 1964 he received the Washington Junior Chamber of Commerce Outstanding Young Man of the Year Award. In addition to his Urban League and civic work, he has also written for professional journals, served as consultant for numerous agencies, and lectured and written for the USIA. He currently lectures at the Washington International Center and the American University School of International Service.

One of his major activities during the past year has been service as chairman of the Citizens Advisory Council to the Superintendent of Public Schools. Among the many committees or boards of which he is a member are: the D.C. Advisory Committee, the U.S.

Commission on Civil Rights, the D.C. Manpower Advisory Council, the D.C. Citizens for Better Education, the Urban Planning Commission, the Episcopal Diocese of Washington, the Chief's Council on Police Community Relations, the Greater Washington Educational Television Association, and the Inter-religious Committee on Race Relations.

WE *SHALL* OVERCOME

by Sterling Tucker

SOME ten years ago, in the balmy July twilight of Bombay, India, I stood on the banks of the Arabian Sea. I longed for the family I had left behind, and for America, the land of democracy and equal opportunity, the land to which I had dedicated my life service toward the achievement of those ideals for which it stands. But even in my loneliness, as I looked around me at the many people from different lands, I experienced a surge of new life, a sense of rebirth: I sensed a feeling of "togetherness" with them as we shared the beauty of nature in the setting of the sun.

Yet, in the midst of all that beauty, just across the street families were bedding down for the night on the sidewalks, with no place to lay their heads, such was the extent of their poverty. As I crossed the street, a small child reached out for my hand and in a weak, fading voice pleaded, "An anna, mister, an anna." Then his tiny hand slipped from mine and his emaciated body crumpled at my feet where he died, his last breath sapped by the malnutrition of a land abounding in poverty, yet awesome in nature's beauty.

It was then that a line I had always remembered became truly meaningful to me: "The brotherhood of man transcends the sovereignty of nations." I knew fully at that precise moment that when I returned home to once again take up the cause of the American Negro in his battle for Civil Rights, I would be fighting a battle not just for the Negro minority in the United States, but a war for mankind all over the world. I would return to my homeland with the knowledge that the constant search for equal opportunity must be our continuing, priority task; but I would also know that it should not be the *sole* concern of Negroes in either community or world affairs. Neither could we continue to feel that the struggle for human rights is the Negro's private war, rejecting or failing to encourage the support of white America. I knew the stake in the battle for equality to be the same for us all, the social and economic health of this nation to be no less significant for one group of people in this country than for another. And I felt somewhat comforted in facing what I knew to be a tremendous battle when I remembered the words of Homer, "Light is the task where many share the toil. . . ." For indeed it is the mission of the Urban League, an organization to which I have dedicated my life's work, to enlist the participation of every American citizen working together to relieve the adversities that face our democratic society, working together to achieve the ideals upon which our nation was founded, working together to make America in truth a "land of the free."

As I reflect on the course of my life and the direction of my career, I can remember growing up with a high degree of social consciousness. I can give no pat analysis of the reason for this. Like most Negroes I was born of humble parentage, my father being a civil servant in the Akron City Government—so I was poor. Yet I never *felt* impoverished. There seemed no need for more than the one suit of clothes I owned when I could wear only one suit at a time. I was well fed and we had always owned our house. So I felt no personal grudges against society; life had done me no wrong. The road map, then, for the course of my life's direction lay within me: had the world been perfect, I would have wanted and worked to make it better.

As a youngster I was always organizing groups for causes. Even as early as grade school I led a group to get a neighborhood playground established, which, when finally completed, I rejected, because I preferred playing on the neighborhood dump amidst the broken glass and strewn bottles to playing ball at the toot of a supervisor's whistle and boxing at two toots of that same whistle. Even then the streak of rebellion in me was emerging, mild though it was, since it was always within the framework of the system. I rather imagine that in my rebellion I was looked upon by adults, not as obnoxious or antagonistic, but simply as a nuisance.

With my penchant for social reform, I was influenced early in life by the Urban League. A group of us young people, in fact, belonged to an Urban League Club. Although the Executive Director of the League, George Thompson, was brilliant, handsome, impeccable in speech and dress, had connections with the power structure and was, reputedly, very influential in the community as a whole, there were few, if any, discernible results of his influence on our group or in the Negro community per se.

During my senior year in high school, there was to be a mass meeting concerning plans for the opening of a Negro Y.M.C.A. The members of our youth group did not want a colored "Y" but desired instead to see a central, integrated Y.M.C.A. established. Since the Urban League had been active in tackling other problems of the Negro minority—jobs, housing, and education—we looked to the League for leadership at that meeting, despite our earlier criticism of the organization. Unfortunately, neither the League nor the "Y" fared well in that meeting—perhaps there was not enough money in the community pocketbook—and we young people left, thoroughly disgusted with the older generation.

It was then that we organized a group called the Youth Forum. I was President of the group and by that time a college freshman. We published a weekly crusading newspaper (which sold for a dime, as I recall), and distributed it in ten neighborhood schools. With all the vitality and impetuosity of youth, we attacked the problems of the community and offered our solutions to them all. And those papers sold like hot cakes.

I recall one editorial in our newspaper that had a very personal, if not traumatic, effect on me. The downtown, white power structure had praised editorially a Negro bootblack and held him up to the Negro community as an example of a man who had raised himself by his own efforts, and hence was to be regarded as a model. Our newspaper refuted that editorial as an insult to every Negro citizen in Akron. While there was nothing wrong, we asserted, with being a bootblack, we considered it unfortunate that the white people of Akron knew so little about our race that they could not select for praise a more representative model for the Negro American.

That bootblack lived only a few doors from my home; and one day, while I was waiting nearby for a bus, his wife invited me in. She wanted to let me know how offended she and her husband were by our attack on the editorial in the white newspaper which had praised him so highly. And as we faced each other in a fierce but polite argument, I shall never forget her words: "You don't care who you hurt, do you?" I could only answer that I had done what I had to do; that our cause was larger than they were; and that often people must stand aside, or be moved aside, for the sake of a cause.

Her husband, I tried to explain, simply was not an appropriate model for Negro youth. Yet I was bothered by having brought grief to that family. I wonder if I would have been comforted had I remembered the words of William Lloyd Garrison: "I will be as harsh as truth and as uncompromising as justice"? I doubt it.

It was during the period when our Youth Forum was active that I met the man who was to have the single most profound influence on my life's work. Lester Granger, Executive Director of the National Urban League, came to Akron to speak, and I sought an interview for our newspaper. I was advised of his tight schedule and was allowed ten minutes to speak to a man who greeted me as though he had known me all his life. And in his characteristically relaxed manner, that great national figure talked with me for an hour and a half, filling me with inspiration as he listened to my views and encouraged my idealism.

I had made no final decision as to a career, though I was majoring in sociology at the University of Akron and was being encouraged by several different department heads to major in their fields. Any success that I may have had as a student should be credited at least in part to the Firestone Company, where I worked evenings as an office boy. Years later in talking to Harvey Firestone, Jr., I apprised him of the contribution his company had made to me in my pursuit of knowledge. Certainly no student ever studied in more elegant surroundings than I, as I sat at Mr. Firestone's desk (having been told to disappear by an understanding foreman), or turned in papers more beautifully typed than those done for me by the secretaries of the Firestone Company.

After graduating from college, I went to Ray Brown, then Executive Director of the Akron Urban League, in search of a position. He created a job and conjured up a salary of $2,400, and I took it on the spot. From that point on, I learned the Urban League upside down and inside out. When the janitor went on vacation for two weeks, I took over his job and changed from my white collar during the day to my blue collar at night.

During those days I was impulsive, impatient, and probably impossible. I am sure that I made a great many mistakes then, some that will never be forgiven. There was so much to be done and I was in such a hurry to do it. Now, some twenty years later, I have learned that *how* things are done is almost as important as *getting* them done.

In the course of my career in Akron, Lester Granger invited my wife and me to be his first guests at his new summer home. During that two-week vacation Lester and I argued regularly and vehemently on issues and approaches; and I am sure that he must have made proper allowance for my lack of discretion in pursuit of a point, for he offered me a job with the National Urban League as a traveling consultant to work with industry in consolidating gains made by Negroes following the Korean War. I accepted his offer and left for five months to travel throughout the country, loving my work, yet hating to be away from my family. Thus, it was with some feeling of relief that I entered Lester's office at the end of that five months, assignment completed. And though he offered me a permanent job with the national office, I chose to return to the local affiliate with the grass-roots people I wished to serve. I felt that I could not tell another how to do a job I had not yet done myself.

Naturally, there came a time in my career when I had to consider the continuation of my academic studies. At one point, at the prompting of a political science professor, I had considered going to law school; but all lawyers in my experience were poor, and I felt that if I were destined to be poor, I did not need the luxury of a law degree. I knew many Negro lawyers who were extremely *capable*, but I knew none who were *prosperous*; and although I had no particular concern for money, I was practical enough to know that I needed economic security in whatever field I chose, to be free to do my job without concern for income. I wanted the freedom to evaluate problems purely on the basis of their worth, not their monetary value. This is a viewpoint (a religion if you please) that I still hold.

In 1950 I knew that I had reached a crossroad in my career and asked my Executive Director for permission to attend law school at night—not with the idea of trying to earn a living as a practicing attorney, but with the notion of widening my knowledge of the legal aspects of social problems. The Board of Directors refused permission, feeling that study in law would not further enhance my work with the League. I have always felt that the agency made a mistake in that decision. It should have encouraged staff members to acquire all the education possible. My disappointment at the

Board's refusal even led me to consider other employment; but instead of changing jobs, I did graduate work in social psychology.

After six months as Assistant to the Executive Director in Akron, I was sent to be the Executive Director in what was then the Siberia of local affiliates—Canton, Ohio; an official of the United Fund thought so little of Canton as to suggest "they lock the door and throw the key away!" I must admit that I felt some great injustice was being perpetrated upon me by those who had considered me the "fair-haired boy" of the Urban League movement. Yet each professional move I have made has been a good one. Though I have never actively sought a job or opportunities, they have presented themselves to me and I have been fortunate in my choices. My only regret is that I was never able to complete what needed to be done before moving on. But a man cannot pick the time and place of his destiny. He can only continue in the service of his cause.

Another crucial point in my career came in the mid-fifties when I entertained the possibility of accepting a foreign service post following a State Department tour of duty in India. Even though I had become convinced that the race relations problem was not solely an American but an international problem, I decided that I could best serve my country and humanity abroad by working with this problem at home.

In the early 1960's, after I had come to Washington as Executive Director of the Washington Urban League, at a time when everyone was caught up in the fever of the New Frontier, I, like many others, received numerous job offers. I could easily have taken a leave of absence from the League, but I think I was afraid I might not return, and I was really happy where I was. I enjoyed being a part of the nation's capital, examining it and prodding it along to maintain its forward motion. While I had enjoyed the grass-roots aspect of life in a smaller community, being in Washington made it possible for me to reach out in unlimited directions—local, national, international. Perhaps I reach too far, grapple too much. Perhaps there should be a younger man directing the work of the local Washington Urban League. Perhaps I am approaching another moment of decision in my life.

There is no limit to the opportunity available to the young person today who wishes to enter the field of community service. With the disappearance of the narrow concept of Civil Rights, we are faced with new and greater challenges: the challenge of providing equal opportunity for all people; the challenge of innovative urban planning for an ever-expanding population; the challenge of designing motivating as well as educational (not simply instructional) school systems; the challenge of building good police-community relations in our urban ghettos. There are so many challenges and opportunities for service for so many years to come—too many years, really—that the youth of today need only prepare for what can be a great and satisfying career.

His preparation lies not only in meeting academic qualifications, but in mastering the technology and skill of his profession, and in building and understanding its language and its goals. He must develop a sensitivity to the problems with which he will cope, a sensitivity that is at the same time objective and subjective: objective, so that he can give calm and rational consideration to all of the issues involved; subjective, so that he can retain the feeling for what he is doing and consequently never work in detached isolation from the people he serves and their problems as he attempts to solve them.

There is a special challenge and reward for the Negro in community service. First, he has the opportunity of bringing other Negroes together in a much-needed unity, for we are yet divided. We must soon realize that our strength lies in organization and that our weaknesses are only exposed and aggravated by disorganization. If this is "black power," so be it. I hear no hue and cry when one mentions the Jewish Community Council or the Greek Orthodox Society or the Italian Federation. Through our own unity we render a service to ourselves and to the general society of which we are a part. Second, the Negro who accepts the challenge of community service has the opportunity to help put into practice some of mankind's greatest concepts in our nation's democracy.

The Negro has made tremendous contributions to American life. He has taught America how to suffer in dignity, how to persevere, how to face insurmountable obstacles. He has *truly* kept the faith. I cannot help remembering an article by John Steinbeck in which he said, "I am constantly amazed at the qualities we expect in Negroes. No race has ever offered another such high regard. We expect Negroes to be wiser than we are, more tolerant than we are, braver, more dignified than we, more self-controlled and self-disciplined.

We even demand more talent from them than from ourselves. A Negro must be ten times as gifted as a white to receive equal recognition. We expect Negroes to have more endurance than we in athletics, more courage in defeat, more rhythm and versatility in music and dancing, more controlled emotion in theater. We expect them to obey rules of conduct we flout, to be more courteous, more gallant, more proud, more steadfast. In a word, while maintaining that Negroes are inferior to us, by our unquestioning faith in them we prove our conviction that they are superior in many fields, even fields we are presumed to be trained and conditioned in and they are not."

I cannot say that I agree completely with Mr. Steinbeck's analysis, but I do say that America has never fully understood how much the American Negro has contributed to the building of this country's ideals and way of life and how fervently we believe in the Constitution and the Bill of Rights. I do not ridicule the words "brotherhood," "freedom," and "equality." If we in America cannot make them truly meaningful, then what else is really worthwhile?

I am unwilling to assign to another generation the indignity and inhumanity that have been heaped upon our forebears and ourselves. Yet, at the risk of being called a gradualist (or worse), I can only say that the solution to our many problems will take more time. But we must not falter. We must remember the words of William Lloyd Garrison, "I am in earnest, I will not equivocate, I will not excuse, I will not retreat a single inch and I will be heard." We *shall* overcome.

H. CLAUDE HUDSON

Dr. H. Claude Hudson, prominent dentist, businessman, and Civil Rights advocate, was born on April 19, 1886, in Marksville, Louisiana, and was educated in the schools of Louisiana and Texas. He attended Wiley University in Marshall, Texas, prior to entering the Howard University School of Dentistry in Washington, D.C. He graduated from Howard University in 1913 with the degree of D.D.S., and was engaged in the practice of dentistry from 1913 to 1923 in Shreveport, Louisiana. Dr. Hudson then moved his family to Los Angeles and is engaged now in the practice of dentistry there.

He was elected to the presidency of the Shreveport, Louisiana, branch of the NAACP in 1921 and served in that capacity until his departure for Los Angeles. Less than a year after arriving in Los Angeles, he was elected to the presidency of the Los Angeles branch of the NAACP, and held this position for ten consecutive years. During his term of office, he developed the Los Angeles branch into the largest and most effective in the nation. Since 1934 Dr. Hudson has served the local branch either as Vice-President or as a member of the Executive Board.

In 1950 he was elected to the National Board of Directors of the NAACP and has served continuously since that date. He is, at present, a member of the Executive Committee of the National Board of Directors.

In 1927 Dr. Hudson enrolled in the Loyola University School of Law and was awarded the LL.B. degree in 1931. His interest in the study of law grew out of a desire to broaden his knowledge and thus serve the NAACP more effectively.

He is President of the Broadway Federal Savings and Loan Association of Los Angeles, an institution with assets in excess of fifty-five million dollars. When Dr. Hudson assumed the presidency of the Association in 1949, it had assets of less than three million dollars.

In 1962, at Charter Day Exercises, Dr. Hudson received the Distinguished Alumnus Award from his alma mater, Howard University, Washington, D.C. In 1963 he was given a Distinguished Citizens Award by the County Conference on Community Relations. He is a Trustee of the Wesley Methodist Church and is active in many social, professional, and human relations organizations.

On the West Coast of the United States, because of a life dedicated to social service, he is known as "Mr. Civil Rights."

ETERNAL VIGILANCE—

THE PRICE OF FREEDOM

by H. Claude Hudson

MY story is that of the rise of a Louisiana sharecropper's son to a successful dental practice, a position of leadership in the Civil Rights struggle, and the presidency of a fifty-million-dollar savings and loan institution.

Son of a former slave, I have known what it is to suffer deprivation and to be faced with seemingly insurmountable odds. I have known, too, that faith and determination can raise one above the level of want, can moderate frustrations, and can dispel the darkness of despair. And I have known that a helping hand at a timely moment can make the difference between hopelessness and fulfillment.

Born in Marksville, Louisiana, and reared in Alexandria, Louisiana, I attended public school in the latter town up to the sixth grade, which was as far as I could go at the time in the Louisiana public school system. No additional public education was available to members of my race.

My father, who was then a sharecropper, saved enough from his meager earnings to send me to a private school that was operated by the District Baptist Churches. The school, with a faculty composed of a principal and two teachers, was housed in a small structure, but had the imposing name of "Thirteenth District Baptist Academy." It was at this school that I first learned that there was such a thing as a higher level of education in other cities.

Although my sights were now raised to higher achievements, I did not perceive the opportunities that might be mine, because my parents were very poor, and I could not see my way clear to pursue my education further. Without the type of fortuitous circumstance which so often plays a meaningful part in the destiny of men, my formal education might well have been concluded at this point.

But when all seemed dark, with no opportunity apparently available to me, I was sent as a delegate from the Newman Memorial Methodist Church of Alexandria to a missionary Sunday School convention. The convention was held at the Liberty Methodist Church in New Orleans, Louisiana, under the sponsorship of the Methodist Churches of the Southeast Area of the United States. My companions and I journeyed by railroad from Alexandria to New Orleans, and almost by fate my party boarded the same train that was carrying to the convention another delegation which included President Dogan of Wiley College in Marshall, Texas. I was introduced to President Dogan by the superintendent of our Sunday School, Dr. I. W. Young, through whose influence I had been elected a delegate.

This was in the year 1906. I will never know what President Dogan saw in me, but before the convention was over, he invited me to enroll that fall in Wiley College in Marshall, Texas. I had just graduated from the Baptist Academy with a large certificate, which seemed magnificent at the time, but which merely certified that I had finished all of the courses of study through the eighth grade.

The invitation from President Dogan to enter Wiley College had for me an urgent appeal. The President had assured me that I would be given an opportunity to work my way through college. This proved extremely fortunate. Although I had saved some money, when I entered Wiley that October, I did not have the cash to pay my way through school to Thanksgiving.

Again as fate would have it, Andrew Carnegie had donated $15,000 to Wiley College for the building of a library. The College had difficulty securing a contractor who would construct the building according to plans and specifications for the limited funds available. Fortunately, I had learned a bricklayer's trade while quite young, serving an apprenticeship in Alexandria, Louisiana. With the confidence of youth and determination to succeed, I told President Dogan that I could build the library with the students' help if he would provide me with an experienced carpenter as an assistant. The President permitted me to proceed for one week until the architect could inspect the work to see whether it had been done according to plans. After checking the amount of construction, the laying out of the foundation, and the preparations being made, the architect told President Dogan that I knew what I was doing.

The construction work assured my four-year stay at Wiley and also gave my two brothers a chance to obtain a college education. The building was successfully completed with student labor and, though quite busy directing the construction of the building, I satisfactorily completed my school work and finished with my class.

Those who are familiar with Wiley College know what I mean when I say we were imbued with the "Wiley spirit." The young people attending the College from 1906 to 1910 knew no such word as "fail." When a generous contributor gave money for a boys' dormitory, that, too, was begun and practically completed with student help during the years 1906 to 1910. Living in Marshall, Texas, we had all the difficulties, all the discriminations, and all the threats of bodily violence that Negroes suffered throughout the Southern sections of the country, but nothing seemed to daunt us.

By this time, I was determined that I would enter the profession of dentistry. Thus, in the fall of 1910, I entered the Howard University Dental College in Washington, D.C. At Howard I was in contact with aspiring young Negroes and students from all over the world. The quality of the education, the proximity to the seat of government, and the fellowship of students with divergent backgrounds broadened my outlook on life and admirably prepared me for the many adversities and struggles that I later encountered in my profession and in the Civil Rights field.

I was able to work my way through Howard and graduated in the spring of 1913 with a degree of Doctor of Dental Surgery. Following graduation, I returned to Louisiana to practice dentistry and opened an office in Shreveport, where I later married and established a family.

In 1913 the outlook for the American Negro was indeed grim, and conditions seemed to be growing worse. In 1909 a group of far-sighted white and Negro citizens had organized the National Association for the Advancement of Colored People. I was greatly impressed by the purposes and policies of this body, for it seemed obvious that a national organization with central direction attacking discrimination and injustice from every angle would be an invaluable aid toward improving conditions for Negro Americans.

In spite of the work of the NAACP, conditions grew worse.

Nevertheless, I became active in all of Shreveport's community business and social efforts and in 1921 was elected President of the Shreveport Branch of the NAACP. To be a member of the NAACP in Louisiana at that time was bad enough, but to be an officer in the Association was almost suicidal. An invitation, for example, to William Pickens, who was then the National Field Secretary for the NAACP, to come to Shreveport to speak produced a mob that I had to face under extremely perilous conditions. Being known as an active Civil Rights advocate in Shreveport resulted in repeated threats upon my life.

Finally, I determined that the fight for equality could be carried to a greater advantage if I located my family in another community where I could be more effective and where my family would be safer. In 1923 I moved to Los Angeles, California. I had been a citizen of that community for only eleven months when I was elected to the presidency of the local branch of the NAACP.

For ten years I served as President of the Los Angeles Branch and was an active leader of the Civil Rights movement, pioneering in the struggle for equality which, for the most part, we take for granted today. As early as 1924, for example, eight of us were arrested for using a segregated beach to swim in the Pacific Ocean. All of us were jailed at Manhattan Beach, California, and were tried and sentenced to ninety days or a $500 fine. As far as I know, this was the first "wade-in," or "swim-in." The Los Angeles Branch won this fight. The convictions were overturned; and from then on, all of the beaches in California have been enjoyed by all citizens without regard to color, race, or other discriminatory factors.

Throughout the years since my arrival in California, I have been actively engaged in the work of the NAACP, the Urban League, the Y.M.C.A., the Community Chest, and the Methodist Church, in which I serve as a trustee. I have also maintained a close interest in political campaigns directly affecting Negroes.

In the mid-1920's, while serving as a member of the educational committee of the downtown Y.M.C.A., I observed that many white businessmen were studying law in order to broaden their educational background. I immediately concluded that if a white businessman needed to study law in order to broaden his education and make him a better citizen, then it was imperative that I do the same. In 1928 I entered the Loyola College of Law, and through night school studies received an LL.B. degree in 1932. During my studies, I continued a busy dental practice and raised the Los Angeles Branch of the NAACP to national influence. With all this I was able to achieve class grades that I could hold up to my children as an example. Needless to say, my legal training has been of inestimable value to me as a citizen, a businessman, and an officer of the NAACP.

Following World War II, Southern California experienced a population explosion and a resulting demand for homes. During this period it was difficult for Negroes to secure financing for homes or businesses. The discriminatory practices of lending institutions prompted a group of us to organize the Broadway Federal Savings and Loan Association. Broadway Federal opened its doors on January 11, 1947. The Association has enjoyed a steady growth and today has assets of fifty million dollars and employs more than fifty people.

This endeavor greatly reduced the financial stranglehold upon the economic lives of Negro citizens in Los Angeles. The home purchaser was able to buy in a better neighborhood and, as a result, send his children to greatly improved schools. Real estate sales by Negro brokers and agents increased rapidly because they were able to secure loans for their customers.

Negro citizens have long been identified with the building industry as mechanics; but with the advent of Broadway Federal, many Negroes built substantial contracting businesses. The building industry, thus strengthened by available funds, gave employment to mechanics and artisans, improving the economic position of our people and of our nation.

In 1949, when I was elected President of the Broadway Federal Savings and Loan Association, its asset strength stood at three million dollars. Loans were still difficult, if not impossible, to secure from other lending institutions, and other savings and loan associations did not hire our young people. Today, I can report that banks and savings and loan institutions in Los Angeles do not discriminate in either their lending or their employment practices.

Through Broadway Federal, we were able to reach and inspire people who had never before done so, to save what funds they could. This increased their value as citizens, since one who saves and invests in America's future is a better citizen than one who is indolent and unconcerned about his own future. While most of us are assured some pension benefits when we reach old age or become disabled, they are minimal at best. The systematic accumulation of money in savings and loan associations and through purchase of stocks and bonds is both easy and wise. The old copybook axiom, "waste not, want not," is as true today as it was a century ago. The profit and income from these investments can provide the good life when we retire.

In retrospect, as I think of the condition of the American Negro when I was a young man, I dread to think of our fate had it not been for the organization and work of the NAACP. There is no part of my life that has been more constructive than the effort put forth, the money expended, and the sleepless nights spent in an effort to carry out in my community the policies enunciated by NAACP conventions, by the National Board of Directors, and the national office. I would also call attention to the fact that all over this country dedicated men and women are working for the same cause superbly directed by the national officers of the Association. They have never failed to exert pressures and influence whenever and wherever they were most needed.

I can recall the open attacks made upon American Negroes in 1910 from the state capitals of the South, in the halls of Congress and the Senate, and in the executive directives from the White House. Such attacks would have crushed people of less ambition. Today I can rejoice at the opportunities available now. Yet we must not think the fight for equal rights and full citizenship has been won. Indeed, in my opinion, there is a long, hard struggle ahead of us. Now our opponents are more insidious, subtle, and clever.

The burden of carrying on this struggle today belongs to our young people, who must not feel that all the battles have been won. Though the problems they face may differ in number and kind from those my generation faced, American Negroes must continue to be vigilant, courageous, and persistent in the fight for full freedom and equality. My generation has opened doors with dignity, courage, and determination. It is the task of our young people to keep them open and to forge ahead.

Life holds many paradoxes, but I have found that a high regard for the welfare and dignity of others is a philosophy that will bring happiness and a feeling of accomplishment when one has reached the evening of life. It is impossible to do something unselfishly for someone else without indirectly receiving benefit oneself.

JAMES M. NABRIT, JR.

President of Howard University and former U.S. Permanent Deputy Representative to the United Nations with the rank of Ambassador, James M. Nabrit, Jr. was born in Atlanta, Georgia, on September 14, 1900. In 1923 he graduated from Morehouse College and in 1927 received the Doctor of Jurisprudence degree from Northwestern University. He began a teaching career at Leland College in Louisiana and subsequently became the Dean at Arkansas State College for Negroes. After six years in Houston, Texas, as a lawyer, he joined the faculty of the Howard University Law School in 1936.

As a practicing attorney in Houston, Dr. Nabrit participated in some twenty-five cases involving Civil Rights, principally voting cases. As a member of the faculty of the School of Law at Howard University, he organized, in 1938, the first formal course in Civil Rights law to be taught in an American law school.

After having served as a faculty member, Administrative Assistant to the President, Secretary of the University, Director of Public Relations, and Dean of the School of Law, he was named President of Howard University in 1960.

In August, 1965, President Lyndon B. Johnson nominated him U.S. Deputy Representative to the Security Council of the United Nations. He resigned that position in January, 1967, to return to his post at Howard.

Dr. Nabrit's broad and continuing interest in civic and educational affairs is reflected in the many and varied positions he has held in local, national, and international organizations. He has served, for example, as Director of the American Arbitration Association, the NAACP Legal Defense and Educational Fund, the United Givers Fund, the Center for Community Action Education, the United Cerebral Palsy Foundation, the North Carolina Mutual Life Insurance Company, and the National Conference on International Economic and Social Development. He has also served as a member of such organizations as the Advisory Council of the American Association for the United Nations, the National Fund for Medical Education, the Advisory Committee of the Negro Actors' Guild of America, the Legal Advisory Committee of the National Society for Medical Research, the President's Committee on Employment of the Physically Handicapped, the President's Committee on Youth Development, the Joint Commission on Mental Health of Children, and the International Institute for Labor Studies. In addition, he has been an Overseer of the College of the Virgin Islands.

James M. Nabrit, Jr. has received the honorary degree of Doctor of Laws from the following institutions: Morehouse College (1955), Lincoln University (Pennsylvania, 1961), Georgetown University (1963), Johnson C. Smith University (1964), Catholic University (1964), Delaware State College (1965), West Virginia State University (1966), Tuskegee Institute (1966), Virginia State College (1966), St. Lawrence University (1966), Morgan State College (1966), and Northwestern University (1966). He has also received the honorary degree of Doctor of Humane Letters from Bates College (1963), and from Yeshiva University (1967). Among his other honors and awards are the Meritorious Award of the D.C. Federation of Civic Associations (1956), the Russwurm Award of the National Newspaper Publishers Association (1962), the Alumni Merit Award of Northwestern University (1962), and the Achievement Award of the D.C. Junior Citizens Corps (1966).

EQUALITY OF HUMAN DIGNITY—

OUR ULTIMATE GOAL

by James M. Nabrit, Jr.

CONSIDERING the question "What do I believe?" an individual must express his convictions in the light of experience, for (apart from religious faith) no belief that remains untested by experience is worthy of the name. The convictions I hold now result largely from the manifold experiences that I have had over a number of years. Since training in the legal field was one of my early experiences and has remained one of my major interests, it is to be expected that this background would have a direct bearing upon my general views.

At the outset, let me say I believe that law is created in order to assist society in achieving and maintaining certain goals and that it is the necessary tool of orderly social growth.

In the development of society, the law is our surest strength *if* we remember that laws are created for the benefit of all. The essence of justice lies in the fact that it is impartial: that it applies to everyone, that "no man is above the law and none below it." But laws alone cannot protect a society from itself: in order to have respect for the law, one must be able to respect the society it protects. Therefore, a good law will not only reflect the present needs of the people it represents, it will also provide for future needs and aspirations and the changes which are inevitable in human life.

All too often the difficulties we have faced in this nation have arisen because of laws which, while possibly serving a purpose at the time they were passed, were attuned to a static rather than a viable society. The decision in the *Plessey vs. Ferguson* case, for example, purported to settle the question of education equitably through the separate but equal doctrine. Subsequent developments, however, demonstrated clearly that this decision resolved the issue to the advantage of the majority group and to the definite disadvantage of the minority group. Any law which works to the disadvantage of one segment of the population is against the best interests of all. Every segregation law has worked against the best interests of all by depriving a segment of the population of opportunities, and hence depriving the nation of potential resources. The makers of such laws were short-sighted and did not look to the future. A society saddled with such laws has no choice but to change the laws to meet the demands of changing times.

Law has been instrumental in the improvement of education and in the enlarging of social opportunity. When I was a child, there were no public secondary schools available to me where I lived; my family had the alternative of sending me to private school or having me forego my education. Were I a child living in Georgia today, a public school would be available to me, and my attendance would be compulsory according to law. Furthermore, that school would be open to both white and Negro students. These changes are the result of legal decisions by those who not only faced an immediate problem but provided for the future needs of the nation. We have entered into an era and live in a society which demands more education of more and more people. As Chief Justice Warren said in 1963 in *Brown vs. Board of Education:*

Today, education is perhaps the most important function of state and local government. Compulsory school attendance laws and the great expenditures of education both demonstrate our recognition of the importance of education to our democratic society. It is required in the performance of our most basic public responsibilities, even service in the armed forces. . . . In these days, it is doubtful that any child may reasonably be expected to succeed in life if he is denied the opportunity to an education. Such an opportunity, where the state has undertaken to provide it, is a right which must be made available to all on equal terms.

None of us would be so naïve as to claim that education is presently available to all on equal terms. The law simply makes this possible. It then becomes our crucial job to make this "equal terms" concept a reality. In 1960 President Eisenhower received a report from the Commission on National Goals, which begins as follows: "A paramount goal of the United States was set long ago. It is to guard the rights of the individual, to insure his development and to enlarge his opportunity." Such a goal cannot be achieved by the state alone; it involves us all. Education has for too long evolved in a happenstance manner, in response to crisis. The result has been an inequality of excellence which is all too apparent. If we would move the majority closer to the standards of excellence so far maintained by the few, we need the intelligence, the information, and the common sense of people who have not yet become involved. We need to establish criteria of excellence and then find the means of making them practicable. Uniqueness—intelligent individuality—and not uniformity is our proper goal.

The emphasis placed on the *quality* of education by the Civil Rights movement has become a central and complex issue because it is recognized that education provides the principal avenue of escape from low social and economic status and a path to integration. It is a complex issue because the achievement of pupils in the schools is the result not only of the quality of the schools but also of the background of the child—of his family, neighborhood, and general cultural milieu.

The general restiveness and the occasional violence which have characterized the 1960's may in themselves be cause for dismay, but I believe the motivations behind them are not. The message of the Supreme Court decision of 1954 rang a bell for change; yet, while the message reached the people, the change has not yet fully occurred: the majority of the schools in the South are still segregated, and it is widely true in both North and South that cases of de facto segregation are still being brought before the courts. The Civil Rights Act raised expectations even higher; again, little of a visible nature has changed. With almost one-fourth of all Negroes in this country possessing less than a fifth-grade education and with the average Negro worker earning only forty-nine percent of the annual wage earned by the average white worker, there is need of much more understanding of the problem, and certainly of much more action. The streets of the slums are filling with idle people—the unemployable of our era—who know no escape, have no hope, and possess little patience; their urge is to strike down what they cannot change. But we must remember that people born in poverty and bred to desperation do not have the patience of those of us who seek redress of grievances in the courts—often a long, drawn-out process. They do not understand the need for peaceful procedures, nor for respect of the law; and this is true in every corner of the world where people, having achieved independence, are still seeking the substance of freedom. We will compound their impatience with distrust if, despite the law, we fail them once again. How can we ask them to respect that which we ignore? The law has given us the goal; it is up to us to implement it in finding the right road.

As a result of my experiences with the United Nations, observing many diverse groups striving to effectuate the Declaration of Human Rights, I think that we should not be discouraged. Clearly, there is a gap between what we foresee as possible and what we realistically recognize as probable. The Declaration of Human Rights is not today's reality, but tomorrow's hope. Without that goal in mind, however, no action is meaningful and no hope is possible.

It is the same with our own national objectives. We have openly made commitments which have been taken at face value by the people they most concern. If these people rise up to propel the nation toward its goal, it is not because they lack respect for law and order; on the contrary, they are literally seeking to strengthen the law by giving it substance.

We have just witnessed an unceasing series of racial disturbances throughout the country. These disorders—call them by whatever name you will—have resulted in large part from the historical treatment of Negroes in America, from the days when the first African slaves were landed to the present time. Slavery, by its very nature as an institution, divides people between the oppressors and the oppressed. These distinctions tend to linger long after the institution itself has been abolished. More than one hundred years after the signing of the Emancipation Proclamation, the Negro people in America, the descendants of slaves, have not been able to shake off completely the shackles of oppression. Racial segregation and discrimination continue to abound. They strike at Negroes in areas which are most critical to life—in matters related to employment, housing, and education. As the white majority knows, neither the Negro minority nor any other people can advance substantially unless genuine progress is made in these areas—not in just one area at a time, but in all three simultaneously. Those who administer our programs of assistance overseas know this well.

At the close of World War II, we instituted immediately a massive program of aid to the war-torn countries of Western Europe. Since that time, we have continued assistance in various forms to countries in Africa, Latin America, and Asia. Unfortunately, many of our country's leaders have not viewed the problems of these latter areas with the same urgency and interest as they did in the case of Western Europe. Our foreign aid program for the present fiscal year is substantially less than it has been in most recent years. I do not wish to dwell on this matter, but mention it simply to suggest that there is something of a parallel with respect to the way in which many of our countrymen view the plight of the developing countries and the situation of Negroes at home.

There must be a deeper understanding among the American people that neither the employment of arms overseas nor the use of troops in the streets of American cities can resolve issues which are not military by nature. Results obtained by force of arms cannot bring answers to problems which are primarily social, economic, and political.

I cannot in honesty say that there is no understanding at all among the American people regarding this essential fact. The very existence of a program of overseas assistance and of various poverty programs at home not only indicates an awareness of the nature of these pressing matters but also demonstrates an effort, for which we must give credit, to bring about a satisfactory resolution of these problems. But generally speaking, all of these programs are inadequate for the accomplishment of the task. These programs, both at home and abroad, have contributed to a wave of rising expectations. To date, however, the American people have not shown the will to carry through to final fruition the programs which they have only recently begun.

I am sure that future scholars studying the history of our country will not fail to note the military precociousness of the American people. We are frequently engaged in military ventures, generally on the victorious side. In such operations, our people show a spirit of tenaciousness and a determination to endure the loss of blood and resources inevitably accompanying a major war. These virtues so evident in times of war, if applied to nonmilitary matters might more quickly ameliorate the social, economic, and political ailments which afflict us.

If we did not know it before, certainly experience should now teach us that a small dose of economic aid is not sufficient treatment for a massive economic ailment. This is as true for the impoverished Negroes at home as it is for the starving millions abroad. It is not enough, for example, to make it possible for a few Negroes to get a better education, a better job, and a better home. These essential matters in life must be brought within the realm of possibility for the masses of the people.

It is in the interest of all to end the perpetuation of the division of the world's people between the haves and have-nots and the oppressors and the oppressed. A world in which every newborn child has a birthright which includes an equality of human dignity and an opportunity to share in the bounty which civilization affords must be our ultimate goal. Until this objective is reached, we are faced with a dismal future of struggle from which neither side will emerge the victor.

There is great diversity among us as to how we should approach the problems which, because of their urgency, demand an immediate solution. With respect to the issue of race in America, there are those who, tired of America's promises and pessimistic about the prospects of genuine integration, propose methods which would in effect enable the Negro people to go their own way. Those who advocate this position include many who have labored valiantly in the vineyard of Civil Rights activity and who have grown weary from what seems to be the futility of their efforts. It is unfortunately true that they have not reaped the full harvest of their expectations. The 1954 Supreme Court decision banning segregation in public education is still resisted in many areas, and there are more Negro children in segregated schools now than ever before. Public accommodation laws make it possible for everyone to be admitted to hotels, restaurants, theaters, and the like which were previously barred to Negroes, but this fact has little reality for those who do not have the means to take advantage of these new freedoms. Voter registration laws have been effective only after long, costly campaigns fought county by county and almost precinct by precinct by the formerly disenfranchised.

In the midst of national affluence, the employment pattern of Negroes grows steadily worse. Their prospects for decent housing and good education are equally grim. White people in the North who supported Civil Rights activists in the South become hostile as the Civil Rights movement reaches the edges of their own neighborhoods. Poverty programs, which once had at least token support, become mired in the swampland of disapproval, neglect, and abandonment when it becomes clear that so many of those to be helped are Negroes and other racial minorities. This is indeed a gloomy prospect which has resulted in disillusioning many of the bright young people in the Negro minority.

It is not surprising that a new militancy has arisen among us, especially among the youth of today. There is a spirit of revolt at work which will not subside until a new order has been established. The new militants will not accept token integration or government-sponsored programs which represent half-hearted approaches to the acute problems of our times. They are tired of studies into which the same data are poured and out of which come the same findings and the same recommendations. It is sometimes said that the nation's circumstances today are similar to those of the Reconstruction period following the Civil War, when reaction set in and a vigorous effort was made to separate Negroes completely from the mainstream of American life. One of the principal differences between the two periods, however, is that Negroes today will not play the role of passive subjects.

While I encourage the "militant spirit," I must define what this concept means to me. To be militant, to encourage change, indeed to provoke revolution, does not necessarily mean to destroy all that pertains to the old establishment. While there are aspects of American society which operate so as to keep the Negro minority in a disadvantaged position, there are other factors which work to our advantage. The distinction between good and bad, between right and wrong, cannot always be made in absolute terms. And whenever possible, it is a part of wisdom to take a position where we can keep our options open, accepting that which we find to be good, rejecting that which we find to be bad.

The struggle of the Negro to achieve his rights in American society, beginning with the close of the Civil War, has been hard-fought and has gone through several different phases. It is indeed a blot on a democratic society that he has had to engage in such a struggle at all. But we must accept the historical fact that such a struggle had to be undertaken and that other minority groups which came to these shores have also had to overcome opposition to their assimilation into American life. It is ironic that the Indians, who were native to the land, have made almost no headway at all in this respect.

One of the recent phases of the struggle has now come virtually to an end. This can be observed, for example, in the case of the sit-ins which were made so effective in the South by students and other young people who broke down barriers in the area of public accommodations. There is also doubt about the continued effectiveness of such demonstrations as the March on Washington and the Selma March. We know, too, that while there is need for new legislation and for the strengthening of certain laws already enacted, there is decreasing interest in the area of legislation, and increasing concern regarding the implementation of laws which are already in operation.

Is the Civil Rights movement dead? This is a question which is frequently asked today. The answer, it seems to me, is both in the affirmative and in the negative. A phase of the struggle as typified by the activities of the 1950's and the 1960's is over. A new phase has begun. The earlier successes of the movement have been in some respects illusory. Solid victories in major engagements are more difficult to achieve than in brief skirmishes. The enemy has been met and some concessions have been made.

Some of the young people who took part in Civil Rights activities in the South became embittered when they found that their work did not produce the immediate results for which they had made such painful sacrifices. Yet they may have achieved much more than they realize, for their efforts contributed immensely to the creation of a climate which made possible the progress of recent years, however small or great.

These young people, filled with a vigorous, restless spirit, have introduced new tactics and are following a philosophy radically different from that of earlier Civil Rights advocates. With their advent now, there is a broader diversity among the organizations principally engaged in Civil Rights activities, and there are deep differences of opinion regarding future courses of action. This is not an altogether unanticipated or unhealthy turn of events. The Negro people in America are not a monolithic group and, like other groups, contain within themselves a broad spectrum of philosophies and judgments.

I am glad to see the emphasis which is being placed upon the importance of discarding the feeling of inferiority on the part of Negroes, which the psychology of oppression has imprinted upon so many of us. Having pride and confidence in oneself is essential to self-development and advancement.

It is necessary that we redouble our efforts to achieve our legitimate aspirations. While we shall continue to have differences of views as to how we should proceed, let us seek to avoid bitterness and hatred both among ourselves and in our association with others. Let us seek to avoid the excesses which have characterized some of those who have been among our oppressors. The cause of the Negro is just and has a strong moral basis which we should endeavor to maintain untarnished.

WHITNEY M. YOUNG, JR.

Whitney M. Young, Jr., Executive Director of the National Urban League, was born in Lincoln Ridge, Kentucky, on July 31, 1921. After completing undergraduate studies at Kentucky State College in 1941, he entered the Army during World War II and served in the European Theater.

Following graduate work at the Massachusetts Institute of Technology and at the University of Minnesota, he joined the Urban League in 1948 as Industrial Relations Secretary of the St. Paul (Minnesota) affiliate. In 1950 he became Executive Director of the Omaha Urban League. While serving in this capacity, he also taught at the University of Nebraska School of Social Work and at Creighton University, which awarded him an honorary Doctor of Laws degree in 1964.

Prior to his appointment as Executive Director of the National Urban League in 1961, he served as Dean of the School of Social Work of Atlanta University for seven years.

During the academic year 1960–61, he was a visiting scholar at Harvard University. A recipient of many citations and awards in the social work profession, he received the Outstanding Alumni Award from the University of Minnesota and has received honorary degrees from several other institutions.

Mr. Young has served on many Presidential committees, among them, the Youth Employment Committee and the Committee on Equal Opportunity in the Armed Forces. He has been a member of the Commission on Technology, Automation, and Economic Progress and of the special Presidential Task Force on Urban Affairs. He is a Presidential appointee on the Commission on Law Enforcement and Administration of Justice. He serves on the National Advisory Council of the U.S. Office of Economic Opportunity, on the Advisory Council on Vocational Education of the U.S. Office of Education, and on the Advisory Committee for the New Model Cities and Metropolitan Development Program of the Department of Housing and Urban Development.

Whitney Young also serves as President of the National Conference on Social Welfare, and as a member of the Board of Trustees of the Eleanor Roosevelt Memorial Foundation and of the John F. Kennedy Memorial Library. He is on the Advisory Council of the New York School of Social Work, Columbia University, and on the Board of the Unitarian Universalist Service Committee. He is Chairman of the Council for United Civil Rights Leadership.

A noted writer, his articles have appeared in a large number of professional journals and national magazines; and his book, *To Be Equal*, was published in 1964. He writes a weekly column by the same name for seventy-five newspapers across the nation. As Executive Director of the National Urban League, he is regarded as one of the foremost spokesmen for equal opportunity in the country.

WHEN OPPORTUNITY KNOCKS

by Whitney M. Young, Jr.

OF all the circumstances which predict a man's life and fortune, it is my conviction that the single most important is the circumstance of birth, defined not by wealth or poverty, aristocracy or serfdom, or by color, but by the nature of a human being's first brush with humanity. And in this respect I was born among the truly privileged.

To be born black in the state of Kentucky, in an age when the life of the Southern Negro was barely more than a form of sophisticated slavery, is a birthright of privilege that is open to question, no matter what the circumstances. But the circumstances of my inheritance, of the daily exposure to the decency, dignity, courage, and compassion of my parents proved to be stronger in composing my image of mankind than all the atrocities and inhumanity perpetrated by the white world outside. It is this inbred belief in the ultimate power of decency over bigotry, of intelligence over ignorance, of truth over fear, that has sustained me in my life and life's work in the fight for Negro freedom and progress.

It is true that because my father was the President of Lincoln Institute and because I was raised on the school campus, I was to a large degree protected from the worst forms of discrimination during my early years. The white people in the neighboring towns were dependent upon the school for business reasons and, for Southerners, were unusually courteous to us. The white teachers in the school were, to some extent, self-styled missionaries, and their manner toward us was, at worst, patronizing.

But no Negro, unless he spent his entire life in a cave, could escape the poisonous influences of discrimination in the South. One of the favorite and most devastating forms of discrimination was—and is—the emasculation of the Negro male. Historically, the Negro society has been a matriarchal one. It had to become so for the pure and simple purpose of sheer survival. Because the

75

Negro male was such a threat to the system, any recognition of him as a man, or any hint of respect for his position, had to be carefully guarded against.

The Negro woman was treated better. It was easier for her to get work, and she often became the principal wage earner. In Negro families, if money and opportunity were available for higher education, it was usually the girl who was chosen to pursue it. (Until the last decade, twice as many Negro girls as boys went to college.) And in the matters of day-to-day living, because there was less chance of her being lynched, the woman became the chief negotiator with the whites.

I remember my first introduction to this particular brand of turpitude; I was eight years old, when my father took me to buy a suit from a white merchant. The suit did not fit me and, when we returned home, my mother insisted that it be taken back to be altered or exchanged. I remember experiencing an acute sense of bewilderment and, later, deep sorrow and shame for my father when I understood that the burden of doing battle with the whites, in even the slightest demand for justice, automatically fell to the Negro woman. Fortunately, in this type of situation my mother was particularly effective. She took me back to the store and, after long and skillful verbal maneuvering, succeeded in obtaining a suit I could wear.

My father, I am proud to say, was a man not easily emasculated —despite the white Southerner's ingenious talents for inflicting senseless human suffering and debasement. Outwardly, he honored the rules of the white man's game. Not to do so in those days was a quick and efficient form of suicide. But privately, he was quietly working and living and raising his family by his own rules: "A man good for excuses is good for nothing."

Because he, to a greater degree than others, had a more commanding view of the terrible human destruction wreaked by ignorance and fear, my father believed that knowledge was the most powerful weapon a man could possess and that education was a principal path to the gateway of freedom. He believed—and it is this belief which has served my life and work—that the most important step in moving toward any goal was to be prepared for opportunity when it presented itself.

To hold such a view in those days in the state of Kentucky—when the Civil Rights movement was not yet even a dream, when the major problems of the black man were how to get food and how not to get shot—was more than radical, more than visionary. It was truly heroic.

My father prepared me well, both in learning and in the determination to pursue a college education. His influence and insight sustained my courage and nurtured my will throughout all the days —the sometimes difficult and harrowing days—of my academic years.

Within the province of his power, he was as determined for the students of the school as he was for me. In his position as President of Lincoln Institute he placed emphasis on the library and the classroom, and on formal academic learning—all of this at some risk. The school at that time was permitted to exist through the good will of the white power structure for the principal purpose of educating ignorant Negro youth to be more efficient and more knowledgeable butlers, cooks, maids, farm hands, and cotton runners.

Whenever the white Board of Directors was scheduled to honor the school with a visit, my father would declare a holiday from the classrooms; and the students would quietly retire to the kitchens and to the fields where they would be viewed busy at the sink in one instance, and driving tractors in the other—learning how better to serve the white community.

From my mother I learned about morality. Morality is simply treating other people with consideration; and in her daily life my mother showed me the meaning of this word in its highest form. At the age of four, I came to understand that I risked a spanking if I were caught being inconsiderate, that is, if I failed to speak to people as I walked along the street.

My mother's love of humanity, her unyielding faith in the power for good in man and her incredible talent for discovering it—in the face of a society malignant with fear and hatred—was a major influence in the development of the views I hold and practice today. These views are founded on the belief that it is possible for men, both black and white, to live together in harmony and in peace, both contributing to, and sharing equally in, the material and spiritual bounties of this land.

It was my early ambition to become a physician, partly, I think, because I had always been struck by the independence with which

Negro doctors moved around without fear of white people. Upon graduation from Kentucky State College for Negroes after pursuing a premedical course, I did not have the means to go on immediately to medical school, and so began to teach in high school in Madisonville, Kentucky, in order to acquire the necessary funds. Then came Pearl Harbor, and I enlisted in the Army.

It was my experience in the armed forces that had the most powerful and direct influence on my decision to enter the field of race relations. After two and a half years at the Massachusetts Institute of Technology studying electrical engineering, I was shipped overseas, where I became part of the American segregated fighting force. In the segregated Army the enlisted men were all Negroes; the officers, all white. The machinery of discrimination was nicely geared.

It was in the Army that I really had my first close-range contact with white Southerners. The foggy childhood superstition of the white man's superiority quickly evaporated in the warm light of fact. The white officers were superior in neither intelligence nor education to many of the Negro men; and they were considerably inferior in sensitivity.

At home, the whites had been able to dominate Negroes on the basis of fear. Overseas, they did not have this weapon. The Negro troops quickly sensed this fact and acted accordingly. The Negro men became openly hostile; the white officers, openly afraid.

Admittedly, in that situation the Negro had a distinct advantage, besides the mere advantage of numbers. In order to survive, the black man has had to cultivate a supersensitivity to people and an instinctive knowledge of mankind; he has had to know when and how factors will work for him, and when against. There has been no historical reason for the white man to cultivate an understanding of the Negro any more than there is reason for a South Carolina farmer to understand the psyche of his hunting dog.

Because of my advanced education, I had quickly been made a first sergeant. And as the top noncommissioned officer and a black man, I found myself acting in the role of liaison between the officers and the men. In return for this service, I insisted upon—and obtained—better treatment for the Negro men. It was at that time that I began to feel the first flicker of hope that if justice could be won for the American Negro in a foreign land, then it could, and must be won for him in his own country. I decided that I could best serve my country by serving my own people in the fight for freedom, and that I would dedicate my life to service in this battle.

I think it is safe to say that service overseas in World War II was KP duty compared with fighting on the front lines in my native land against discrimination, despair, disease, joblessness, homelessness, bitterness, and hard-core cynicism. The fight for human and constitutional rights is the longest war in the history of the world—and it has only just begun.

Former Vice-President Hubert Humphrey has observed that many Negroes today "still experience the crisis conditions of the Great Depression." It is my belief that if these same conditions prevailed in the total community, we would be threatened with a shooting revolution, as at times we were during the 1930's.

It is my fervent hope that the war of racial justice will be won through peaceful means since, like the overwhelming majority of Negroes, I neither believe in nor condone acts of violence or extremism. But without massive and immediate action by the whole of American society to end the daily psychological and economic lynching of the American Negro, the risk of violence and bloodshed mounts, and the welfare of the nation lies in jeopardy.

It is a harsh and bitter fact that despite the dramatic victories won through the Civil Rights movement and despite all the heartening signs of progress in the last decade, the gap between nonwhites and whites is not narrowing. It is widening.

Since 1954 Negro unemployment has doubled; and today it is two and a half times the rate of white unemployment. The gap between the white and Negro median income has broadened. Sixty percent of all Negro youth of the nation live below the government's poverty line. There are more Negro children in segregated classrooms than ever before; and eighth-graders in Negro slum schools commonly read at sixth-grade levels.

Seventy-three percent of the American Negro population live in the cities. According to the U.S. Civil Rights Commission, if all of New York City were as jammed with people as are several of the worst blocks in Harlem, the entire population of the United States could fit into three of the city's five boroughs, with two left over.

In terms of human suffering, the cost of this social and economic strangulation can scarcely be imagined, let alone measured. The cost to the nation, economically and culturally, is more definable. The educational, social, and economic deprivation and bondage of the Negro costs the nation an estimated $27 billion a year (four percent of the gross national product) in purchasing power. It costs the nation billions of dollars a year in welfare monies.

The great and timeless contributions to America and to mankind made by outstanding Negroes in every aspect of life—science, government, the arts, literature, medicine, industry—in the face of overwhelming handicaps merely hint at the vast potential that would be released for the enrichment of American life, if the Negro had equal opportunity by law and freedom of choice by practice. A culture is as great as its capacity for diversity. Stagnation, mediocrity, and cultural dry rot are the products of sameness. The growth of people and of nations does not proceed from similarity. It proceeds from the embrace of difference.

The young Negro today faces a much more difficult life than the Negro of my generation. From the time we learned to perceive the difference in color, we were simultaneously educated about the law of the land—discrimination, its attendant rules, and above all, its dangers. There were two simple formulas for staying alive: silence and acceptance.

The young Negro today finds himself in the midst of a national racial struggle, engaged in front-line fighting. He is not concerned with mere existence, but with a full and equal life of opportunity and freedom of choice. Equality, democracy, and freedom are the spoils of this battle, a battle in which he must have total victory. The young Negro today cannot appreciate how far we have come, nor assess the bitter costs of even small historical victories. He is not placated by progress, by our emergence from the days when Negroes were herded into the balconies of theaters, into the backs of buses, and into the segregated ranks of the American Army. He is concerned only with the ground yet to be covered.

Although the forces of freedom have gained strength, numbers, and some ground, the truth remains that the Negro has achieved only token equality. The enemies answering to the names of bigotry, fear, and inhumanity still thrive in abundance, and the situation worsens. Moreover, the Negro youth today faces the perils of an increasingly complex society, in which even the most affluent and privileged are uneasy and anxious before the monster god of technology.

In the fight for freedom through the Civil Rights movement, the Negro engaged in some of the most magnificent demonstrations of faith, courage, and dignity the world has ever seen. The freedom rides, the sit-ins, and the marches on Washington, Selma, and Jackson were events which all decent Americans watched with pride and exhilaration—and the world, with wonder—as the American Negro people offered dramatic reaffirmation of the indestructible power of the human spirit, too often confused, maligned, and forgotten in the daily life of mechanized man.

The Negro revolution does not seek the destruction of American society or a separate, guarded place within it, but full and equal partnership in that society under the nation's Constitution.

The best advice I could offer to young Negroes today is the same advice my father gave to me. That is, be prepared to meet the challenge of equal opportunity and freedom of choice which must inevitably come to all Negro people of this country. I would also advise them to be prominently visible in every phase of the fight for freedom—as visible at the ballot box, in the library, in the PTA, and at Scout meetings as in the marches.

The Negro must move, and will move, in the mainstream of American life. The American dream is the just and lawful heritage of Negro Americans, who have labored and died to defend their country and to help build the economic, educational, and cultural life that makes it great. It is not through the withdrawal of any group, but through the fervent, united efforts of decent people of good will of every race, color, and creed that the system can be made to work for the benefit of all men.

The true worth of any nation is determined by that nation's treatment of its most disadvantaged citizen. It is determined also by its success or failure to honor its own bond, which, for the United States of America, is nothing less than total freedom of opportunity for every citizen. It is a bond long overdue American Negroes, and today, the American credo faces its gravest challenge. How this challenge is met will not be measured in terms of the gross national product or progress to the moon, but in terms of national morality.

I believe absolutely that the success or failure of this country will be measured by the success or failure of the Negro American to win the opportunity, equality, self-respect, and self-sufficiency which are his constitutional and God-given rights, and by the willingness of the white American to meet his obligations to the principles of democracy, to his country, and to mankind.

The Arts

SAUNDERS REDDING

Saunders Redding, currently Director of the Division of Research and Publications in the National Endowment for the Humanities, has had a long and distinguished career as an author and as an educator. Born in Wilmington, Delaware, he was educated in the public schools of that city, and later at Brown University, where he received his undergraduate and graduate degrees, including the Ph.B., M.A., and Litt.D. In addition, Hobart College has conferred upon him the honorary degree of L.H.D.

Following the publication of his first book, *To Make a Poet Black*, in 1939, he was awarded a Rockefeller Foundation Fellowship, in 1940, which enabled him to spend a year traveling through the South "to see"—in the wording of the grant—"what he could see." These travels resulted in the book *No Day of Triumph*, which won the Mayflower Award "for distinguished writing." After the appearance of this work there came a number of noteworthy publications of various types. These include several books, among which the most significant are: *They Came in Chains* (in Lippincott's "Peoples of America" series); *Stranger and Alone* (resulting from one of the two Guggenheim Fellowships he has received); *An American in India* (the result of a State Department assignment to India); *The Lonesome Road* (in Doubleday's "Mainstream of America" series); and *On Being a Negro in America*. His latest book, *The Negro*, was published in the fall of 1967.

A former Head of the English Department at Southern University, and later a longtime member of the faculty at Hampton Institute, Saunders Redding was for ten years, until 1963, on the Editorial Board of the *American Scholar*. In 1964–65 he was a Fellow in the Cooperative Program in the Humanities at Duke University and at the University of North Carolina. He has been a Visiting Professor at Brown University and has served as Rosenfeld Lecturer at Grinnell College and as a lecturer in Africa under the auspices of the American Society of African Culture (AMSAC). He is a member of the Executive Council of this organization, and also holds memberships in several civic organizations, including the NAACP and the Urban League.

A WRITER'S HERITAGE

by Saunders Redding

I DID not set out to be a writer. I doubt that anyone sets out to be what he eventually becomes—a lawyer, politician, priest, or pimp; a good person or a bad; cruel or compassionate; strong or weak. We become what we are by a complex of conditioned instincts first, then by circumstance and chance, and then—but always last, and only sometimes—by taking thought. Circumscribed by natural inheritance, one has almost no choice as to the *kind* of person he will be, free will notwithstanding, and really damned little choice as to *what* he will be. Fitting together the disparate elements of model-image, talent, opportunity, training, motivation, and desire, and getting an answer as to what to be is not easy, and most people never attempt it. Most never "set out" on a predetermined direction. Most drift.

One might be lucky and have some wise, deeply interested person (parent, teacher), who is also patient and commanding, discover what his bent or hidden talent is, and then proceed to motivate, train, cajole, and whip him toward what he can best be. But how many youngsters are that lucky? And what one can best be is not necessarily what he wants to be. He's more than lucky—he's some kind god's favored child—if what he can best be is also what he wants to be. Besides, students of adolescent psychology and high school counselors tell us that the time when youngsters should begin preparing to be what they have greatest aptitude for and can best be is the very time also when they want to be so many things that if they had a real choice they couldn't make it.

I wanted to be a lot of things before I wanted to be a writer. I wanted to be a detective, a traveling evangelist, a hobo, a prizefighter, and a merchant. I had a model-image for each of these, and even now could describe the circumstances under which each one inspired me to emulation. The wish to be a merchant stayed with me longest. A merchant was an acquaintance of my father's, intimately known as a frequent caller at our house. "Merchant" was my maternal grandmother's word, and the household adopted it. Anyone who sold anything was a "merchant," who might also be defined by what he sold and where. There were, for instance, street merchants (whom everyone else called hucksters) and commission merchants, fish merchants, candy merchants, coal merchants, and dry goods merchants. (My maternal grandmother had a lot of language, and all of it was elegant and precious. My paternal grandmother had little language, but all of it was earthy, strong. One spoke of her *limbs;* the other of her *legs* and *shanks.* One spoke of *passing;* the other spoke of *death.* We did not see much of Grandma Redding, but Grandma Conway-Holmes we saw for a month at a stretch every year and at least two weeks every summer.)

Anyway, my model-image merchant, Mr. Raikes, had an establishment called an "emporium," and he dealt in every conceivable second-hand thing—including, my mother used to say, soap. But how my mother would have known this I can't imagine, since Raikes' Emporium was way down on the east side in the "Bridge District," where, so far as I know, my mother and my sisters never went. Mr. Raikes sold clothing and footwear, furniture, beds and bedding, stoves and cooking utensils, sporting goods, and hairpieces —all second hand, but, his monthly handbill said, "guaranteed like new." "Mr. Raikes," my father explained, "sells what colored people can afford to buy."

But Mr. Raikes himself seemed to buy—or at least to acquire— things even few white people could afford. In winter he wore an overcoat collared and lined with luxurious fur. His suits, my father said, were made by Delgrano Brothers, the custom tailors, where the lowest prices were sky-high; his shoes were hand-sewn. He bought the first Peerless Six automobile—a dark green beauty—I ever knew a colored man to own. I thought he was matchlessly wealthy, in a class with the DuPonts; and I thought, too, that the admonitions that rolled off his tongue were matchless gems of wisdom. "Perseverance, that's the winning ticket," he would say, and tapping me on the forehead with a long finger, "Early to bed, early to rise makes a man healthy, wealthy and wise." For weeks I nearly killed myself getting up before dawn.

One day—and for several days—there was dinner-table talk between my mother and father about things which I did not understand—"creditors," "litigation," "collateral," "mortgages overdue" —except that they somehow pertained to Mr. Raikes. It was at about this time that the emporium was boarded up, and Mr. Raikes himself disappeared, and I stopped wanting to be a merchant.

It did not occur to me to want to be a writer even after an essay of mine won a prize given by the short-lived Negro weekly, the Wilmington *Advocate*, for the "best essay written by a high school student." Since the contest was closed to whites, there couldn't have been much competition. I was a high school junior then—one of fourteen classmates—and there were only fifty-one students in all four-year high school classes, and even if all these had entered the competition, which of course they hadn't, it couldn't have been called tough.

I can't remember what my essay was all about. Indeed, I can't now imagine what subject could have moved and interested me so much as to make me write on it. I remember that my father had just bought an Oliver typewriter for us, and a likely explanation is that my interest was less in *writing* than in *typewriting*. It is more than likely, too, that a good bit that went into that essay was simply a crude reflection of my reading—was, in short, cribbed. But if it was, Alice Dunbar Nelson, who judged the contest, did not discover it.

Mrs. Nelson was my high school English teacher and a family friend. (Lest it be thought that friendship had a bearing on her literary judgment in the essay competition, let me hasten to say that the writers' names did not appear on the essays. Each was identified by a number designating a name known only to the contest director.) A flaming redhead of statuesque figure, she was quite a woman. She might have been my model-image of a writer, had I been perceptive enough to have wanted one or to have felt the need for one (and if I could have disregarded the fact that she was a woman). She was a writer—a poet, and, although not widely known as such even locally, a published poet. A slim, autographed copy of her poems graced the bookcase in our back parlor, along with most of the volumes of her late first husband, Paul Lawrence Dunbar. One other writer who could be identified as Negro was represented in our bookcase, and to this day I treasure first editions of *The Souls* of *Black Folk* (which my father owned before I was born), *The Quest of the Silver Fleece*, and *Dark Princess*.

My mother was also something of a poet—though "rhymester" was the word she used. She would compose rhymes for special family occasions, such as birthdays and holidays, and she would make up new lines to go with old tunes, and many a dinner time was made gaily raucous with all of us singing—each in a different key—"Gimme some old time molasses, gimme some old time molasses, it's bound to cure me. It was good for Uncle Rastus," etc., to the tune of "That Old Time Religion." My mother hated sad songs and solemn words. Her wit ran to the satirical, the amusing, and only rarely to the reverent.

When I fell irrevocably in love every fifth or sixth day in my fourteenth year, I tried writing poetry. (Doesn't every boy?) And of course I wrote letters by the ream to my heart's ephemeral liege, pledging undying love. Love was sweet, but love was very painful, and I suppose I realized in some subconscious way that writing about love to my love modified the pain and made it bearable. Also, I enjoyed the responses my letters drew, when they drew them, which was seldom. It seemed that none of the girls I loved cared a thing about me. The quest was fun. Conquest, I'm sure, would have troubled me.

Nothing troubled me until I went to college in New England. I turned seventeen that fall. There were three other Negroes. Two of them were seniors, and one a sophomore, who did not return after Christmas and who killed himself a few months later. We Negroes were aliens, and we knew it, and the knowledge forced us to assume postures of defense and to take on a sort of double-consciousness. It was not a matter of real ambivalence, or a question of identity: we knew who we were. But we feared to act ourselves, feared to "act the nigger," whatever that meant. Where the knowledge that induced this fear came from—for certainly it was a knowledge unconsciously learned—we did not know. All we knew was that it was deeply troubling, and that neither the cramming for high marks (for a sense of competition with the whites was fierce, psychotic), nor the ritualistic excesses of our race-brotherhood, nor the hysterical bouts of party-going in New Haven, Springfield, and Boston was exorcism. It was then that I began to write out of what I have since called my "Negroness." It was all I had, and all I still have, and all any colored person born and reared and schooled in America has to write out of if he pretends to honesty; and all any colored person so born and reared and schooled has to act out of too. To think otherwise is a delusion; to feel otherwise is fakery.

LENA HORNE

Lena Mary Calhoun Horne, celebrated singer-actress, is one of the outstanding female personalities in the entertainment world. Through the years she has thrilled audiences on the Broadway stage, on television, and in motion picture theaters with her voice, her acting ability, and her distinctive "mode" as an entertaining artist. She has been regarded by many as "the most beautiful woman in the world."

Miss Horne was born in Brooklyn, New York, on June 30, 1917, and began her public schooling there. After attending various one-room schools in Miami, Atlanta, Birmingham, and Cincinnati, she returned to Brooklyn, where she attended Girls' High School.

Displaying artistic abilities at an early age, Miss Horne won public acclaim for her singing and dancing skills as an adolescent. At the age of sixteen she was a dancer in the famous New York Cotton Club chorus, and at eighteen she went on tour with Noble Sissle's orchestra and remained with that organization until her marriage a year later.

As early as 1940 Miss Horne was the featured vocalist with the Charlie Barnett Orchestra. It was while she was with this orchestra that she made her first recordings, including the well-known songs "Haunted Town," "Stormy Weather," "Blues in the Night," "The Lady Is a Tramp," and "Mad About the Boy."

She later appeared at New York's Café Society Downtown, and subsequently went to Hollywood, where she was the first Negro woman to sign a term contract with a major studio (M.G.M.). Her Hollywood achievements include starring roles in "Panama Hattie," "Cabin in the Sky," "Stormy Weather," and "Meet Me in Las Vegas." Returning to New York, she appeared in several Broadway shows, among them, the musical hit "Jamaica."

Today, in addition to her busy schedule of personal and TV appearances, she is both interested and active in the Civil Rights movement and in civic affairs.

BELIEVING IN ONESELF

by Lena Horne

AS rewarding as they sometimes are, books can teach you only so much. The best you can hope for is to strike some sympathetic note in somebody else when you write, or to see something a little clearer when you read because you're viewing things through another person's eyes. There are some things you just have to live through before you can understand them; books alone are not enough, although the vicarious experiences gained from them can certainly be helpful. This idea was in my mind when I "wrote" *In Person*, my first autobiography, which came out in 1950. (That is, I talked, and somebody else did the writing. People who call that the lazy man's way of writing a book don't realize how much talking you have to do.) I certainly don't feel like bragging about that book, but the fact is it *did* seem to fill a need at the time. That book was not designed to give people a penetrating look at my mind and soul; I was far too unaware of myself and far too self-protective then to permit that. It was written for my fans, especially the young ones with anxious mothers, who wanted to know what it was like to be a Negro woman in show business. Frankly, it capitalized on my success in Hollywood; and it reinforced the new idea that Negroes were no longer restricted to bit parts in Tarzan movies, or to parts in which they rolled their eyes and spoke in fearful tones of ghosts and other superstitions, or to parts depicting them as servants. I was a new Hollywood "creation"—the Negro glamor girl. Although I was what I've called "pinned to a pillar" in most of my movie roles (I stood there looking as provocative as possible and sang), the point was that I didn't play any "mammy" roles full of patient suffering and good-heartedness; and in those days that was something of an achievement. The stereotype image had cracked, even if it hadn't completely broken.

Ironically enough, the stereotypes still persisted in my real life:

I was walking a very narrow path most of the time. I had become one of the "first Negroes who . . ." people, and I was advised to be very careful. I had always to be on my best behavior so as not to spoil things for those who might follow. I had become a symbol, and symbols are not supposed to act like people: they are just molded to fit a pattern that everyone can find acceptable.

It still pleases me to think about my father's role in connection with my first big contract. I had called and asked him to help me, and he did. I still wish that that particular scene could be put into a real movie: my father, absolutely unimpressed and unmoved, telling the moguls that he didn't want his daughter to work anyway, that all the colored performers he'd seen in movies were waiting on white performers, and that he could hire somebody to wait on me if that was what I wanted. He was magnificent and gave me just the confidence I needed. And I'll bet that not many professional performers have pulled a stunt as effectively. It was just one of several times that my Dad crashed through on my behalf. I scarcely saw him during my childhood, but when I was touring at nineteen we were very satisfyingly reunited, and since then have had some memorable times together.

When I look back over my life, my sharpest impressions are of the many ways in which I have been segregated, the many kinds of prejudice I have experienced. It is hardly surprising that I have only within the past few years begun to consider myself as a whole person, as an individual rather than a segment. When I was little—in fact until well after I was sixteen and got my first job, at the Cotton Club—my life was one of extreme contrasts, conflicts, and constant moving. I was either in the home of my father's parents in Brooklyn, where I was a member of one of the "first families" and segregated not only from white people but from the majority of my own people; or I was on the road with my mother, an aspiring but hardly very successful actress; or I was being taken care of by strangers in a succession of vastly different settings. Everywhere I went, with a few rare and happy exceptions, I was somewhat out of place. I lived in an adult world, although I was a child; I lived in the Southern world, although I was a Northerner; I lived with my father's family, although my mother was not welcome there. It was a life of dramatic upheavals and changes, and whatever stability I had was pretty much of my own creation. My vision of the house in Brooklyn sustained me on many occasions; and after I married and had two children, I went back there for what turned out to be an idyllic—but brief—period.

When I started to work, I was too young to be included in some social affairs. In others I was fiercely chaperoned by my mother. I was separated from friends of my own age by my work. And when we went on tour, I was not only segregated from the other performers by my mother and her second husband—a temperamental Cuban—but I learned the facts of life about segregation in America. These were about the only facts of life I knew anything of during those years. I had been so much removed from any kind of normal development, any kind of consistent upbringing, that I was really existing in a dream world. Perhaps that was why the unreal world of segregation didn't come as any great shock: it matched the unreality I lived with day by day. My stepfather once brutally pointed out to Noble Sissle, with whom I was touring, that his calling us "ladies" didn't mean that we could enter the building through the front door. Unconsciously we all knew it already; the shocking thing was to hear it said right out loud. My stepfather was just being honest, and furious—but that kind of honesty you had to learn to live without in those days, because nobody had the energy to work and fight at the same time. We had to make a living, and we did it according to the available terms, trusting that if we behaved well we'd be allowed to continue. Being on tour was a bleak enough business without being reminded continually of the conditions you had to face; you hoped to avoid patronizing kindness as well as stark ugliness, because anything that upset the balance destroyed the flat level of endurance and the forced poise you had achieved.

Young and naïve as I was, I inevitably married to escape what seemed to me an unbearable grind, and to attain the kind of happy domestic closeness I dreamed that marriage would bring—why, I don't know, since I had seen little enough of it in my own family. I met my first husband through my father. He was a minister's son, which in the Negro hierarchy of that time meant that he was just as spoiled and inexperienced as I was; we simply could do nothing for each other, because we had not yet done much for ourselves. I was married long enough to have two children; but we were

existing side by side, not as a unit, and we were both painfully disillusioned.

The birth of my first child, my daughter Gail, presented me with
the first really excruciating realization of the extent to which segregation dehumanizes us. I had a Negro doctor, whom I naturally
trusted implicitly—I had to, knowing nothing myself and being
really frightened of this new thing that was going to happen to me.
When the time came and I was taken to the hospital, the doctor
met me there; and then he said goodby, wished me the best of
luck, and said he was sure I'd be all right! I was absolutely speech-
less with fright and shock—in fact, I was so paralyzed by my emotions that I could not give birth for two days—as it slowly dawned
on me that he was not allowed to practice in that hospital because
he was a Negro. The Negro maternity cases were clustered together
in a special little place of their own; the doctors were white.

One other incident gave me the same kind of shock, but on this
occasion it was at least followed by a cleansing kind of anger, and I
was at least able to do something about it. During the second World
War, I did a good deal of USO work, traveling to army camps
around the country and entertaining troops. It always galled me
that the officers got the front-row seats, and it further annoyed me
that the Negro troops had to be entertained separately—this involved two kinds of segregation. On one occasion we were required
to do two shows—one for white troops and one for Negro troops—
which meant extending our tour an extra day. At the second show,
presumably for the Negro soldiers, there were white men in the
front rows. When I asked who they were, I was told "German
POW's." I nearly exploded in anger. Imagine! The enemy we were
supposed to be fighting had front-row seats at a show that was intended for our own men. I couldn't believe it! I went right out past
those prisoners and sang to the soldiers, but the whole situation
made me so sick that I just couldn't continue. As a result of that
incident I quit the show, called a cab, and went to the nearest
NAACP office. I introduced myself, and the lady behind the desk
said, "I'm Daisy Bates. What's on your mind?" I didn't realize how
close I was to history at that moment; but I sent off my telegram
and made my public comment, and that was pretty much where
the incident ended. It was certainly not the first public statement

I had made, but it was probably the most heartfelt and necessary one from my own point of view.

I've been married to my second husband, Lennie Hayton, for twenty years now—a long enough time, it would seem to me, to prove that we get along well. Yet when we married we felt it was necessary to go to Europe to do it; and even at that we received mail which would make you sick to read (I was not allowed to read most of it), for the very simple reason that Lennie is white and I am not. Many Negroes are every bit as prejudiced about inter-marriage as whites are; to them, a Negro woman who marries a white man is rejecting her own men and her own people. This attitude is the grand accomplishment of prejudice and segregation: of hypoc-risy so powerful that it can destroy individual private lives as well as public reputations. It can mean that in some places a husband and wife cannot be seen together, much less share the same room; that they have to be concerned about a thousand trivial things which ordinarily would never be noticed. In some states they can't even be husband and wife legally. Yet you have to bear with this kind of arrogant interference and ignore it if you can. You have to realize that the people who attack you don't even think of you as a person: they see the symbol, the threat to their way of thinking, and they strike at it blindly because they have never learned to react to people instead of symbols.

For most of my life I have been a symbol. The role of Public Object has brought me many rewards, but none of them can take the place of self-knowledge. Knowing yourself is very difficult under these circumstances, and being yourself is probably even more difficult, but it seems to me the only worthwhile thing a per-son can achieve. In the past few years I have really begun to feel an awakening as an individual. An urge to be a person has taken hold of me, and I frequently think of what Paul Robeson said to me many years ago: "You are Negro, and that is the whole basis of what you are and what you will become," and he added, "when you live and learn some more, you will be Lena Horne, Negro." I must have known then that he was telling me the truth, because I remembered his words even though I wasn't sure what he meant; just as I said earlier, there are some things you have to live through before you can understand them. The Civil Rights movement, more than any other one thing, has given me the urge to find out who I am and what I'm doing here.

In 1963 I was invited by James Baldwin to take part in a meeting in New York, which had been called by Robert Kennedy. I was on the verge of committing myself to *something*, of identifying myself with my people if they would have me, but I was not interested in acting out the role of Public Symbol any more. I had come to the conclusion that all of us—the "first Negroes who . . ."—had outlived our usefulness, that all we had ever done was to make it possible for the whites to postpone any kind of real justice. We were tokens, that was all: concessions to the white conscience, concessions to the aspirations of Negroes.

That same summer I accepted an offer from *SHOW* magazine to write an article about myself and about being a Negro in America, because I thought it was about time I gave serious thought to such matters. I had scarcely ever "been" a Negro, although my skin makes clear that this is what I am. I hadn't lived as most Negroes live, and I had rarely thought as a Negro. I was beginning to be Lena Horne, Negro, at last. In that article I said that while I couldn't sing protest songs or suddenly take up the guitar, or describe Southern atrocities with any kind of integrity, I thought there was something I could do: I could stop singing about penthouses up in the sky, with rents to match, when we couldn't even afford them, and I could stop singing those old stereotypes from musicals; and, if someone would help me out by writing some new songs, I thought I could sing things that would still be true to me and yet be more realistic, more in keeping with this generation.

Much to my surprise, I got a very prompt reply to that article from Harold Arlen; the outcome was the song "Silent Spring," dedicated to the four children murdered in the bombing of the Birmingham church. I had my wish: I had a protest song that I felt was true to me and true to the times. And I felt that I had come home—to myself and to my people. The symbol had been useful in its day, but now it had helped me to create something much larger than a symbol, much larger than myself.

I'm mature now, and a grandmother, and I have to confess that I've written another autobiography. People have commented that it is very different from the first one. I'm glad it is, because it was meant to be. There comes a time in your life when you have to talk straight to yourself, and that's what I'm trying to do. I don't feel the need to protect myself any longer; instead, I feel the strength of *being* myself, let the chips fall where they may. If I were to give any advice to young persons beginning their careers, I would urge them to choose their goals carefully, to believe thoroughly in themselves, and to always remember that in reaching for that ultimate freedom—the freedom of the individual—one's inner self is strong enough to make the choice of being human (in its better sense) or of merely being a beast.

NOBLE SISSLE

Born in Indianapolis, Indiana, in 1899, Noble Sissle, composer, singer, and orchestra leader, has been prominent in the musical world for more than half a century.

At an early age he received from his mother, a public school teacher, gesture and diction lessons which were to prove beneficial to him in his later professional career. It was in 1908, while still a sophomore in high school, that he had his first professional engagement, singing in a quartet on a summer tour. Following attendance at DePauw University and Butler University, he organized his first orchestra in 1915, and soon thereafter became associated with other musical organizations, among them Joe Porter's Sextet, Bob Young's Royal Poincianna Sextet, and James Reese Europe's Society Orchestra.

After service in Europe in World War I, Noble Sissle returned to America and toured with James Europe's Hell Fighters Band. After Europe's death in 1919, he formed a partnership with Eubie Blake in a vaudeville act which opened at the Palace Theater in New York and toured the Keith Circuit as a featured attraction.

In 1921 Sissle and Blake opened on Broadway with Miller and Lyles in *Shuffle Along*, which enjoyed a fourteen-month record-breaking run. In 1927 Noble Sissle appeared in the music halls of England with Harry Revel as pianist, and with Revel wrote several songs that later became favorites. For the next four years he played engagements in such centers as Paris, Monte Carlo, Cannes, Deauville, and Ostend, Belgium. Returning to America in 1931, he resumed his band career, which reached its high point during the years he spent at Billy Rose's Diamond Horseshoe Café from 1938 to 1951. In 1953 his orchestra was chosen to play at the Inaugural Ball of President Dwight D. Eisenhower.

Mr. Sissle has continued his active career in music and entertainment up to the present moment through orchestra engagements and special concerts often given with his veteran partner Eubie

Blake. He has been a member of the Entertainment Committee of the National USO since its inception. He also founded the Negro Actors' Guild and served as its President for twenty years.

In a long and illustrious career Noble Sissle has received numerous honors. One of the most recent tributes paid to him and Eubie Blake came in 1965 from the American Society of Composers, Authors, and Publishers (ASCAP), the American Guild of Vaudeville Artists, and other groups on the occasion of their fiftieth anniversary in show business.

EUBIE BLAKE

Eubie Blake, born on February 7, 1883, in Baltimore, Maryland, was christened James Hubert, but at an early age he was affectionately called "Hubie." This eventually resulted in "Eubie," by which he is professionally known today.

Once, while shopping with his mother in downtown Baltimore, "Hubie"—then a five-year-old child—disappeared into a musical instrument store where an organ was on display. Before his mother realized what was happening, "Hubie" had climbed up on the organ stool and was fingering the keys. Since he appeared to have a definite interest in the instrument, he was given piano lessons as a direct result of this incident. Later he was taught musical composition by Llewelyn Wilson, an accomplished musician who at one time conducted an all-Negro symphony orchestra which was sponsored by the City of Baltimore.

At the age of seventeen, Eubie Blake began playing piano professionally. In 1915 he and Noble Sissle formed a partnership as lyricist and composer. They later became the well-known vaudeville team of Sissle and Blake. The year 1921 brought Sissle and Blake together with Miller and Lyles, and from this combination of talent came the pioneer Negro show on Broadway, *Shuffle Along*. One song from this show has retained its popularity for almost fifty years—"I'm Just Wild About Harry."

In the early 1930's Eubie Blake collaborated with Andy Razaf and wrote the musical score for Lew Leslie's *Blackbirds*. From this association came the still popular hit "Memories of You." Razaf and Blake wrote at least twenty floor shows.

During World War II, Mr. Blake was musical conductor for the USO Hospital Unit and toured the United States continuously for five years, playing in every state which had a USO camp show.

Still an active man after his retirement in 1946, he went "back to school" and completed a course in music at New York University at the age of sixty-six.

He is a charter member of the Negro Actors' Guild and a member of the American Society of Composers, Authors, and Publishers (ASCAP), and the American Guild of Authors and Composers.

In May of 1965 Sissle and Blake were honored in Town Hall in New York City by ASCAP, the American Guild of Vaudeville Artists, and a number of other organizations for their fifty-year contribution to musical entertainment. In August of the same year they were honored guests of the *Chicago Tribune* at the thirty-sixth Annual Chicagoland Music Festival. The Museum of the City of New York honored Eubie Blake in May of 1967 at an unveiling of a bronze bust of him by the sculptress Estella V. Wright who had done a similar bust of his partner Noble Sissle.

HAVE FAITH IN YOUR TALENT

by Noble Sissle and Eubie Blake

"EUBIE, this is Noble Sissle. He's the new singer who just got in from Indianapolis to replace Russell Smith."

The rehearsal for the opening at Riverview Park had just broken up and the group was heading out of Joe Porter's house. Joe introduced us as we stood on a pair of those white steps which are so famous in Baltimore. We shook hands and the conversation was little more than cryptic. It went like this:

"Sissle? Didn't I see your name on a song sheet?"

"Yes."

"You're a lyricist. I need a lyricist."

The date was May 15, 1915. The handshake then had little significance to either of us, but it marked the beginning of a show business team which was to last for more than half a century. At the time, it seemed to be no more than a meeting between a struggling pianist-composer and a struggling singer-lyricist—a perfunctory gesture between two guys who would be working together during the summer season in Baltimore.

Our summer engagement at Riverview Park was a pickup job. In the days before air conditioning, the humidity forced entertainment to move out-of-doors, from the clubrooms and supperclubs to the garden, from the ballrooms to the hotel roofs, from the concert halls to the parks. It was during that summer season that the new team of Sissle and Blake collaborated to write their first songs. Among them was "It's All Your Fault." It was written for Sophie Tucker, who was appearing at the Keith Theater in Baltimore. She liked it and worked it into her act, and the team of Sissle and Blake was off to a flying start.

Of the more than two hundred songs we've collaborated on since Sophie Tucker made "It's All Your Fault" the rage of Baltimore that season, perhaps one of the tunes people remember best today is "I'm Just Wild About Harry." To clear up a point with the younger generation: "I'm Just Wild About Harry" was not written as a campaign song for President Harry S Truman. After surviving a last-minute plan to cut it out of our Broadway musical *Shuffle Along*, "I'm Just Wild About Harry," originally written as a waltz, became the hit of the show.

Until *Shuffle Along*, which we wrote in collaboration with Flournoy Miller and Aubrey Lyles, opened its fourteen-month run on Broadway in 1921, no other Negro show had been successful in breaking into the legitimate theater—that is, the legitimate theaters in metropolitan areas of the United States and Canada. At that time the team of Sissle and Blake was a toddling six years old. Over the years we have continued to write music and to perform our works.

On the stage of Town Hall in June, 1965, our career was highlighted when the American Society of Composers, Authors, and Publishers and the American Guild of Variety Artists paid tribute to us on the occasion of our fiftieth anniversary as a team.

Among the participants at the Town Hall event were Ed Sullivan, Dr. Ralph Bunche, Joey Adams, Sammy Davis, Jr., Damita Jo, Timmie Rogers, Smith and Dale, Connee Boswell, Arthur Tracey, Joe Williams, Jayne Mansfield, and Harry Hershfield.

It is important to point out that we didn't make it to that night, to that tribute in Town Hall all on our own. We received a lot of help on the way from a great many people. Our most illustrious benefactor was James Reese Europe, whose influence was felt by so many struggling musicians in New York in the years before World War I. Jim Europe, who had organized Negro musicians in New York to form the Clef Club, a protective organization and booking agency, used us as drawing-room entertainers soon after we joined his group.

He had a personal interest in our career that gave us faith in our own talents, and he let us share the gleam he had in his own eye. As an orchestra leader, Jim Europe felt that the Negro had within his power a greater contribution to make to the cultural heritage of of this country than dance music. He felt that our Negro composers and lyricists of the day could, and eventually would, create a beautiful, classical music from the deeply emotional themes of the spirituals, as a monument to the people who had labored in slavery for this nation. He had visions of the Negro, using his talent for music, breaking into the mainstream of show business.

Shortly before we entered World War I, Jim talked the Midwestern half of the Sissle-Blake team into enlisting in the 15th New York Regiment of the National Guard as a drum major for the regimental band he was forming. Jim Europe, who had been commissioned as a first lieutenant, was a dedicated and accomplished musician. However, he took the assignment of organizing a regimental band reluctantly. But he perked up when his drum major (Sissle) argued that the National Guard band could be used as a training ground for musicians who might eventually form the symphony orchestra that Jim had in the back of his mind, for the performance of Negro classical music.

The Baltimore half of the duo did not join the peacetime National Guard unit. Although the clouds of war were gathering when the regiment was federalized, Blake was not affected, since he had to support his wife, his aged mother, and his father, a Civil War veteran.

When the regiment, which had become the 369th Infantry, went to the battlefields of France, the regimental band's organizer, Lieutenant Europe, was in charge of a machine-gun company. All during the war he was able to perform only occasionally with the band. However, before the ink was dry on the armistice, plans were afoot to arrange a ten-week tour for the now famous 369th "Hell Fighters' Band" headed by Lieutenant James Reese Europe.

The "Hell Fighters" received rave notices at every stop along the way. The final concert of the tour was in Boston where, for Jim Europe, the dream ended abruptly. He was stabbed by a drummer in the band during an intermission at the Boston concert while a half dozen witnesses, including the famous Roland Hayes, looked on in horror.

Jim Europe's tragic death left both of us in a state of shock. We, too, dreamed his dream of laboring toward that day when Negro entertainers—composers, musicians, singers, and actors—would break through the color barrier stifling our talents. In picking up the pieces caused by Jim Europe's slaying, Eubie and I decided to team up as a vaudeville act.

Initial discussions for the new act took place in the Broadway offices of Pat Casey, the chief booking agent in the giant Keith

Theater organization. Casey was familiar with our parlor entertainment act with the Jim Europe organization prior to World War I. He agreed to handle our bookings. As a matter of fact, his office had booked the 369th band's national tour.

The discussion got pretty far out when some of Casey's assistants started to talk about the way we should dress for the vaudeville stage. One wag suggested that we dress like waiters and use the setting of an empty nightclub for our act. The routine, though, was to go something like this: dressed as stevedores, we'd come on stage pulling a dolly to take a piano off the pier, and, upon seeing no one around, go into our act.

That latter suggestion caused Casey to shout, "Gentlemen, this discussion is nonsense! Dammit, Sissle and Blake are drawing-room entertainers who've also performed in some of the finest clubs in this country. So, for this vaudeville act they will dress the way they've dressed in the past. Sissle, you and Blake will wear your tuxedos."

Casey decided that we should open out of town and then come into New York and appear at a break-in house as a kind of showcase for the large midtown theater owners. We opened in Bridgeport, Connecticut, and after three days we returned to New York for a booking in the Harlem Opera House. This was a real testing ground. A Keith vaudeville house on the subway circuit, the Harlem Opera House was located in a white neighborhood. We had to play to a segregated theater because residents of the community were beginning to resent having Negroes move into the area. And to top that, we opened on amateur night, when entertainers were fair game for the audience. The first five acts of the eleven-act bill were nonprofessionals.

The audience was having a ball chasing offstage the acts which preceded us. We were number seven and the only Negroes on the bill. When the curtain went up on the Sissle-Blake duo, there we stood in tuxedos with a palace backdrop, fancy piano, and a floor lamp. That Harlem Opera House audience had never seen the likes of us—a couple of Negroes in fancy getups without blackface makeup.

"Congratulations," boomed Pat Casey in his office the next day. "You fellows did a damn fine job. You'll be all right. You knocked them cold last night."

Our booking agent then went over a few more out-of-town appearances he'd lined up for the act. He suggested that we get some tuxedos made to order because "those you have are not styled for your appearance at the Palace Theater." After the agent mentioned the Palace Theater a second time, Sissle turned to Casey and Tim O'Donnell and asked innocently, "What city is this Palace Theater located in?"

Pat Casey burst into a hearty laugh.

"Tim," Casey said, "Sissle wants to know where the Palace Theater is that they're supposed to play."

Tim O'Donnell, smiling, pointed across the street to the building at Forty-seventh Street and Broadway which housed the famous Palace Theater, the dream of every vaudeville act in the country.

Our opening at the Palace on that Fourth of July week in 1919 skyrocketed us into the theatrical whirl. There, and in the cities that we later toured, we used our own compositions in the act. Our publishers, the Witmark Music Publishing Company, sent our sheet music to the Woolworth and Kresge five-and-ten-cent stores in the cities where we appeared.

We had been on the Keith vaudeville circuit for more than a year, when in August of 1920 we appeared in Philadelphia for a National Association for the Advancement of Colored People benefit at the Dunbar Theater. On that same program were Flournoy Miller and Aubrey Lyles, the famous comedy team.

It was at that time that the four of us began talking about cracking the Broadway legitimate theater. After additional discussions in New York and Boston, *Shuffle Along* began to take form. Miller and Lyles wrote the book and we provided the score. Up to the time the show opened out of town, we continued our separate acts in order to have ready cash to advance to members of the cast while the show was in its eight weeks of rehearsal.

Financial woes haunted us from place to place all during the out-of-town tryouts in such places as Washington's Howard Theater, Philadelphia's Dunbar Theater, and the one-night stand legitimate theaters in Coatsville, Reading, Allentown, and Trenton.

After what appeared to be a lifetime of frustrations, we finally opened our musical in New York City at the Sixty-third Street Theater in 1921. Many distinguished Negro artists had attempted to crash Broadway and had failed. We'd achieved the impossible.

To *Shuffle Along*, conceived at an NAACP benefit, went the honor of blazing the trail for Negro entertainers to the Broadway and legitimate stages throughout America.

Miller and Lyles had leading roles in the musical. Other show business greats appearing in the pioneering effort included Gertrude Saunders, Florence Mills, Lottie Gee, and Josephine Baker, who was a member of the chorus line. She demonstrated a flair for comic dancing. Sissle appeared in the cast, and Blake conducted the orchestra; and we also performed a specialty act in the show.

Luck played its part in the success of *Shuffle Along*. Even today we still shudder at the thought of what almost happened to "I'm Just Wild About Harry." We called in Lottie Gee, who would sing the song in the show, to get her reaction. We played it for her.

"I can't sing that song," she said. "It's a waltz. Whoever heard of a waltz in a colored show?"

We looked at each other and then at her. Blake said facetiously: "Why not? There was a waltz in one show I can mention and YOU sang it."

"Yes," she said, "but how many copies did it sell? Maybe half a dozen, and that's about all. If you could change it to a one-step. . . ."

"I'm not going to change a thing," was Blake's reaction.

But Sissle said, "Oh, yes, you are."

We discovered during the out-of-town tryouts that "Harry" wasn't getting the kind of audience response we'd hoped for, and we were about to throw it out of the show when a member of the male chorus line won a reprieve for the song. The six male dancers who went through their dance routine around Lottie Gee as she sang the lyrics had trouble making their exit because of an obstruction in the wing. The last man in the line, quick-witted Bobby Lee, who wasn't the greatest of dancers, was trapped on stage longer than he should have been. Improvising until he could make his exit, Bobby Lee went into a high-stepping strut which sent the audience into an uproar. It saved the song. Bobby Lee's routine remained in the act and helped "I'm Just Wild About Harry" become the biggest hit of the show.

Flo Mills got the lead role after Gertrude Saunders became ill and had to leave the show. Flo's show-stopper was "I'm Craving for That Kind of Love." She began the song on the apron at stage right, and the soulful restraint of her delivery was felt throughout the audience. While singing the verse, she appeared not to move a muscle. She wove a spell around the audience by her stillness and the sparkle in her eyes. As she reached the chorus, she crept slowly toward center stage with arms outstretched towards Eubie, who was conducting the orchestra in the pit. Clutching her hands, Flo chanted the words, "I'm just craving for, craving for, craving for that kind of love." And the audience went wild.

Flo Mills put such a personal stamp on the song that she killed it for sales. She was so good that nobody else wanted to do it.

Many performing artists used to attend the special Wednesday midnight show. One night, Frisco, a white comedian who came again and again to watch the Miller and Lyles routine, spotted Florenz Ziegfeld in the audience. Ziegfeld was seated in the last row with his hand covering his mouth. He would occasionally bend over. After watching him from the other side of the aisle for some time, Frisco, who stuttered, walked over to the Broadway producer and said: "Z-Z-Z-Ziggie, you know it's funny. Go ahead and l-l-laugh out loud."

Many ingredients went into making *Shuffle Along* a success. It moved fast and it was fun. It had good music, a good story, and above all, it was clean. A white patron who took the same first-row orchestra seat three or four nights a week, summed up *Shuffle Along* better than we can.

The patron said: "I bet you wonder why I come to see this show so often. I've been waiting to hear one double entendre, one 'hell' or one 'damn.' I didn't hear one. Now, I can bring my wife and daughter to see the show."

After the fourteen-month run on Broadway, two *Shuffle Along* companies toured the country for two years. The tour proved conclusively that a show by Negroes, about Negroes, and with music based on Negro rhythms could be just as salable to the general theatergoing public as any other show. Until that time, producers had used the excuse that the public just wouldn't buy this type of show, especially the downstairs society clientele, and it was this attitude that had kept Negroes out of the legitimate theater—until *Shuffle Along*.

Our success certainly made the path easier for the second Sissle and Blake Broadway venture, *Chocolate Dandies*, which opened in

1924 and featured such stars as Inez Clough, Josephine Baker, and comedian Johnny Hudgins. We were able even to revive *Shuffle Along* during World War II; it was one of the former Broadway hits sent by the USO to entertain our boys who were waiting for the ships to take them home from the European Theater of Operations.

Over the last decade, several musicals starring Negroes, though written and produced by whites, have attracted audiences to the Broadway theater. During that period, Sammy Davis, Jr. has been seen in two shows, *Mr. Wonderful* and *Golden Boy*; Lena Horne starred in *Jamaica*; *No Strings* was written for Diahann Carroll; and Leslie Uggams made her Broadway debut in *Hallelujah, Baby*.

This recent resurgence of interest in Negro entertainers on the Broadway stage is a good sign. We foresee even more opportunities opening for talented composers and lyricists, musicians, performers, and writers. In order to take advantage of these new vistas, young people who feel the need to pursue a career in the theater should first get the very best training available to them. During our career, we learned that it helped immeasurably to conduct ourselves in such a way that people just had to respect us regardless of our race. We found that there would always be people here and there who would deny us respect, because there are always people here and there who don't respect themselves. We learned to forgive them.

Another thing we learned: as in all professions, you must be businesslike. Professional deportment inspires, on the part of people to whom you hope to sell, confidence in your abilities.

Together, we had a very unusual career. We started out in 1915 during the dance craze when the music of America was going through an exciting metamorphosis. Together, our knowledge of this metamorphosis in music spans one hundred years, when you consider that many of the fellows we played with in those early days had been on the scene already for fifty years or more and that we ourselves have been in the business for fifty years. Our point here is that training and a profound familiarity with the area in which you hope to succeed are essential.

We smile knowing smiles now when we hear some Johnnies-come-lately state with such finality that jazz "came up the river from New Orleans." At the time that jazz was starting in New Orleans, we heard Negro musicians playing syncopated riffs in Baltimore and Indianapolis.

We can agree with the experts, though, who argue correctly that the Negro has put his indelible stamp on American music. Those haunting rhythms you hear in sophisticated songs today had their genesis in the Negro spiritual, field hollers, folk tunes, and the blues. The rhythms of America, which we have contributed to the culture of the new world, are a product of our African heritage.

MARGARET WALKER

The author, Margaret Walker (Mrs. F. J. Alexander), was born in Birmingham, Alabama, on July 7, 1915. After completing her undergraduate work at Northwestern University, she earned the M.A. and Ph.D. degrees from the University of Iowa.

Throughout her career, she has taught at several institutions of higher learning, including Livingstone College, West Virginia State College, and Jackson State College.

As an author she is known both for her poetry and her prose. Her poems have appeared over the years in such periodicals as *Crisis, Poetry, Opportunity, Phylon,* and the *Virginia Quarterly.* She is widely represented in several anthologies, such as *The Negro Caravan, Negro American Poetry,* and *Famous American Negro Poets.* Her short stories and articles have been published in *Creative Writing, Common Ground,* and the *Negro Digest.*

Margaret Walker's honors and awards include the Yale Award for Younger Poets, given in 1942 for her volume of poetry *For My People;* a Rosenwald Fellowship for Creative Writing in 1944; and a Ford Fellowship at Yale University in 1954. Her first novel, *Jubilee,* resulted from a Houghton Mifflin Literary Fellowship in 1966.

In addition to writing, teaching, and rearing four children, Margaret Walker has made numerous appearances as a radio, television, and platform speaker.

WILLING TO PAY THE PRICE

by Margaret Walker

HERE in America "Success" with a capital "S" is measured in materialistic terms of fame and fortune. An artist is not basically concerned with this kind of success. A creative worker dealing with the fiery lightning of imagination is interested in artistic accomplishment, and I have spent my life seeking this kind of fulfillment. As long as I live, this will be my quest; and, as such, the superficial trappings of success can have no real meaning for me. I do not really care what snide remarks my confreres make nor how searing the words of caustic critics are. Life is too short for me to concern myself with anything but the work I must do before my day is done.

If there are any single factors which have blessed my life with the best, they are: intelligent parents who not only fired my ambition and demanded that I set my sights high and be judged by standards of excellence, but also insisted that I seek spiritual values and crave righteousness and integrity more than money; remarkable teachers in three of the nation's finest academic institutions; and lessons learned from bitter experience and from fellow writers. Linked with these factors has also been an indispensable element of luck and good fortune.

True, I have faced obstacles and have been forced to run every race with a handicap: I am a Negro born in America. All my life I have been poor in the goods of the world. I am a woman. And since birth I have been dogged with ill health. Yet each of these could have been worse. Despite these handicaps and race prejudice in America, which I discovered early and have lived with all my life, I was able to complete my education, attending, while doing so, some of the nation's finest institutions. Yes, my lot might have been worse; I have often heard poor whites speak of their lack of opportunity to get such an education. As a woman I have known great personal freedom to do as I pleased and to further my career whether single or married. I have the complete fulfillment of being wife and mother and having a happy home.

Despite poverty and ill health, my needs have always been met in the nick of time. Once in a Chicago slum I was startled while riding on the elevated train and looking over the very neighborhood where I lived, to hear a woman say, "I wonder how in the world people live there!" Often it was difficult for me to obtain the twenty-five-cent fare to ride the elevated train to Evanston and classes at Northwestern during my senior year, but I managed somehow, and with the help of my wonderful teachers made A's just the same. Other Negro students often did not speak to me because they were embarrassed about the way I looked—wearing dresses and coats which had seen better days and ragged stockings. When I was working on the WPA Writers' Project, my sister and I lived on eighty-five dollars a month, but we got along because the cost of living was not high. We paid five dollars a week for a room with kitchen privileges, and mostly we cooked and ate at home. Ten dollars' worth of groceries provided staples for two weeks. A favorite meal was a can of mushroom soup, a can of corn kernels, and four weiners. On paydays we splurged on steak or oysters. I still think nothing tastes as good as porterhouse steak tasted then in Chicago. But there were days when we did not have a nickel for a White Castle hamburger, and I can remember feeling faint with the smell of food cooking and going home to sleep off my hunger. Friends often fed us, and always did so on holidays. Yet those days in Chicago give me some of the most wonderful memories in my life.

About that time a renaissance was developing in the arts: painting, acting, music, and writing. Studio parties were held in smoke-filled rooms, with much intellectual or political conversation going on; and although I never learned to drink the beer, the food was wonderful—cold cuts and rye bread and lots of pickles. On the Project many writers were struggling, some of whom were destined to become famous; among these were Willard Mottley, Richard Wright, Frank Yerby, Nelson Algren, Arna Bontemps, and Jack Conroy. This Writers' Project turned out to be one of the best writers' schools I ever attended. It was Nelson Algren who asked me the question, "What do you want for your people?" That query motivated me to finish my poem "For My People." Later, Nelson reviewed the book *For My People* when it was published. Wright and I met my first year out of college. We became fast friends and corresponded for two years after he went to New York. While I was writing poetry, he was writing the novella in *Uncle Tom's Children*, and *Native Son*. I am sure that this friendship made an indelible impression on my writing career. Marxism was the intellectual fad then, and those who were not Stalinists were Trotskyites. It was the time of the Memorial Day Massacre and the beginning of the C.I.O.; Roosevelt was our hero, the man of our Age, as youngsters in the sixties considered John F. Kennedy. Bravely, I sought to repudiate my academic background, for in this crowd it was no recommendation.

Pride in my folk heritage as a Negro was, however, very much the rage. Race pride was something I was taught as a child. My father went to Tuskegee for a few brief months in the days of Booker T. Washington, but he found what he wanted in Atlanta in the days of W. E. B. Du Bois. My mother had heard as a girl the words of Kelly Miller and Roscoe Conklin Simmons. She read poems by Paul Lawrence Dunbar to us along with John Greenleaf Whittier's "Snow-Bound." I can never remember when *Crisis* and *Opportunity* magazines were not in our house, along with the Methodist Church papers like the *Christian Advocate*, and such Negro newspapers as the *Chicago Defender*, the *Pittsburgh Courier*, and the *Louisiana Weekly*.

Later, after moving to New Orleans, we attended as many cultural programs as possible. Thus, long before my hegira to Northwestern I heard Marian Anderson, Langston Hughes, James Weldon Johnson, and Zora Neal Hurston, and saw *Green Pastures*. Throughout my high school days I made a scrapbook of famous Negro Americans, whether they were athletes, politicians, or blues singers. At school there were my mother's spring musicales and recitals and the memorable times when she accompanied a visiting artist who sang or played the violin. On Sunday afternoons in the chapel, with its rich patina of wood wainscoting, I listened to wonderful music, looked out at the sun setting, and wondered if ever there would be such a golden moment again. In Chicago during the late thirties my sister and I had such moments: in Grant Park during the summer concerts under the stars, at Orchestra Hall hearing her play with the Symphony Orchestra, and at Northwestern University hearing Harriet Monroe or Carl Sandburg read poetry.

When I was a little girl and some lady asked me what I wanted to be when I grew up, my father answered for me, "Tell her you are going to be an elocutionist!" Most people don't talk about elocution these days, and I smile now to remember the puzzled look on many people's faces when I responded to my father's suggestion. My parents were convinced early that I would become a public speaker, and I was standing before audiences by the time I was five.

I cannot remember when I learned to read; my mother taught me by the time I was four, and I in turn read the comic strips and *Tales of Uncle Wiggly* to my younger sisters. I loved books, and by the time I was eight I knew I wanted to learn to write books. My father had many volumes in his library, and I grew up believing that with the exception of human personality nothing in the world could be finer than a good book. The hope that I could become a poet seemed impossible at first, for I was laboring under the general illusion that the poet has some special mystique beyond the knowledge of ordinary human beings. In my adolescence I lost that illusion, for I wrote poetry or some kind of jingle almost every day. Earlier, when I was ten, I became enamored with the story of my great-grandmother's life, as told to me by my grandmother and as recorded in *Jubilee*, so that I nurtured the secret hope that I would learn to write prose—fiction and nonfiction—as well as poetry, free verse and traditional forms. My education and much of my environment accordingly were geared to that purpose. My parents taught school. My sisters, my brother, and I teach school. We are teachers in spite of ourselves and despite any other ambition we may have had. Yet we teach different things. One sister teaches little children because that is what she has always wanted to do. My brother teaches mathematics and social sciences in a high school despite his fervid interest in Progressive Jazz, and I teach college English because I had decided that if I ever taught school it would be on the college level.

My father must have gotten his ideas of education from Whitehead, for he followed a definite theory about our education. I never was good in arithmetic, algebra, or any form of mathematics, but I loved literature and history and I concentrated on those subjects. Once in college I thought I might switch my major to the social sciences, particularly sociology, but my father said, "No, you cannot swap horses in the middle of the stream." He strictly forbade my taking any courses in philosophy because he insisted that in my teens I was not mature enough and, besides, I lacked the logical mind. So I have learned philosophy, both idealistic and materialistic, by reading the major works of great philosophers since I left college. My father had a tendency to choose courses for all of us, and we never went wrong if we followed his advice. He also insisted that we study foreign languages early, so I had studied four languages before I was twenty. He was convinced that once a person was mature it was a mistake to try to learn a new language.

Father also believed that my writing poetry was only a puberty urge. My mother did not agree and neither did I. When I was eighteen and had completed my junior year in college, I asked him if he still thought my writing was only a puberty urge. He laughed and said, "No, I guess not, you will probably continue writing for the rest of your days." It was my father who first bought me a permanent notebook for my poems and told me to keep them together. He was a scholar, as fine as any teacher I have ever known in three great universities. He won every prize available in college and seminary for English, Greek, Latin, and Hebrew, and took his M.A. degree from Northwestern in Biblical Literature. I realize that his ambitions for me were very great despite the fact that I had disappointed him by not being a boy. If I had been a boy he would have made a preacher out of me, but since I wasn't a boy he decided to make the most of it. It was his desire that I have a Ph.D. in English before I became twenty-one, but luckily for me, neither health nor finances would permit it. Once out of college I went to work on the Writers' Project, and I was twenty-five the summer I received my M.A. degree. My father did not live to see me get this degree, but I know he would have been happy about it. He did live to enjoy For My People.

Early in my life my parents instilled certain principles and beliefs in all their children, and these principles remain thoroughly ingrained in all of us. First, they provided us with a deeply religious background. For them the Protestant ethic was Puritan to the core, a stern moralistic code of duty and responsibility, and prayer was a daily occurrence in our home. We grew up in Sunday School and church, and I was amazed when I went away from home to discover that everybody did not go to church. We were taught that we were expected to achieve and that the achievement must be one of excellence. However, we were taught not to expect excessive praise for a job well done. Even on the day my parents received a copy of *For My People*, my mother wrote a prim little note saying, "You have made us very proud." And that was that.

I do not believe in giving advice, since most people don't want it, and I am loath to set myself up as an authority on any subject, but I can pass along some of the things told to me and some of the things that I have learned from other writers:

1. Write what you know about, not about something of which you know little or nothing.
2. Work hard and revise and never be weary of trying to achieve perfection. Above all, try never to print anything of which you may be ashamed in the future.
3. Never pay to have your work published.
4. Study the masters and learn from them. Read the great writers and imitate them.
5. Become your most severe critic. Don't be easily satisfied and know when you have done the best you possibly can.

Writing poetry is not, as many people think, something that strikes one as a bolt from the blue. It is a skill that must be developed as a result of patient practice, hard work, and study.

Every spare moment of my early years was devoted to learning and developing this skill. In those years I benefited greatly from the advice and encouragement of teachers whom I shall never forget. I was also inspired and helped by a number of writers and poets whom I was fortunate enough to know, and who left an indelible impression on me. I was sixteen years old when I had the first opportunity to talk directly with a living poet, Langston Hughes, who read some of my verses one night and encouraged me to continue writing. In Chicago during my WPA days I met the writers George Dillion and Peter DeVries. George Dillion helped and encouraged me and suggested that I read all the French Symbolists. As a result, I read Baudelaire, Rimbaud, Verlaine, and Mallarmé.

I never met a writer with more drive than Richard Wright. Even though he was an intellectual giant of his time, talented to the point of genius, it was his drive that compelled him to achieve. In the workshop at Iowa University I had the firming-up that I needed to become a professional writer. All of those days were not easy, but they were very profitable. At Iowa I began writing to Stephen

Vincent Benét, and I have a small handful of letters in which he gave me good advice about writing poems, particularly ballads. Naturally I prize these letters, along with those of Richard Wright and Langston Hughes, that mark those early years.

From these random notes I think my philosophy of life should be clear. I believe anybody can achieve regardless of the handicaps —if he is willing to pay the price. Some people are born to achieve, but writers, while born talented, must work hard to develop their talents. It has always been my thesis that writing grows out of living, and not living out of writing, so that living comes first. I realize, however, that writing for many is a reason for existence.

My *raison d'être* is to express life as I see it. Everything in life comes with a price. Hard work is a foregone conclusion. Some of us as Negroes were born in slums, uneducated, mistreated, and deprived, but we have achieved in spite of this. I have always heard it said that writing is a difficult and lonely business. I would not say that I have been exactly lonely, but I do know that any writer worth his salt has had to work hard. One thing I always wanted to avoid was becoming a dilettante. I have always wanted to be a serious, full-time writer. I have been instead a full-time teacher, and nobody really writes effectively while teaching full time. Therefore, in one sense all my books are not written, and I am in that sense a failure, since I never sacrificed anything for writing. Rather, I sacrificed writing to have a family, to keep a job, to make a living. The best writers have given up everything for the sake of their art, and therein lies part of their success. Now as I face retirement from teaching, I look forward to full-time writing. It is a lifelong dream, but who knows whether it will ever come true? Perhaps I have been too late. Have I really put first things first?

I am not one who believes that my writing and my being a Negro are related purely by accident of birth. All I have ever written or desire to write is motivated by the fact that I am a Negro living in America, one of a minority group unrecognized or rejected by the dominant group. We Negroes are America's stepchildren, as Langston Hughes has so beautifully said, and we have a need to express our feelings of being rejected, of being oppressed, of being denied, and of being brutalized and dehumanized. Being a Negro in America is my central theme, with the concomitant problems of being a Negro woman, being exploited and scorned, being hated and despised. The meaning of my life is tied up irrevocably and inextricably with this theme,

All my life I have longed to see the signs go down—the signs of segregation, of degradation, and discrimination. Even as a child I wondered if I would live long enough to see this happen. For I never doubted that it would; I just wondered how long it would take, and if I would live to see the day. Now I have lived to see the signs go down, the signs I sat behind on street cars and buses, the curtains I rode behind on trains, ropes I stood behind in theaters and restaurants. In bewilderment and pain I grew up looking at the signs, and now, thank God, most of the signs are down.

I never shall forget hearing Judge Hastie say in 1952 in Jackson, Mississippi, when someone questioned whether men's hearts and minds could be changed by laws, "We are going to make segregation illegal, against the law, and then we will proceed from there." The Supreme Court and the Congress of the United States have declared segregation illegal and unconstitutional. Yet we also know that men's minds and hearts have not entirely changed. We cannot be satisfied, for school integration is still only tokenism and threatens to remain thus as long as residential segregation prevails; but we know that the start has been made.

The Negro Revolution of this decade came like a breath of fresh air blowing through America, but it has only been a light breeze, not a storm. The fundamental facts of segregation still remain. I think all of us must have held our breath when the Reverend Martin Luther King began his noble adventure in Montgomery. But when Martin Luther King went to Birmingham, I think the whole nation knew we were on our way.

We became increasingly proud of the later "sit-ins," "wade-ins," "stand-ins," and the like. All of these events, however, did not complete the change in men's hearts and minds. The earlier murders of Emmett Till and Mack Charles Parker and other shootings and attacks were followed by still other heinous crimes. The tragic death of Medgar Evers saddened us all. He was our neighbor and friend, as well as a brave young leader of the Negro people in Mississippi. As an intrepid young fighter against discrimination and segregation he gave his life, but he did not die in vain. His death shocked the world and aroused the conscience of this nation. His death and the deaths of others give us hope that there will be a better nation and a better community because they died.

As a Negro, I am perforce concerned with all aspects of the struggle for Civil Rights. As a writer, however, my commitment has to be to the one thing I can do best, and that is to the business of writing. Richard Wright used to say that nothing should come before a writer's art but his writing. Civil Rights are part of my frame of reference, since I must of necessity write always about Negro life, segregated or integrated. In the twenty-first century, perhaps, there will be no need for this view, but I belong to the twentieth century, and there are a few things left on the agenda, a few pieces of unfinished business where the Negro is concerned in America before this century ends.

I believe firmly in the goodness of the future, and that in the final analysis right will prevail—not through goodness and optimism, necessarily, but through stress and travail. I believe that man's destiny is a spiritual destiny and that God is not merely transcendent but also immanent, deeply involved in the affairs of men since men are made in His image, each with a spark of the divine and a human personality always maintaining that divine potential. Sometimes in America the future of the Negro looks hopelessly dark, but against all evil this divinity and the human spirit or human personality will shine like a light.

Am I a gradualist, an activist, a segregationist member of the Black Establishment, or where do I stand? I do not believe any Negro in good conscience can acquiesce in the vicious evil of segregation, but I also believe that not everyone is brave enough to die—yet everyone has his role. I believe my role in the struggle is the role of a writer. Everything I have ever written or hope to write is dedicated to that struggle, to our hope of peace and dignity and freedom in the world, not just as black people, or as Negroes, but as free human beings in a world community.

I know segregation has seemed to benefit some Negroes who have battened upon the oppressed, but these are not in the majority. I am a firm believer in the value of education in this struggle. It is what my great-grandparents believed. What I have in mind is not necessarily formal education. I have seen many intelligent and educated people who never went to school; however, I believe it is important to cultivate the intellect. Our schools and colleges should not strive merely to turn out graduates as we turn out goods from factories.

Perhaps I do not understand fully the meaning of the slogan "Black Power." Sometimes I think I do and then again I wonder. Richard Wright's book *Black Power* concerned the emerging nations of Africa and social ferment in Asia. "Black Power" as a slogan for Negro Americans is something else.

On one issue I am clear. I do not believe that hating any man solves the problem of race or any other problem. The failures of a capitalistic society in the final stages of high financial imperialism need not be imitated by the victims of such a materialistic system. I firmly believe that hatred, like anger, works on the physical glandular system as well as on the moral fiber of our nation and, in doing so, can bring no positive good. Although I do not believe in servility, I do not believe that we should insult our friends or say we do not need them because they are white. Perhaps our genuine friends will overlook our bad manners, but I wonder if our children will do so and not imitate our precept and example?

What the white man has done to us through centuries of oppression is patently clear. He has brutalized and stigmatized us and tried to dehumanize us, but we, like Job, have nevertheless maintained our own integrity. The mechanistic system itself makes for dehumanization, impersonality, and depersonalization, but the system also is doomed to change as all things change.

The Negro has a great spiritual role to play in America. He has already evidenced that role in his folk contribution to the literature, music, and religious life of America. Negroes helped to build America, and a full knowledge of Negro history reveals that all American life has been influenced by them. We do have a special mystique, and it has not come from hatred. In the deep welter of Negro emotion, suffering, and pride we have a profound spirituality to offer America on the road to the fulfillment of her great destiny. If she refuses and turns away, we cannot use that as an excuse for our not offering this precious and rare gift.

I do not deny, however, the importance of political action and of social revolution. I know that the thinker is slow to act and that fact may damn him; but I also know that before action can implement thought, there must first be an idea. I believe that as a teacher my role is to stimulate my students to think; after that, all

I can do is guide them. In a century since freedom, our great job as black people has been to develop intellectuals who could lead us and who, in turn, could transform ideas into action. This, I believe, is the way, the truth, and the life.

If Western civilization steadily declines and the twenty-first century finds the balance of power to lie in Asia and Africa, the destiny of Negro Americans will nevertheless be bound up with the destiny of America. White America may very well be ending Western civilization as the nonwhite people in the world ride a high road to destiny. But unless Negroes quit these enslaved shores, we are still Americans, unrecognized though we may be. Perhaps there is hope that our black cities like our black art and black pride and black suffering will change the political course of America and alter her social system so that justice and brotherhood may prevail before it is too late. I am not sure we can depend on that. White people ask Southern Negroes daily, "Don't you think race relations are better? Don't your people feel that they have made progress?" In Mississippi, where I am now, these are hard questions in the face of all the violence we have seen. Just as in Montgomery, Birmingham, and Selma, Alabama; New Orleans and Plaquemine, Louisiana; Memphis and Clinton, Tennessee; Little Rock, Arkansas; and Albany, Georgia—we have many problems still in Grenada, Natchez, Jackson, and McComb.

Segregation has been outlawed and made illegal, and the United States Government no longer gives legal sanction to Jim Crow, but all the people's hearts have not changed. The violent, ignorant, rabid, and unjust are still among us. Whether they will gain political and economic control and thus continue to poison our lives as well as their own is an open question. Whether the men of good will who have been afraid to speak out or stand up and be counted on pain of economic pressure, political reprisal, or violent death will come forward now and assert their strength is another question. But we Negroes know that America stands at the crossroads of Western civilization and that we black people are truly the test of democracy. We are the conscience and the soul of America. Either we must all perish together or we must all learn to live together, and white citizens essentially must make this decision. Scientists tell us that in this new Space Age man has his self-destruction already in his own hands. Perhaps we are on the verge of annihilation, and the grasping materialistic economy behind the hypocrisy of spiritual idealism will go down in ashes to defeat.

But if we are not on this verge, and if America can weather the Negro Revolution and successfully meet the test of genuine American democracy, then the twenty-first century will usher in the millenium with social justice, international understanding, and peace for all members of the human race.

LOUIS ARMSTRONG

Born on July 4, 1900, in New Orleans, Louisiana, Louis Armstrong —musician, showman, stage, screen, and television star—has been called by Hugh Panassié "the greatest of all jazz musicians," and "one of the most extraordinary creative geniuses that all music has ever known."

His interest in music began at an early age when he and some of his boyhood friends formed a quartet and strolled the streets of the Storyville section of his native New Orleans, singing new jazz songs and passing the hat for pennies. His formal introduction to music, however, came in his early teens, after he had been sent to the Waifs' Home for a year's discipline on the charge of firing a pistol while celebrating New Year's Eve. It was here that he learned the rudiments of reading music, and by the time he left the institution, he had become the leader of the Home's brass band.

Still only fourteen years old, he was too young to obtain a regular job in a band, but sold newspapers and worked in a dairy, earning an extra dollar a night on occasion by playing in one of the smaller night spots.

It was about this time that "King" Oliver, a musician and local idol who was known for his powerful and original trumpet work, began giving him lessons. When Oliver left for Chicago in 1917, Louis Armstrong took his place in Kid Ory's Band. Two years later he was playing in an orchestra on the Mississippi excursion boat *Dixie Bell*. In 1921 he left the *Dixie Bell* and obtained a job at the Orchard Cabaret in New Orleans at a salary of twenty-one dollars a week.

On these modest beginnings Louis Armstrong built a career which—while not without its ups and downs—has carried him to the heights of show business. He has not only been associated with such well-known names in the field of music as "King" Oliver, Fletcher Henderson, Erskine Tate, and Lew Russell, but has had during his career several bands of his own.

131

It is as a personality in his own right, however, that Louis Armstrong has made his greatest contribution. Throughout a long and illustrious career he has made more than one thousand recordings, many of which are considered collectors' items today, and has also written approximately two dozen songs. He has, in addition, been featured in a number of motion pictures.

One of the brightest stars in the entertainment field—both nationally and internationally—his name and fame are legendary, not only as a recording artist, but as a stage and television personality as well. His showmanship is known in practically every part of the world, and through his music and his creative genius he has become one of this nation's most effective ambassadors of good will.

BLOWING MY HORN

by Louis Armstrong

AS an American born in the year 1900, I have observed many changes that have occurred in the world—changes that have affected people all over the globe—and particularly changes that have touched the lives of my own people during these past sixty-eight years. I am not a writer and don't pretend to be one. I generally express my feelings by doing what I do best—blowing my horn— just as other people with different abilities express theirs in their own way, a poet with his poetry, for example, or an artist with his brush. So I don't know whether this is an essay or not, but I do know that the little I have to say will attempt to describe my feelings with respect to the part Negroes are playing today, both in international affairs and affairs at home, and the part they have yet to play in this exciting period of history. From where I sit—I've said before that I'm not a writer, and I'd like to add that I'm not an orator or a politician either—I'm proud to see the interest that young Negroes, as well as those not so young, are taking in what is going on today. I'm even prouder of the fact that they are actively participating in today's events.

There was a time not too long ago when our race was limited in the areas in which we could make a contribution, but that period in our lives is now history. Doors are opening now that my contemporaries and I never dreamed would open. Our young men and women are turning to other fields besides law, teaching, medicine, the stage, and music. Of course, we still need and will always need good lawyers and doctors and teachers, but we also need to take full advantage of America's many other opportunities and encourage more and more of our young people to go into science and engineering, and into all the newer fields that are developing, such as electronics, data processing, and space technology. It gives me a nice warm feeling to note also the progress that our race is making in politics and foreign service. This is as it should be in a democracy, and I'm sure that many Negroes in these new fields will eventually replace people like me in the Hall of Fame. Today we can point with great satisfaction and a large measure of self-respect to Negro mayors of great American cities, to Negro ambassadors and others of high rank in the nation's diplomatic service, and to congressmen in both the House of Representatives and the Senate.

I believe that the greatest contribution the Negro has made to our country up until now has been in the arts. This is particularly true in the field of music because of the efforts of so many famous performers in the past and because of the talents of such present-day artists as Duke Ellington, Harry Belafonte, Dizzy Gillespie, and the many others who enjoy world-wide reputations.

What has been done by the Negro composer and theatrical artist is irreplaceable. It is a part of our history and culture and has long expressed what the Negro feels inside—all the happiness and un-happiness and yearning for a better and more understanding world. And certainly today, with the world torn apart by conflicts between nations, between races, between classes, and with strife even among those who should be united in a common cause—there is nothing more important than developing an understanding between dif-ferent groups and peoples. One of the most effective ways of achieving this understanding is through the arts, and especially through music. Music is a universal language, the one language in which individuals can speak to individuals and races can speak to races without need of interpreters or translators and without fear of misunderstanding.

It is the musical world that I am most informed about, and I don't think that any other race or group has contributed more than the Negro to music—to its writing or its performance. And the Ne-gro, I am sure, will continue to make his contribution in this area. But today, with new doors opening, our talented young people are not restricted to the limited choices available to their parents. Years ago—in 1929, to be exact—I wrote a song, "Go South, Young Man." Today I would express my sentiments by saying, "Go any-where your talent takes you, young man. The barriers are falling, and our race's future is up to you!"

DIAHANN CARROLL

Diahann Carroll, prominent singer-actress, is a frequent guest on television's leading variety shows. She is regularly featured in headline engagements in the nation's most celebrated places of entertainment and has achieved stardom on Broadway. Miss Carroll has been hailed by critics, fellow artists, and the public alike for her exciting performance abilities.

Born in the Bronx, New York, in 1935, Diahann Carroll always wanted to be a singer. When she was ten years old, she won a Metropolitan Opera scholarship, which subsequently led to her attendance at the High School of Music and Art. After her graduation, still uncertain of a show business career, she entered New York University to study sociology.

By this time, however, performing had become so increasingly important to her that she auditioned for a part in the revue *Jazz Train*, which was being assembled by showman Lou Walters. Although the show never materialized, Walters was so impressed by her performance that he described her as "the greatest natural talent I've heard in twenty-five years" and arranged for her to appear on the *Chance of a Lifetime* TV show, on which she set a record for female artists by winning for three consecutive weeks.

These appearances on the *Chance of a Lifetime* show led to more engagements in television. In this medium she has become an international favorite, winning great success on British television screens as well as on those at home. She was one of the first American stars to make a guest appearance on the BBC's variety program *International Cabaret*. Among the better known American programs on which she has been featured are *The Danny Kaye Show*, *The Hollywood Palace*, *The Ed Sullivan Show* and *The Dean Martin Show*. She has also appeared in such special TV productions as *The Strolling Twenties*.

Her Broadway career was launched in 1954 when she impressed critics and audiences alike in *House of Flowers*. Later, as the star of

Richard Rodgers' *No Strings*, she again won critical and public acclaim. Turning from Broadway to Hollywood, Miss Carroll co-starred in *Porgy and Bess* and in *Paris Blues*. She also played a straight dramatic role as a star in Otto Preminger's Paramount release *Hurry Sundown*.

Now one of the leading entertainers on the show business scene, Diahann Carroll was recently signed to a long-term contract by Columbia Records and is looking forward to a busy recording career in addition to her many other activities. She is currently starring in her own NBC-TV series, "Julia," one of the most popular new shows on television.

CHANCE OF A LIFETIME

by Diahann Carroll

IN show business today there are many young people who are making successful careers for themselves, and I see a great many others who hope to do the same and are eager to begin. I often wonder if they realize the kind of sacrifices they will have to make to maintain this kind of life. I know I didn't. Perhaps none of them would get started if they could see what it was going to mean! Actually, I didn't have any real desire to be a performer, at least not until I had been heading that way for quite a while. My biggest ambition as a child was to be roller-skate champion of the world. Every afternoon when I had finished my homework and my chores, I took off down the street on my roller skates. It was probably very good for me—most children need some kind of strenuous exercise—but I think the reason I loved it was that I felt as free as a bird and could take in the sights and sounds around me as I skated along. It's a feeling you don't have often after you have committed yourself to a career.

In my childhood I was surrounded by music—our neighborhood was full of it—and my parents often took me to Radio City or to local theaters, so that I saw a great many live performances while I was very young. As colored entertainers were not uncommon, Negro performers became familiar to me early in my life. Realizing that I was interested in music, my parents permitted me to decide which instrument I would like to play. Like most middle-class Negro children, I chose piano, but later grew to hate the long hours of practice. I first discovered I really liked to sing when I joined a children's choir called The Tiny Tots at the Abyssinian Baptist Church in New York. To be truthful, I loved all kinds of music. In my neighborhood we heard mostly what was then called rhythm and blues. It is no wonder then that I leaned toward popular music, because that was what I heard the most. Later, when I began thinking about an audience, that kind of music seemed to be what people wanted to hear, and I wanted them to listen to me.

The turning point in my life came in junior high school, when a guidance counselor advised me to apply to the High School of Music and Art in Harlem. I began to realize that if I were to take a musical career seriously there would be things I'd have to give up: going to a different school meant being separated from my friends, for one thing, and I was quite reluctant to make that decision. I realized that I would not have time to play with my friends and be a part of neighborhood goings-on. It was a lonely decision, and a lonely goal; but my mother felt it was important that I change my environment, so I decided to go. It was a new life for me, and for the first time I was made aware that I was not playing a game. I had responsibilities which were beginning right away and could not be put off until I felt ready for them.

The work at my new school was difficult. I had never experienced such concentration, and it was a little frightening to realize how hard I had to work if I wanted to stay. At the same time it was exciting because the students really cared about the work they were doing and the teachers really cared about the students. You can't help but develop a strong sense of loyalty for a place where you find such enthusiasm and encouragement, and since I graduated I've been back there many times.

I went to college at New York University. In the evenings I did my school assignments and was employed at the same time answering the telephone at Ophelia de Vore's Modeling School, where I had done some modeling during my high school days. One evening a call came through from a man named Lou Walters, who was trying to package a show to take to Europe. Even though I had no intention of quitting college and going to Europe, I thought I would attend the auditions; and while I was sitting in the audition hall, I began to feel confidence in myself and thought, "Maybe I can do that." My fear dwindled. I got up and sang, and was asked to sing again. I noticed that everyone had not been asked to sing a second time, and I'm sure I sang the next song much better just because of that. Within a few weeks I found myself with a contract and a manager, and not long after that I went on a TV show called "Chance of a Lifetime"—a show for people who were in the business but who had not really "made it." I won the $1000 prize on that show three times, giving me total winnings of $3000, and that was the real beginning of my career, as my father at that point felt that I should drop out of college and see what I could do in show business. I began singing in night clubs, which was a very strange and very difficult experience. For a while I tried to keep on going to school, but I just couldn't continue because I was falling asleep in class every day. Once more I had to make a choice and accept the consequences.

When you're young and inexperienced, you think you can do everything and still have some time left over. I soon found out that the kind of time show business demands doesn't leave room for much else. I was learning how to perform, finding out what kind of music I wanted to sing, learning how to use the talent I had and how to refine it—I worked much longer than an eight-hour day, and the glamour that people associate with show business was all very far away.

I hadn't realized what it was like to work such long hours. I would leave my home in the morning, go over to a rehearsal hall on Ninth Avenue in New York City, and work all morning until the break for lunch. After lunch I would go back and work until evening. As often as it could be managed, I was taken still later in the evening to see other performers in order to study their techniques. Usually I would get home thoroughly exhausted around two or three o'clock in the morning. The working hours in show business are simply incredible. There is no such thing as the comfortable life; there are many sacrifices to be made, particularly for a woman.

In spite of my earnings, I was always broke: every dime that I made went into my music, more lessons, and my on-stage clothes. Show people are supposed to be rich, but even in the last two years I've only been able to keep a little of the money I've made. Even if you do make money, you can't expect to have leisure. If you have leisure it's either because you aren't working or it means you won't be working in the near future. There is no limit to practicing and rehearsing unless you're at the end of your career.

My advice to young people who want to be performers is that they understand from the beginning that show business is *business* more than it is *show*. Don't start out with the illusion that you're going to have a good time and take it easy, because this is one of the most difficult careers you can choose, and you have to be prepared to give everything you have. When you have to sacrifice so much, the only satisfaction that makes it worthwhile is your own sense of dedication. The more you give, the stronger that sense becomes, and this is your best reward.

The kind of "inner peace" that most people strive for is not one of the automatic rewards of show business, either. To achieve this kind of peace, I think you have to be honest about what you are and what you want to be, or hope you can be. For me, the hardest thing to be honest about, to make a decision about and to become "peaceful" about, is the kind of mother I am. I am not—and cannot be—always the kind of mother I want to be, and I can never be the kind of mother that mine was, always at home for me. Show business is especially hard on a woman when she wants to take on the role of wife and mother, because she is primarily a worker and traveling performer, and it is not a situation that makes it easy to create a family life. I've had to deal with this because I've tried to be a wife and mother. I can give my daughter, Suzanne, many things my mother could not give me, but there are also things that Suzanne will miss because of my career. I mean, after all, I'm a vaudevillian, I'm a strolling player, I'm a constant traveler—and none of these connote "the proper mother." But no parent is perfect, and no childhood is perfect. If I were to give up my career in order to live up to somebody else's standards of motherhood, I would be unhappy; and that would make my child unhappy, too. So we've had to work it out, and it can work, if it is not a lie. The head of my daughter's school says that Suzanne is a happy child, and that although I am what they call an "absentee mother," my presence and influence are felt. I am content with just that. And Suzanne is part of a generation that seems to me to have a wide-open future.

What do I think about race relations in the world today? The black-white relations have taken a very interesting turn, and I'm glad that I've had the chance to witness it. I've seen my country come around to recognition. I say that things have changed, that it's a wonderful time to be alive, and to be black. In earlier years, I saw silent black people who took blows and never thought of organizing to plan a way out. It is touching to look at my parents and see the expressions on their faces, and then so gratifying to look at young people and see the new confidence in *their* eyes, the new expressions on *their* faces, and to know that black children coming along will have this new expression, this new attitude about themselves. It's exciting! It's exciting to be alive NOW.

Science

PERCY L. JULIAN

The present Director of the Julian Research Institute in Franklin Park, Illinois, and President of Julian Associates, Inc., Percy L. Julian was born in Montgomery, Alabama, on April 11, 1899. He received the A.B. degree from DePauw University in 1920, the M.A. degree from Harvard University in 1923 as an Austin Fellow, and the Ph.D. degree from the University of Vienna, Austria, in 1931.

He began his academic career at Fisk University, where he was Instructor in Chemistry from 1920 to 1922. As a Harvard Fellow, he engaged in research from 1923 to 1926. After serving as Professor of Chemistry at West Virginia State College during the academic year 1926–27, he became the Head of the Department of Chemistry at Howard University. From 1932 to 1936 he was a Research Fellow at DePauw University. During the period from 1936 to 1953, he was employed by the Glidden Company as Director of Research, Soya Products Division, Vegetable Oil and Food Division, and Manager of Fine Chemicals. In 1954 Dr. Julian became the Founder-President of the Julian Laboratories, Inc., and of Laboratorios Julian de Mexico, S. A., Mexico City, both of which he headed for ten years until his retirement in 1964.

A scholar and a prolific writer, he has approximately 160 scientific publications to his credit and has obtained more than 100 patents, not only in the United States but in Switzerland, Guatemala, Australia, Great Britain, South Africa, Mexico, the Netherlands, France, and Canada, as well. The late Professor Arthur Beckett Lamb of Harvard University stated, "His papers were the first from the pen of a Negro as senior author ever to be submitted to a reputable journal of chemistry in this country."

In spite of his numerous scientific activities, Dr. Julian has found time to render distinguished public service. He is a member of the Board of Trustees of Howard University, Fisk University, DePauw University, Roosevelt University, and Southern Union College; of the Board of Directors of the Chicago Theological Seminary; and of the Board of Regents, State of Illinois Colleges and Universities. He is also a member of the Executive Board of the Chicago Chapter of the National Conference of Christians and Jews and of the Board of Directors of the NAACP Legal Defense and Educational Fund, and the Center for the Study of Democratic Institutions.

His numerous honors and awards include the following: the Spingarn Medal Award, NAACP (1947); the Distinguished Service Award, the Phi Beta Kappa Association of the Chicago Area (1949); the "Chicagoan of the Year" Award, the *Chicago Sun-Times* and the Junior Chamber of Commerce (1950); the "Old Gold Goblet" Award, DePauw University (1951); the Honor Scroll Award, the American Institute of Chemists (1964); the Annual Silver Plaque Award, the National Conference of Christians and Jews (1965); the Founders Day Award, Loyola University, Chicago (1967); the Merit Award of the Chicago Technical Societies Council (1967); and the Chemical Pioneer Award, American Institute of Chemists (1968). He is also a Fellow of the American Institute of Chemists, of the Chemical Society of London, and of the New York Academy of Science.

ON BEING SCIENTIST,

HUMANIST, AND NEGRO

by Percy L. Julian

FEW scientists in our nation over the past fifty years have enjoyed the distinction of being recognized humanists. The few who tried the tightrope intellectual maneuvering of embracing both science and the humanities have been suspect in their own discipline and ignored by the chauvinistic devotees of the humanities. Indeed, since the early years of the century, the latter group has considered science the greatest threat to the essential curriculum of the ideal university.

The simmering battle between science and the humanities was hotly joined in 1920 when Professor Irving Babbit of Harvard wrote that delightful little book entitled *Literature and the American College*. In it he warned, "The humanities must today be defended against the encroachments of the physical sciences, even as they once had to be defended against the dogmas of theology." As scientific knowledge expanded, as scientific literature multiplied, as scientific technology modified old industries and spawned new ones hitherto never dreamed of, as the possession of things became the dominant obsession of the twentieth century, and as the colleges and universities found the kaleidoscopic array of science courses crowding into near oblivion the traditional liberal arts balance between the two major sets of disciplines—as all of these occurred, the conflict increased in bitterness.

Robert Maynard Hutchins, in his article "Science, Scientists and Politics," thinks of most scientists as men of fractional or pseudo-culture and warns that the problems facing our world are not going to be solved by such men. "I wish, at the outset," he says, with one of the charming darts that only Hutchins can throw, "to repudiate

C. P. Snow, who intimates in one of his books that scientists should be entrusted with the world because they are a little better than other people. My view, based on long and painful observation, is that professors are somewhat worse than other people, and that scientists are somewhat worse than other professors." These denunciations, though obviously unfair in many respects to the scientists—who are but products of the shifting emphases of their times—do, nevertheless, have some basis in fact. The fruits of the controversy may certainly enrich the totality of our educational process.

It is ironic that in this controversy the Negro scientist has been overlooked, for he has bridged the gap between humanism and science, if not always by choice, certainly then by circumstance. Living in a segregated society, or ghetto in the broad sense of the term, he has had to concern himself with the problems of his fellow-men as a humanist, while at the same time pursuing his career as best he could as a scientist.

Historically the Negro student of science has not been able to enjoy the luxury of exclusive devotion to his discipline. The American ghetto and the American brand of apartheid made the Negro with genuine scientific talent and scientific yearnings probably the most poignantly tragic intellectual schizophrenic of the first half of the twentieth century. The inviolate seclusion of the laboratory was never vouchsafed to him, even for a few hours a day. The problems of the ghetto trespassed mercilessly upon his "scientific privacy." He was expected, strangely enough by his colleagues of both races, to be a humanist by becoming involved in social problems, which no one expected of his white fellow scientists. Moreover, up to just a few years ago, the ghetto was his total life abode; he lived there and he worked there. Ghetto life demanded that he be an "all-round man," no matter how "flat on some sides" his love of science might influence him to be. Hardly had he thrown himself into an all-absorbing scientific problem when a racial situation ruthlessly demanded his presence on a human relations committee, or on a study committee to make protests to some establishment that was attempting to make miserable his life and the life of his people. Moreover, apartheid exclusion from the society of his peers (since no outstanding college or university of the majority race even in the North dared or even desired to offer him a post) made his doctor's degree much of a farce: he usually taught students of the ghetto, most of whom knew neither arithmetic nor elementary English. Even public libraries of his field were denied to him in the Southern areas where he lived and worked. Of course, industry excluded him almost completely from an exploitation of his education or his latent scientific talent. Ghetto poverty was so devastating that it required a dreamer and almost a fool to think of education in any other terms than the development of marketable skills, and thus latent scientific talent almost exclusively went into medicine.

The Negro physician and the undertaker in earlier days were among the few who could provide at least some of the aspects of low-middle-class living for their families. The Negro pharmacist, if he could scrape together the means for funding his own business, fared well until the chain drug stores virtually drove him out of business.

But there were a few dreamers or fools who dared to follow their urges toward pure science. Ernest Just, who somehow found his way to a Phi Beta Kappa Key and a Dartmouth College degree with a major in English in 1907, went back to the ghetto to teach. Years later, we find him at the University of Chicago, earning a Ph.D. degree in Zoology under the tutelage of Frank Lillie. Just's beautiful papers, dealing mostly with artificial parthenogenesis, represented the first respectable scientific contributions from the pen of a Negro as the senior author. Going back to the ghetto to teach, after securing his doctor's degree, he suffered the nine months' isolation of the school year until the surcease of a summer's retreat at the Woods Hole Marine Biology Center gave him the opportunity to bury himself in creditable investigations.

It was in 1916 when St. Elmo Brady became the first Negro in American history to receive a Ph.D. degree in chemistry. What happened to this brilliant student and why, is not only an important part of the cultural history of the Negro American; it illuminates the Negro intellectual's struggles for an understanding of his lot by the majority race.

The awarding of this advanced degree took place in a day when almost every aspiring young Negro student could read in Negro newspapers or in Crisis (the NAACP organ) the names of every man of his race who had won a degree at colleges and universities throughout the nation. Young people awaited their local newspaper, or particularly Crisis (whose list was nationwide), with eagerness. Few announcements have ever meant more to the Negro youngster.

The inspiring news of St. Elmo Brady's degree reached me in the summer of 1916, at my home in Montgomery, Alabama, just as I was applying for admission to college without ever having attended an accredited high school. With only one public high school (in Birmingham) for hundreds of thousands of Negroes in all of Alabama, I had gone to the State Normal School for Negroes in Montgomery.* Brady's accomplishment strengthened my determination to attend college, and—what was a miracle to me— I was subsequently admitted in 1916 to DePauw University in Greencastle, Indiana, on probation and as a "sub-freshman." I remained a "sub-freshman" for two years while I carried high school courses in the remnants of the old Asbury Academy, along with my full program of freshman and sophomore work. The junior year records my first emancipation from college anonymity to full-fledged college standing.

As I recall those days of racial blight, and what they have done for our nation, North and South, I cannot but cite other miracles: the accomplishments of Joe Bibb from the same community, who went to Harvard and achieved eminence in the field of law; of Myles Paige, who went to Columbia and became an eminent New York judge (just recently retired); of Nat King Cole, who, with his persuading personality and winning voice, sang himself into the hearts of millions of Americans; of Joe Louis, who, with poor grammar but with gentlemanly determination, made the hearts of Americans stand still as the radio blared forth his victories; of Willie Mays, who still continues to dazzle baseball fans with his spectacular feats—all of these and many more from the "dark, grey towns" of Alabama!

* Founded in Marion, Alabama, by a Scotsman, William Burns Patterson, who had enlisted the services of some brilliant young Northern white men and women as teachers, the school was burned to the ground by whites in 1888. Patterson, on the advice of a benevolent governor of that time, the Honorable Thomas Seay, moved his school to the capital, where he could receive more "protection." Earlier, when his funds had neared exhaustion, Patterson had appealed for and received state aid. But in 1915 the legislature of Alabama passed a law prohibiting any white person from teaching in a Negro school receiving state aid. Thus, the school was crippled at a time when Negro college graduates throughout the nation, to say nothing of Alabama, were few indeed.

Like many others who had come from Alabama, the brilliant
St. Elmo Brady, A.B., A.M., Ph.D., was blissfully ignorant of what
the future actually had in store for him. When he left the University of Illinois he decided to go back to the ghetto, indeed to
Alabama (Tuskegee) to teach. How can anyone completely describe the American ghetto and what, in particular, it has meant to
a people recently emerged from a slavery that kept them in total
ignorance and, in fact, in total isolation from those influences of
Western culture that created the so-called "melting pot" for
European immigrants? The description of this ghetto is as difficult
for the Negro American as is the understanding of its real devasta-
tion by the uninitiated. There has been no other ghetto like it in
the history of mankind.

In 1917 Brady went to Tuskegee, an institution for which Booker
Washington had been compelled to request state aid, and which,
therefore, fell under the 1915 statute, making it "off limits" to any
real assimilation into Western culture. Who was to be taught and
from whom could fellowship in imaginative and creative thinking
be garnered? Where was there in the state even a university chemistry department that would let him use its library—to say nothing
of its equipment—even if he had been willing to do so in a segregated room? Nowhere! Where was there even enough money to
provide him with journals in which he might read the findings of
creative men—men like him with a gift from the gracious God of
destiny, but a gift that would only perish like the finest flower in a
society of weeds?

This man, Brady, was an inveterate reader of his science; he was
hungry for knowledge and actually spent bread money for journals.
He could have been guided by wiser and more fearless teachers into
a creative life that would have done great credit to his country.
Instead, even well-meaning leaders in American thought were so
convinced in that day of the virtue of two severely monolithic racial
and cultural structures within a so-called democratic society moni-
tored by the majority race, that men like Brady had no place to
go but the ghetto. Granted, he was needed there to train other
Negro students, and that he did; but the fact of the matter is
that the apartheid concept destroyed the greatest possibility at
that time of getting Brady and others on the scientific creative

roster. Those teachers could not grasp what it would have meant in inspiration to hundreds of intellectually hungry Brady admirers, if his own alma mater or another major university had given him an instructorship and perhaps later a professorship in an atmosphere where his latent creative talent might have blossomed. Most of all, they knew nothing of the slow death that came to creative impulse in the ghetto of that day. Brady's really brilliant students could readily discern his plight and did not choose his path; they went into medicine.

Indeed, it is a wonder that Brady himself ever got to Illinois. A wise old man of his race, Thomas Talley of Fisk, knew well the ghetto and wanted his brilliant student out of it. He literally hounded him until Brady gave up the idea of studying medicine and went to the Illinois graduate school. I call it a wonder, because I shall never forget a week of anxious waiting in 1920 to see if I could get to graduate school. I had worked hard for four years with the inspiration of Brady's degree always in mind. My father wanted me to study medicine (my two brothers are physicians), and though I wanted to please him, I desired to study chemistry. The Phi Beta Kappa elections were over, and I had won my key—with it, I understand, the highest grade rating in my class. It was tradition in that day at DePauw—and still is—for the head of the Department of Chemistry to find graduate fellowships for all of the majors who wished to go on to the Ph.D. I stood by as day by day my fellow students in chemistry came by saying, "I am going to Illinois"; "I'm going to Ohio State"; "I'm going to Michigan"; "I'm going to Yale." "Where are you going?" they asked, and they answered for me, "You must be getting the Harvard plum!"

I could stand the suspense no longer. I went to Professor Blanchard from North Carolina, as staunch a friend as he knew how to be then, and certainly later my most unforgettable friend, and asked timidly, "Professor, did you possibly get me a fellowship?" And then this dear fellow with resignation told me, "Now, now, Julian, I knew you would be asking me that. Come into my office." And there he showed me numerous letters from men who had really meant "god" to me—great American chemists of their day. And they had written him, "I'll take your Mr. ——, but I'd advise you to discourage your bright colored lad. We couldn't get him a job when he's done, and it'll only mean frustration. In industry, research demands co-work, and white boys would so sabotage his work that an industrial research leader would go crazy! And, of course, we couldn't find him a job as a teacher in a white university. Why don't you find him a teaching job in a Negro college in the South? He doesn't need a Ph.D. for that!"

And so the good Professor, with a deep sigh, said, "Don't be discouraged, Julian. I think I have found just the place for you. The President of Fisk University will be here tomorrow to see you, and I'm sure he will give you a position. You are going to make a great teacher." There went my dreams and hopes of four years, and as I pressed my lips to hold back the tears, I remembered my breeding, braced myself, and thanked him warmly for thinking of me. And the next day, Fayette Avery MacKenzie of Fisk did come, and I went to Fisk to work as an instructor in chemistry under Professor Talley, the same wise, old man who had sent Brady off to graduate school!

I went back into the ghetto blissfully ignorant of all the descriptions I have just given of it. Fortunately, I found brilliant students who challenged me, forcing me to work long past midnight to keep a step or two ahead of them. It was the greatest challenge I had ever had up to that time; it was a challenge that only increased my yearning to complete my formal education. Two years later I was admitted to Harvard on an Austin Fellowship for one year, during which I earned a master's degree. This fellowship stipulated that I return to teaching. Fisk had been a place of great inspiration, but I began to have fears for a future only in the ghetto.

By and large, the American ghetto has been, as far as the nourishment and blossoming of Negro talent is concerned, little more than a desert. While a few outstanding men have found it fruitful—most of these in the social sciences where source material was rich indeed—many scholars in its environment have suffered a strange and regrettable intellectual death. In the most generous terms, I have come to see it as a society of "one-eyed men in the kingdom of the blind." While some have been relatively one-eyed, and most have been relatively blind, the definition still stands. Certainly one-eyed men, or relatively one-eyed men, have been kings in the ghetto kingdom. Many of us have been too loyal to one another, or too fearful, to dare face up to the stark, degrading truth of the ghetto. The brilliant young man just out of school, with his honors glittering about him, walks into this kingdom anointed as a god by many of the less brilliant. The older, once quite brilliant, but now almost totally dead members of the intellectual community do not even view him with that kind of skepticism that might prod him on to proving himself. Tired and weary, they join in the hosannas to the young giant. Perhaps they sincerely want to encourage him, but they have forgotten how it should be done. They have forgotten that as they, years earlier, looked around and recognized their own superiority, they became victims of a strange psychological law: they began to feel that they must be gods; they ceased the rigid introspection that sustained scholarship demands; they stopped looking for truth; and they fell prey to self-worship.

It is rare for such a "god" to closet himself with his other self and ask the latter, "Who am I and what am I anyway?" Rather, the next step is a gradual but definite erosion of his intellectual honesty. He begins to make believe; he *talks* of what he is doing until he really *believes* that he *is* doing, while indeed he is already impotent. Soon there is no turning back. He has crowned himself *king*, and literally signed his own intellectual death certificate. Such has been and still is, to a great degree, the heritage of the American ghetto. There are a few brave souls in it who have remained aloof from its destructiveness; many—and too many, alas—are caught in its clutches without wondering, "Where went the glorious hopes of my youth?"

And there is a by-product of apartheid: the *raison d'être* and rationalization mechanism of the ghetto. Eager to calm the grumblings of their consciences, members of the establishment seek some way to make amends to the obviously talented whom they know they have plagued by blocking them from advancement. When a talented person comes up with an above-average accomplishment, they praise him with exalted exaggeration—all out of proportion to the real value of his contribution. This provides a dangerous temptation for the young achiever. Unless he has enough character and foresight to be coldly objective and to keep himself subjected to rigid self-examination, he may suffer the fate that comes to many vain men. If he yields to the plaudits and crowns himself a king, his self-destruction has begun—it is only a question of time before he, too, becomes an intellectual sham and a faker.

For the young would-be scholar of integrity whose sensitivities are deeply wounded by this uncalled-for exaggeration, such moments are often painful and costly embarrassments. Well do I remember two such incidents in my own scientific career. I had just brought to completion my first small industrial "triumph." My co-workers and I had put into production, on a daily multiple-ton output, a process for the isolation, with controlled properties, of the major protein species of the soy bean. It was the product of hard work, and it was already proving its industrial potential for the coating and sizing of book and magazine paper, the coating of labels which permitted improved printing, and the waterproofing of cartons. Moreover, one could foresee its ultimate significance for feeding millions of protein-starved people in backward countries. I had some right to be proud of earning my way with a company that exhibited great courage in making me its director of research. One day, a prominent protein specialist, in the company of one of my superiors, visited the laboratory. Naturally, the congratulations of this recognized chemical authority warmed my heart. We began to talk of the micelle size of this unique protein, of its content of amino acids essential to life, and of its comparison in various characteristics to casein, the principal protein of milk. Imagine my surprise when my superior broke in and said, "Dr. Julian has just completed the synthesis of *insulin*," and noting my bewilderment, he added quickly, "He is too modest to talk of his accomplishments, but we will soon be announcing this historic contribution."

"But," said my scientific hero, "this is Nobel Prize work!"

What could I say? I could not contradict my superior. Rather weakly, I stammered, "We are very interested in proteins like insulin." I died a thousand deaths in those few minutes.

The other experience was connected with my laboratory's contribution to the chemistry of what is known today as cortisone. We had succeeded in effecting a commercially adaptable synthesis of cortexolone, just about the time the Mayo Clinic made the historic announcement of the beneficial effect of cortisone for rheumatoid arthritic patients. Now cortexolone differs from cortisone by just one lone oxygen atom; moreover, it is found in the adrenal glands with cortisone; and with structures so similar, the demand on us to supply it for testing purposes was naturally universal. To add to the drama, it was evident that our synthesis could ultimately provide cortexolone at a few cents per gram, while cortisone at that time was valued at several hundred dollars per gram. In one of my reports to superior officers I made the comment, "even if Substance 'S' [cortexolone] does not have the unique properties of Compound 'E' [cortisone], its occurrence in the adrenal glands could mean that nature has a mechanism for introducing into cortexolone the missing oxygen atom, thus producing Cortisone, a procedure not yet known to chemistry, but which is certainly in the offing." And indeed it was not long thereafter that most of the world's hydrocortisone was so prepared.

Again, our chemistry had been honest, hard-earned, and respectable. No one would deny us today a permanent place in the chemical and economic history of the cortisone family of drugs. When the American Chemical Society held its Symposium on Cortisone, naturally I was one of those invited to speak on the panel of contributors. But here again, the press and the general public exaggerated our findings all out of proportion to their worth. We were going to "put out of business all other producers of cortisone." I had to deny then, and have innumerable times since had to deny that I was "the *discoverer* of cortisone." Indeed, when I was made "Chicagoan of the Year" by the generous gesture of the Chicago *Sun-Times* and the Junior Chamber of Commerce, I had begun to feel a bit weary of "over-exaltation." One of the few times in my life, I perhaps seemed ungrateful and ill-mannered, as I opened my acceptance remarks with, "Friends, I appreciate deeply all this outpouring of good will, but I don't know why you should so honor me, except that I belong to a race which hangs heavily on your consciences, and you are deifying me before I actually become eligible for the Kingdom of The Gods!" And then I proceeded to talk about the tragedies of the ghetto. Certainly it was bad taste, as I look back upon it, for the many friends who have since forgiven me were but expressing a prayer for the future, and the wishes of prayers have often indeed no relation to the reality of the present.

It seems an age since the memorable March on Washington in 1963. Despite the tragedies of Watts, Newark, Detroit, and other riot areas; despite extremists and cynics who may seem to be apostles of doom, our great country and its people have, in the words of our old spiritual, "set their faces to the sun, and never will turn back." The ghetto gloom of apartheid is slowly but surely fading on the horizon. And a completely new day is dawning for the hitherto schizophrenic Negro scientist. As he is finding his way into university faculties, where his creative talents may find uninhibited outlet, his total intellectual integrity is taking mastery over the frustrating necessity to bolster his own waning spirits. He is slowly arriving; he has faith in himself; and he is becoming a calm, determined scholar—eager, anxious, and definitely destined to write new chapters in the history of his discipline. Indeed, he is already doing so!

And a strange compensation is appearing out of his schizophrenic history. He has developed a priceless historical consciousness that is directing his view beyond the readily visible portion of life's spectrum. His first century of partial freedom has found him wriggling out of almost insuperable prisons of containment and confinement. As a result of the necessity to find ways out when others could either give up or find other openings, his imaginative powers have been broadened and strengthened. Thus, he is finding new internal strength and valid ground for intellectual self-respect.

I have been recently watching Negro scientific talent at work, and I am pleased beyond bounds at this evident liberation of imaginative faculties. Add to this the two inescapable practical considerations, that the Negro scientist now need neither starve nor be condemned to a frustrating intellectual ghetto if he chooses pure science as a career, and one can see a promising future for this fresh and highly uninhibited imaginative power. Moreover, instead of developing a stultified human heart, his own trying experiences will generate deep human compassion. It will be exciting to see the success of this new Negro intellectual in passing this experience and rebirth on to the less fortunate among his fellow-men.

SAMUEL M. NABRIT

Dr. Samuel M. Nabrit, former President of Texas Southern University, was appointed in 1966 by President Lyndon B. Johnson to a four-year term on the Atomic Energy Commission. He has recently resigned from that post to become Executive Director of the Southern Fellowship Fund.

Dr. Nabrit was born in Macon, Georgia, on February 21, 1905. He earned the bachelor's degree at Morehouse College and the master's and Ph.D. degrees from Brown University. His honorary degrees include the Doctor of Laws degree from Morehouse College and the Doctor of Science degree from Brown University, Howard University, and Atlanta University.

After having taught for six years at Morehouse College, he was appointed Professor and Chairman of the Department of Biology at Atlanta University—a position which he held for twenty-three years. During the last eight years of his appointment, he served concurrently as Dean of the Graduate School of Arts and Sciences. In 1955 he was named President of Texas Southern University and remained in that position until his resignation in 1967 while on leave for governmental service.

Dr. Nabrit is a noted scientist who has spent ten summers in research at the Woods Hole Marine Biological Laboratory in Massachusetts and who has directed a number of major research projects. His scientific articles have appeared in such scholarly publications as the *Biological Bulletin*, the *Journal of Experimental Zoology*, the *Journal of Parasitology*, *Anatomical Record*, and the *Handbook of Biological Data*.

Dr. Nabrit has held a number of significant posts. He has been President of the National Institute of Science, and Vice-President and subsequently President of the Association of Colleges and Secondary Schools. He has served as a member of the Board of Directors of the American Council on Education, the Southern Education Foundation, and the Center for the Study of Liberal

Education of Adults. In 1956 Dr. Nabrit was appointed by President Dwight D. Eisenhower to a six-year term on the National Science Board; and, in 1963, by President Lyndon B. Johnson to the Committee on the Study of Higher Education Needs in the District of Columbia.

His interest in education has led to membership on the Board of Trustees of Benedict College in Columbia, S.C., the Board of Directors of Maryville College in Maryville, Tenn., and the Library Board in Houston, Texas. As a result of his interest in business affairs, he is a member of the Board of Directors of the Afro-American Life Insurance Company of Jacksonville, Tennessee, and Vice-President of the Standard Savings and Loan Association of Houston, Texas.

THERE BUT FOR

THE GRACE OF GOD GO I

by Samuel M. Nabrit

THE hereditary information coded as *gene loci* in a section of a string of nucleotide pairs, and the role of DNA in activating enzyme-systems which act through RNA or directly upon responsive cytoplasmic areas and are distributed in a time-space sequence during our development, could not have been understood by my parents. I am sure that they were not the least concerned about particulate or molecular theories of transmission of hereditary traits. Seven of their eight children still survive, and the story that I propose to relate about these seven will be indicative of the fact that Lady Luck was with us when the dice of destiny were tossed. None of us had discernible congenital defects, and all of us had an environment which made it possible for us to demonstrate the wide range of responsiveness of the healthy human brain when it is properly nurtured in a climate of high aspirations and expectancy.

With the exception of my maternal grandmother, I knew my grandparents quite well. All three of them lived until they reached the age of at least seventy.

My father's mother had learned the fundamental alphabet and had attained a very elementary reading skill while a servant-slave in her master's house. Records reveal that after Spelman College was founded in the basement of Friendship Church in Atlanta in 1881, my paternal grandmother was enrolled in an early class under her married name in 1886. My grandfather, her husband, was a skilled craftsman. He was a well-digger and designer, and could erect the superstructure of a well from wood or stone. My father's brother learned, from his father, to lay brick and to plaster. It was my grandmother, though, who encouraged and aided her son's education.

When my father completed elementary school, his mother took a job in the laundry at Morehouse College so that her son could go to high school and college.

My father was graduated from Morehouse College, which was founded in the parsonage of Springfield Baptist Church in Augusta, Georgia. He served this church as pastor during nine years of my elementary and secondary school experience. Subsequent to its establishment in Augusta, Morehouse moved to Atlanta, where my father had been born and where he had studied.

Morehouse, like so many of the early institutions of the Reconstruction era, was supported and staffed by the American Baptist Home Mission Society. Though the white scholars of the Society could not qualify for faculty positions in Northern universities in most cases, they had had college education in the North. In addition, they sympathetically related to and lived with the students and provided for them a sense of human worth and dignity that could not have been matched elsewhere. At this period of development all of these institutions had grade school and secondary school departments. They gradually evolved into colleges, and my father was in the second graduating class at Morehouse, finishing in 1898. Subsequently, he taught school in the rural areas during the winter and summer months, as the public schools were closed in the spring and fall because of the cotton culture. On weekends during the winter he also worked as a baker.

My mother's father was the half-white son of his owner. Thus he was permitted to learn to read and write and was given freedom of entrance and egress to and from the plantation at will. It is not surprising, then, that he later owned a farm, a grocery store, a restaurant, and a furniture store and served as the postmaster of his town on the public square in Cuthbert, Georgia. When, as a little boy, I visited him, I was impressed that each day he received the *Atlanta Constitution* and would not permit anyone to touch it until he had had a chance to read it. (This was always at five o'clock the next morning over his coffee.)

While my paternal grandparents were devoutly religious and patient in their belief that God would make everything right in time, my mother's father believed that economic security was the basic ingredient in "getting along." This notion of economic security, however, frequently got him into difficulties. In spite of the business acumen evidenced by the many enterprises with which he was connected, he was at times victimized by his white cronies who used and exploited him to their own advantage. As I look back now, I believe it is well that we spent so little time with Grandfather West, for we might have become a cynical lot, rather than a family that was not easily taken in or beguiled by flattery, praise, or false friendships.

My mother was trained in the public schools and in Professor Henderson's private school, which qualified her to teach in school systems that required only an elementary school education. She married while quite young and used all her talents in providing a suitable home for her eight children. Sometimes she did plain sewing, and my father, who had become a minister, supplemented her income by giving her the fees from weddings he performed. There was never an emergency when we could not borrow from her to tide us over. To me, my mother was all that I believe any woman could be and more than any of us had a right to expect. There was nothing that her children needed that was not granted before she ministered to her own wants. The only time that we vexed her to the point of tears and a desire to swear, she blurted out, "You all make me so hell mad!" For a long time you could have heard a pin drop anywhere in the house. (Eight youngsters can wear out one's patience!)

My grandparents came out of the period of slavery, the internecine War Between the States, the Reconstruction period and early backlash, without bitterness or rancor, with a feeling that our lot should be better than theirs, and a willingness to assist us in the broader struggles for liberation of the human spirit. There was never any indication that they had ever heard of Frederick Douglass and the efforts of Negroes in the North, or of whites in the North who promised freedom. After the Emancipation Proclamation they frequently visited the descendants of their previous masters and never reflected bitterness over their former lot.

In the South, where I was brought up, the Negro family was—and to some extent still is—predominantly matriarchal in character. This was partly due to the slave tradition of nonrecognition of family, partly to the broken home condition which is encouraged by support programs for dependent children in the city (where children are not entitled to aid if there is a male in the home), partly to the fact that unless a Negro male was educated professionally there was no special benefit in continuing school beyond the high school level, and partly to the fact that only women existed as teachers in the public schools, with the exception of an occasional principal. There but for the Grace of God go I. For I and my brothers and sisters were spared, since we had not merely a man in the house but a central figure in all of our lives—our father.

My father was an athlete, a really great baseball player—a catcher and a long-ball hitter. His college and semiprofessional records were not nationally known because Negroes were not "good enough" athletes to make the professional league—at least that is what the press of our day told us. We boys in the family were fortunate that he also had time to play ball with us.

He was, in addition, a scholar. He read Greek, Latin, and Hebrew with facility—as if he were reading English. He knew the classics, and algebra and trigonometry were easy for him. He taught at Georgia Baptist College and at Walker Baptist Institute, and was later President of the Baptist Theological Seminary at Nashville. He was pastor of churches in Americus, Augusta, and Atlanta, Georgia, and in Memphis, Tennessee. He taught me Xenophon's *Anabasis* and Virgil in high school and thought that he had successfully launched me into the ministry.

We loved and respected him. We listened attentively to his sermons in church and observed his examples of Christianity at home. He was tolerant of my early views on evolution, discussed around the dining-room table, and often participated in our debates. We made the final choices about our careers, but he provided a good climate for decision-making.

All eight children had some exposure to a public school education, although the major part of our education was received in private schools. This private school education was not, by any means, a sign of affluence. There was simply no choice, since Augusta and Atlanta, Georgia, provided no public secondary school education for Negroes until the time I was a junior in college. Moreover, upon graduation from church-related colleges, all of us except one had to go North for graduate study. Today, it appears that that was a fortunate circumstance, because in those days there were few Southern graduate programs of great strength.

The one thing that I am quite sure of is that there was never a day in our lives when there was a question whether any one of us would go to college. It was taken for granted that the three boys would go to Morehouse. Two of the girls went to Spelman, two to Fisk, and one to Talladega. There were two valedictorians, two salutatorians, and an honor graduate among the five girls.

After completing college and graduate work, two boys served as deans of graduate or professional schools, one at Atlanta University and the other at Howard University School of Law. These two boys subsequently became college presidents—one at Texas Southern University, the other at Howard University. They both also served the federal government; one, as Deputy Ambassador in Chief to the United Nations; and the other, as a board member of the National Science Foundation and as a member of the Atomic Energy Commission. The youngest boy served as Religious Education Secretary to the colleges of West Virginia, taught in two colleges, and now has succeeded his father as a pastor in Memphis. He also holds the political appointment of Deputy Jury Commissioner of Shelby County, Tennessee.

One girl married upon graduation from college and served subsequently as a postal clerk. One girl is chief accountant and director of personnel for the Sunday School Publishing Board, and co-owner of a mortuary establishment. Another is a graduate librarian, a former English teacher, and now head of the library at Knoxville College. The fourth, a graduate professional social worker, directs a community center and has served as field supervisor for trainees enrolled in Atlanta University's School of Social Work. The fifth and eldest is a retired dean of students and history professor of Spelman College after forty years of service.

By some miracle our father was able to pay all of our fees through college. This was that something of value that was worth the sacrifices and strivings of the entire family.

Although I had not consciously resisted the idea of a career in the ministry, which my family had assumed I would pursue—in fact, I preached at every opportunity in our back yard to the other children in the family and on our block—another circumstance completely changed the direction of my life. After graduating from high school, I worked during the summer in the Southern Cotton Oil Regional Laboratory. The assistant chemist of the laboratory, Mr. Blackburn, lived on the next street, so that his yard abutted ours at the rear. He gave me a job as "porter" and taught me to run approximately thirty-three Kjeldahls (chemical experiments) daily for protein in seed and meals through nitrogen determinations. It was in this laboratory that I learned how to use a nickel-cobalt catalyst and how to hydrogenate the unsaturated bonds to make lard out of cotton seed oil. Despite the pleading of Mr. Blackburn and the glowing picture that he painted for me in chemistry through apprenticeship, my father packed me off to college. To his surprise I enrolled as a major in chemistry, with the idea of ultimately going into medicine. My experience in the laboratory and the fact that the college was recruiting for its first class to qualify for a B.S. degree in what was then the only building in any Negro college completely devoted to science set my course. When educators speak of the desirability of coupling formal education with an on-the-job real life experience as a part of career preparation, I understand the full significance of this view.

During my junior year in college I was given the opportunity to serve as teaching assistant in biology, chemistry, and physics during the summer session. I believe that this was when I first understood the significance of the "other side" of the desk. I gained the teacher's point of view, but what was more important, I gained a greater knowledge of those subjects in trying to explain to other students the fundamental assumptions and structures of the disciplines involved.

In my senior year I was recommended for a teaching position in biology in my own college, Morehouse. The President, in a kindly manner, advised me to accept the appointment for at least a year in order to ease the financial strain on the family caused by the expense of my brother's senior year in law school. He suggested that after I had taught a year I would have the necessary money and would be much "sharper" for the study of medicine. He further suggested that I spend the intervening summer months at the University of Chicago. This I did.

The well-known Scopes trial was being conducted that summer and had evoked a great deal of interest in scientific circles—particularly among geneticists. I was extremely fortunate that the eminent scholar H. J. Muller was scheduled to teach that summer the course in genetics that I planned to take. This was the summer in which he completed the work on mutation in Drosophila (for which he subsequently won the AAAS thousand-dollar prize, and later the Nobel prize). It was my first opportunity to study under a teacher who had received a Ph.D. degree. It was like starting from the top to be taught by one of the world's great scientists before formally beginning a program of graduate study.

The next summer at Chicago, Dr. Elliott, then a recent Ph.D. graduate of Chicago, taught me embryology; and at the end of the course he suggested that I go to Woods Hole the following summer to take additional work in embryology. My anatomy teacher at Chicago, Carl Moore, was editor of the *Biological Bulletin*, which, incidentally, later published my first research paper. The two summers at Chicago had a formative and a directive influence upon my future.

I found that my academic preparation was quite adequate for general course work at Chicago, but left something to be desired insofar as seminars were concerned. I had never been exposed to any honors-type program or to any program in which the student presented his findings in the literature or laboratory to others. I learned how to do this at Chicago the hard way. When I became a teacher, I saw to it that all of my majors learned this technique early in their academic careers, without traumatic shock.

Woods Hole, in its lectures and in its rigorous seminars, exposed me to a feeling that I had not before experienced for the structure of biology as a discipline. Here, for the first time, I sensed what it was that biologists did, and followed them from problem to hypothesis, through evidence, to proof and to generalizations. I saw many examples of totally different conclusions which were legitimately reached from the same scientific evidence. I came to understand something of the kind of educative experience that unconsciously conditions one's efforts to attain disciplined subjectivity or complete objectivity. Here was a culture which had eluded all but a few Negroes and, at the time, most whites throughout the South.

After a summer's work at Woods Hole I applied for graduate study at Brown University, convinced that I was capable of earning a doctorate. Brown, at first, did not wish to admit me because I was a Negro; the department was small and enjoyed a family-like relationship that a Negro might disrupt. Because of John Hope, a distinguished Negro graduate of Brown, and his communications with President Faunce, Brown did admit me and I became the first Negro to be graduated there with a Ph.D. degree.

Generally speaking, my academic opportunities at Brown were unrestricted. There were, of course, occasions when the matter of race might have led to difficult and embarrassing situations. There was, for example, the occasion when I was asked by my Department to serve as a graduate assistant—at a time when, I am sure, the University was not ready to face the problem of a Negro instructor. Fortunately, this problem never came to a head, since the terms of the General Education Board Fellowship which had been awarded me required that I study full time. As a newlywed, I did not create a social problem. I had recently married Constance T. Crocker, who has been my forty-year companion and a constant inspiration and helpmate. She, too, taught at Morehouse, and she also served as Executive Assistant to the President and as Assistant Treasurer of Atlanta University.

I found at Brown a type of humanity in the faculty that transcended all expectations. When Professors Walter and Wilson assured themselves that I was already a mature, independent scholar in biology, they shared with me their rich interests in German language and culture and in symphonic and operatic music. They perceived that these kinds of educative experiences had not been available to me. This was their contribution to the education of the culturally deprived.

As a teacher I endeavored to emulate these two men. I met my students at their own levels, and I instructed them until I was sure that they satisfied the minimum standards in any master's degree program. My college majors were able to move easily into professional or graduate schools. I have been privileged to see the opportunities afforded me as one individual duplicated many times for my students. To have averaged at least one doctoral student for each year that I spent in the classroom was adequate compensation for the mere subsistence-level income I received for teaching. The visible change in a youngster whom one leads into discovery of knowledge is a remarkable experience for a devoted teacher.

When, in 1944, the General Education Board gave me a third study grant to spend five months at Teachers College in science education, I developed new insights into training secondary school teachers for science and began to sense for the first time the great disparity in knowledge and techniques between ghetto teachers and those in suburban communities. My colleagues and I visited New Trier and Oak Park schools and compared the techniques used in them with those employed in the inner-city schools. The experience motivated us to initiate the movement for the formation of the National Institute of Science. We were so isolated in professional life in the South in those days that we could not attend regional scientific meetings and exchange ideas about research and teaching. We hoped to provide opportunties for young Negro teachers to continue to grow by having a forum for the discussion of their ideas.

I entered administrative work after a visiting committee from the American Association of Colleges and Universities reviewed Atlanta University. As useful and as important as it was for our students to know themselves, this committee feared that we were overly preoccupied in our graduate theses in sociology, education, literature, history, and languages, with the relatively minor achievements of Negroes. Thus, the members of the committee felt that we had permitted our students to veer away from the mainstream of thought and the important movements in their special disciplines. They found, on the other hand, the science and mathematics theses unslanted and suggested that the next dean be named from one of these disciplines.

I worked with the faculty and trustees when they set out to afford, somewhere in the South, a graduate program which provided compensatory and developmental experiences for young Negroes. We wanted to be so thorough in our training and education that our graduates could successfully continue toward their doctorates in step with graduate students from any other institution. This we achieved at a time when no Southern white graduate school would admit a Negro.

I spent the semester of 1949–50 at the University of Brussels in research at the Medical School with Dalcq and Pasteels. Upon my return I became so completely removed from research by the administrative camel that I was vulnerable for a presidency in a college that promised nothing but an opportunity to move it forward.

From 1955 to 1966 I served as President of Texas Southern University in Houston, Texas. I tried to develop there the kind of creative climate for faculty and students that I had learned to appreciate. I felt that it was possible to have a community of scholars and escape from the paternalistic pattern so often encountered in the smaller colleges. I had not fully succeeded in this, but we were moving in that direction when I was appointed to the Atomic Energy Commission.

In addition to my administrative duties at Texas Southern, I was fortunate in being able to help channel positively the aspirations of people striving for human rights and to assist in changing the patterns of discrimination in Houston. These were unanticipated by-products of involvement with my students, who "sat-in" restaurants and other places of public accommodation that maintained a policy of racial discrimination. My alignment with the students in articulating the basic desires of Negroes for making a practical example of a functioning democracy in America was a most important experience and related me more to the students than anything else that we had attempted to achieve in our formal educational adventures. Although the climate for change had been developed by arrests, law suits, student sit-ins, major efforts by the NAACP, CORE, the Urban League, and other newer Civil Rights organizations, the major changes in Houston were brought about by Texas Southern students and by individuals in the power structure of the Negro and white communities without the direct action of Civil Rights organizations.

In different sections of the country and at different periods during the Negro's quest for freedom, the procedures used have had to vary. The goals and objectives, however, have always remained the same: full freedom with all of its rights and privileges.

Both Du Bois and Booker T. Washington saw education of the Negro as *the* important factor at the turn of the century. Du Bois advocated an elitist culture which could demonstrate through literary and scientific scholarship the worthiness of the acceptance of Negroes. These cultured few, or talented tenth, would provide the indigenous examples around whom racial pride could be developed and from whom leadership could be obtained. These achievers, at the same time, could abolish the racial stereotype which had been used to justify slavery and discrimination on the American scene. Washington believed that, in addition, skilled artisans needed to be developed so as to provide a middle-class economic structure upon which America would depend and which could support a cultured class. They were not so different in their views that Washington could not offer Du Bois a job at Tuskegee or assist him in obtaining funds for his researches and studies on the Negro during his first period of service at Atlanta University. Both attempted to obtain support for education of some kind. While Washington wished to have us "let down our buckets where we were" and be patient, Du Bois was one of the 1906 marchers at Harper's Ferry and one of the founders of the Niagara movement and the NAACP.

Today, when we are concerned about identification and our cultural and historical roots which make us worthy of acceptance, and about an opportunity to move into the mainstream of life in America as Americans, Negro leadership still is groping for the proper strategy. It is not sufficient to have a few tokens, in individuals or families, of success in America. We cannot afford a caste system which equates race with unemployment, the ghetto, poor schools, underachievement, delinquency, crime, disease, and a high death rate. We have sufficient examples to illustrate that a good start, family aspiration and expectancy, and opportunity for quality education at a cost level that can be afforded can provide the escape mechanism into a fuller life for the trapped masses at the bottom of our economic ladder.

If it is impossible for suburbia to understand or to care about the opportunities for education in the ghetto, where the achievement level upon graduation from high school is from two to six years below the average expectancy, then it will be necessary to unify and galvanize the ghettos into action committees for change. This is quite likely to be a less disciplined approach to a solution than one could obtain through enlightened, traditional community leadership.

Now that the laws have been enacted or clarified, joint, not separate, racial efforts should be exerted to improve educational opportunity for every American. Preschool education is needed for many of our children. Involvement and understanding are necessary for many parents if they are to relate school aspirations to job success and vertical mobility in the society. Continuing education for adults in the processes and problems of an urban setting and in job training is an essential. Assignment of the best teachers and allocation of larger per capita expenditures to the ghetto schools are necessary. If we are not willing to spend more in the ghetto because it is necessary to spend more, then we must abolish the ghetto for all educational purposes. This can be achieved by the establishment of educational parks and by the redistribution of students, or of students and their parents, through changes in the housing pattern. Education is the most important factor in vertical mobility today. The opportunity for it must be extended to all.

The Federal Government must continue to enact those laws which direct the behavior patterns of our society into positive channels. The outlet for the underprivileged must not be restricted antisocial action patterns that provide only emotional release. The Negro who, by the Grace of God, has managed to escape should place his energies and experiences at the service of the masses with a willingness to relate with, and assist in, finding solutions to their problems. The Negro must not be alienated from those in the white community who can, and are willing to, assist in his liberation.

We must believe in individuals and in America until we are deceived. Then we must find the wisdom to distinguish between those who would use and abuse us, and those who genuinely wish to serve us and our society. We must not make the mistake of stereotyping all people because of inconsiderate action by the few.

Success, to me, is not determined by whether or not I have achieved any set goal, but rather by the inner serenity that I experience when I know that I have done my best. The competition in life is with oneself, and one alone knows whether he is a winner or not. I have never worried about the achievements of others or the plaudits of others. It has been truly said, "One who depends upon the applause of others, puts his happiness in their hands."

Business

ASA T. SPAULDING

Asa T. Spaulding, who recently retired as President of the North Carolina Mutual Life Insurance Company, was born in Columbus County, North Carolina, on July 22, 1902. He received his undergraduate training at the School of Commerce, Accounts, and Finance of New York University, from which he obtained the B.S. degree in 1930, and his graduate training in mathematics and actuarial science at the University of Michigan, which awarded him the M.A. degree in 1932.

A recognized authority in his profession, he has been active for many years not only in business affairs but in civic affairs as well. He holds directorships in such organizations as the Mechanics and Farmers Bank, the Mutual Savings and Loan Association, the James E. Shepard Memorial Foundation, the John Avery Boys' Club, the Chain Investment Corporation, Realty Services, Inc., the W. T. Grant Company, the Durham Chamber of Commerce, the NAACP Legal Defense and Educational Fund, Inc., and the National Council of Christians and Jews.

Among the offices he has held are the following: Chairman of the Board, Bankers Fire and Casualty Insurance Company; Vice Chairman and Chairman of the Durham Bi-Racial Human Relations Committee; and Vice-President and President of the National Negro Insurance Association. He has served as trustee of Howard University, Shaw University, the National Urban League, the North Carolina Council of Churches, and the American Freedom from Hunger Foundation.

His significant awards include: a Presidential Citation (1946) "for his unselfish devotion to the task of helping stabilize our economy . . ."; honorary L.L.D. degrees from Shaw University (1958) and from North Carolina College at Durham (1960); an honorary D.B.A. degree from Morgan State College (1961); the Frederick A. Douglass Achievement Award (1963); the American Academy of

Achievement Golden Plate Award (1964); and the National Urban League's Equal Opportunity Day Award (1964). In 1966 he was selected by the National Newspaper Publishers Association to receive the John B. Russwurm Award.

IN RETROSPECT AND

IN PROSPECT

by Asa T. Spaulding

ONE century ago our nation went through the tragic era of Reconstruction in which the Negro played a central role as the victim of a fate he could neither entirely understand nor hope to control. He was the victim of racial prejudice which only became more violent when he began to realize the hopes that emancipation had inspired. He was the victim of the clash between large economic and class interests. From the period of the early 1870's through the turn of the century, he lost his newly won franchise in all the Southern states, and a terrible era ensued which is still painful to describe. Despite the noble principles upon which our nation was founded and the high moral ideals and purposes of the Emancipation Proclamation, anyone making the most cursory review of our progress towards social justice will be impressed by the fact that we have traveled a weary road often drenched with our own blood and tears. Social justice is not, and never has been, in the words of Martin Luther King, "a lavish dish passed out on a silver platter by the privileged to the underprivileged, with the underprivileged merely furnishing the appetite." The struggle was so great in its beginnings that to the American people, wearied by a quarter century of economic strife, the Spanish-American War came as a welcome relief. The decade of the 1890's seemed deeply tinged with red, with the dread menace of social upheaval and revolution. The panic of 1893, the lengthening bread lines, the pitched battles between capital and labor, the threatening growth of Populism, and the class war preached by the Bryanites in 1896—all these made the dying years of the century a time of sober thought and grim endeavor.

The centripetal movement which culminated in the first decade of the twentieth century produced two results of outstanding importance to American civilization: it shifted a large portion of operation and ownership of the common industries from the actual producer to the banker and nonresident stockholder, and it speeded the concentration of wealth in the hands of a few, thus creating a class more powerful than the people, and even than the government.

About the same time, labor was facing a new era. The right of the wage earner to organize was no longer seriously challenged by either the courts or the employing class. The bitter industrial struggles of the 1880's and 1890's had been a rough school of experience in which American workers learned many lessons which they found useful later. Among the labor unions of the period, the American Federation of Labor, headed by Samuel Gompers, was the most outstanding. Then came the National Civic Federation, with Marcus A. Hanna as President and Samuel Gompers as Vice-President—a strange combination. One labor historian called the period from 1898 to 1904 "a honeymoon period of capital and labour." This period, however, was again followed by many gigantic and bitter struggles both in and out of court, and even by physical violence, finally resulting in the Clayton Act, referred to by Gompers as "Labor's Magna Charta." The Socialist party and the IWW Union were also quite active during this period.

Certainly it is not difficult to draw a parallel between those times and the period through which we are now passing—a period which has already been given the designation of the Second Reconstruction.

To many thoughtful men in the opening years of the twentieth century, it seemed that in making her fortune America was in peril of losing her soul. The question was being asked as to what had become of that precious concern of our forefathers, "the general welfare," when matters of far-reaching social significance could be settled outside legislative halls by contests between big business and little business, capital and labor, urban merchants and embattled farmers—contests in which the bribery of legislators became common practice.

As the new century advanced, the Negro race, comprising a substantial part of the population, entered the most discouraging period since its emancipation, with disfranchisement through various malicious devices on the one hand, and economic oppression on the other. To keep the Negro in subserviency, it was considered necessary to consolidate poor and middle-class whites politically, and these groups found themselves endowed with new political importance. While the abler Southerners threw their energies into economic development, an inferior type seized the reins of political power, producing such "rabble-rousing" politicians as Vardaman of Mississippi, Jeff Davis of Arkansas, Hoke Smith of Georgia, and Cole Blease of South Carolina, who perpetuated the Negro question as a political issue and deprecated movements for the uplift of the race. By such devices as intimidation, literacy and character tests, taxation requirements, and the Grandfather Clause, Negroes were effectively disfanchised in most Southern states. The tenant and credit system had developed with the breakup of plantation slavery, and—in combination with the widespread custom of allowing fines for petty crimes to be worked out in service for the person who paid them—had reduced rural Southern Negroes to virtual peonage.

Two world wars, with their inevitable social ramifications, somewhat altered the racial climate in the United States; but it was not until 1954 and the significant Supreme Court victory of the NAACP legal staff, led by Thurgood Marshall, that daylight really seemed to break upon us. Other court decisions had helped to light the way, but with the declaration that the separate but equal policy of public education was no longer to be considered constitutional, the Supreme Court declared the Negro's emancipation anew in the twentieth century.

At such a time, when so many chiefs of state and other leaders were so silent in the South, it was heartening to have a man like Attorney Irving S. Carlyle of Winston-Salem, North Carolina, say: "The decision of the Supreme Court of the United States on May 17, 1954, holding unconstitutional the compulsory segregation of the races in the public schools, is one of the *historic* decisions handed down by that Court . . . Upon the pages of that Court's epic decisions, national destiny has been written so that all could read and understand, whether they agreed or not." Carlyle continued, "Along with many other Americans, I have come to the conclusion that the decision was right and inevitable and will be so regarded by history." He further asserted that "Truth is on the side of the Court and its decision against segregation . . . The core of the truth is that all men are entitled to freedom. As more men become free, the stronger becomes the freedom of all." It was also the opinion of Carlyle that "Through the compulsion of law and the power of religion, the abolition of racial discrimination in this country in due course is certain and that this will come about because law and religion operate irresistibly upon the conscience of men."

Emancipation, however, is the beginning and not the end: a man once freed must act thereafter in accordance with his freedom, or it becomes a worthless decoration useful only for special occasions. Shortly after the Emancipation Proclamation Centennial Reception in 1963, President Kennedy made clear the Negro's situation in America with the following words: "The Negro baby born in America today—regardless of the section or state in which he is born—has about one-half as much chance of completing high school as a white baby born in the same place on the same day—one-third as much chance of becoming a professional man—twice as much chance of becoming unemployed—about one-seventh as much chance of earning $10,000 per year—a life expectancy which is seven years less—and the prospects of earning only half as much."

It is obvious that at present we are faced with monumental problems both at home and abroad. Our times and conditions demand that we put forth greater efforts to bridge the gaps not only between the haves and impoverished Negroes and other have-nots here in America, but also between our peoples and those of other nations, if we are to hope to live in peace and harmony as a nation and as a world. Those who have resisted social evolution too violently have unwittingly invited, encouraged, and even perhaps hastened a social revolution. For without social *evolution* in our drastically and rapidly changing world and civilization, there is bound to be some form of *revolution*. Man cannot hold back the tide of change. And we cannot have such drastic changes in our physical world, in our body of knowledge, in our means of communication and transportation and maintain an absolute status quo in our society. The unfortunate thing, however, is that man, in the words of Norman Cousins, has "exalted change in everything but himself. He has leaped centuries ahead in inventing a new world to live in, but he seems to know little or nothing about his own part in that world." He does not seem to know how to adjust or how to accommodate himself to changes in human relationships. There is a strong desire and effort on the part of many to maintain the obsolete mores, customs, and traditions of an outmoded society in our new and more sophisticated world. They are still trying to put *new wine* into *old bottles* and *new patches* on *old garments*. And this just will not work.

Modern advances in communication and transportation and other scientific achievements, as well as new court decisions, have brought people of different races, nations, cultures, religions, and political creeds into closer contact with one another than ever before. These contacts will of necessity bring about either cooperation or conflict; and keeping conflict at a minimum, and cooperation at a maximum, should be the aim and objective of all in constructing our new society. In our efforts to do this, we must remember that the ego in man and nations is a relentless, motivating force, driving him and them ever onward. And in our ever shrinking world, the manner and channels in and through which this ego expresses itself must be the concern of all. Otherwise, we could have a catastrophe which would make anything we have seen, including Hiroshima and Nagasaki, appear mild indeed.

No nation or people can achieve true greatness through hate, intolerance, indifference to and exploitation of the weak. Greatness comes through love, neighborliness, interest in and consideration for others manifested through the practice of "The Golden Rule." The greatness of a nation depends upon the moral and spiritual life and force of its people. Indeed, the Bible has words for it: " 'Not by might, nor by power but by my Spirit,' saith the Lord of Hosts." Power, force, and might alone will not hold people or nations together indefinitely. These elements have no cohesive qualities. Moral and spiritual qualities are the ones which have enduring ingredients. The imbalances between our moral and spiritual development, and our achievements and disciplines, pose some of our most serious threats today individually and collectively, interracially and internationally. These imbalances also affect the vital matter of social responsibility. The concept of social responsibility is not new, but never before have so many businessmen and so many scholars of leading universities supported it to the extent they do today. This does not mean, however, that there is no divergence of opinion among businessmen on this matter. Nevertheless, businessmen are beginning to understand, perhaps as never before, their role in American society. Many of them are becoming keenly aware of the social character of their decisions and are calling on the whole business community to commit itself to a doctrine of social responsibility. These appeals may prove to be the most significant force in changing business practices to a closer conformity with the ideals of our democracy. Equal opportunity is also a much emphasized issue, and one that is all-important to a minority group hoping finally to achieve its rightful share of the country's many benefits. From the viewpoint of a Negro employer, I would say that equal opportunity requires a two-way street on all levels.

Heretofore, Negro employers could and did attract a considerable portion of the best trained and qualified Negro white-collar workers. Other doors were not as wide open to them as they are today. Now the giants in business and industry are not only in fierce competition for the "Negro Market," but are also seeking the best trained and most qualified and experienced Negro personnel. The government is also following this trend. This puts the Negro employer at a decided disadvantage. For some time to come, because of the size of his business and other factors, he will find it difficult to attract the qualified and experienced white employee. The Negro employer will, therefore, not only have to "lift himself by his own bootstraps," but will also have to "make bricks without straw" to survive as a Negro employer. Many feel, however, that the bell has already tolled for the all-Negro employer as we know him today.

The Negro employer absorbs the cost of training and developing competent employees, only to lose many of them to larger and stronger competitors without the likelihood of comparable replacements. The competitors obviously save in the process considerable costs in training and development. This siphoning off, by white employers, of the "cream of the crop" from the Negro "manpower pool" compounds the problems of the Negro employer.

Of course, Negroes must prepare themselves thoroughly for the new opportunities that are opening up rapidly in almost every phase of business activity. Young Negroes, especially, must study hard, learn well the essential skills in their chosen fields, and become highly qualified for the positions they seek whether from white or Negro employers. This is particularly true since a disproportion exists in unskilled and semiskilled occupations. The scarcity of Negroes in skilled jobs is due in part to their exclusion from labor-union-controlled apprenticeship training programs both in the North and South. Almost equally exclusive are such unions as those of the printers' and plumbers' trades. This probably accounts for the following statement attributed to Senator Wayne Morse: "There are more American Negroes with doctorates than Negro plumbers and electricians."

The movement toward an integrated society requires many new adjustments and much new thinking now—not tomorrow—by all employers. Perhaps, we need a new breed of businessmen. President Johnson summed it up this way: "Great social change tends to come rapidly . . . I believe we are in the midst of such a period of change." The change will bring new challenges requiring new responses, but it has been man's response to challenge that has influenced his civilization and progress, and fixed his place in history. It has taken him from a cave to a palace, from savagery to civilization, from poverty to wealth, from disease to health, and from slavery to freedom. And I believe the enlightened American employer today will face up responsibly to the challenge of equal employment opportunity. Certainly as Negroes, we must assume our share of the responsibility.

In retrospect, we find faith. In prospect, we find hope. In our new day begun, we find challenges. In proportion as we meet these challenges successfully, we will give more meaning to democracy, help save America, and vouchsafe her continued leadership of the free world.

A. G. GASTON, SR.

Born on July 4, 1892, in Demopolis, Alabama, A. G. Gaston has become one of Birmingham's most distinguished citizens and one of the nation's leading businessmen, widely known for his business acumen and his many and varied civic contributions.

A substantial number of business ventures, ranging in assets from one quarter of a million dollars to more than nine million dollars individually, owe their success to his perception and financial expertise. Among the businesses to which he gives personal direction as President are the following: Smith and Gaston Funeral Directors, a chain of modernly equipped and well-staffed funeral homes throughout the state of Alabama; the Booker T. Washington Insurance Company; the Booker T. Washington Business College, offering complete clerical and business administration courses, including IBM electronic machine accounting; the New Grace Hill Cemetery; the Finley Park Garden Apartments; the Vulcan Realty and Investment Corporation; A. G. Gaston Motels, Inc.; the Citizens Drug Store; the Citizens Federal Savings and Loan Association; and the A. G. Gaston Home for Senior Citizens.

A. G. Gaston's civic and community activities are equally extensive. He has served as member of the Board of Trustees of Tuskegee Institute, Daniel Payne College, and the Y.M.C.A. Other service includes membership on the Board of Directors of the Jefferson County Survey Committee, the Coordinating Council of the City of Birmingham, and the Citizens Committee of Birmingham. He has held the post of President of the Birmingham Negro Business League and has served on two occasions as President of the National Negro Business League.

His humanitarianism has brought him a steady stream of honors and awards. Particularly significant are awards for achievement from the Citizens of Birmingham, the Alabama Newspaper Association, Tuskegee Institute, the 4-H Clubs of Alabama, the National Association of Colored Women's Clubs, and the U.S. Commission on

Civil Rights. Several awards have been given him by various churches, business enterprises, fraternal organizations, and by the Y.M.C.A. He is the recipient of the Russwurm Award from the National Newspaper Publishers Association and of a special award from President Harry S Truman.

A graduate of Tuggle Institute, he has received honorary doctoral degrees from Tuskegee Institute, Daniel Payne College, Paul Quinn College, Allen University, and from Monrovia College in Liberia, West Africa.

INVESTMENT IN LIFE

by A. G. Gaston, Sr.

IN my struggle to attain the "pinnacle of success" generally accredited me by members of the press and my good friends—but which I myself view most cautiously—I have been described as "a John D. Rockefeller, a Commodore Vanderbilt, and a Barnum and Bailey wrapped in one package of dynamic human energy." This conception of my rise in the business world is entirely out of focus with the real story. Any success that I may have attained has come from hard work, from my desire to fulfill a need, and from the school of experience and hard knocks. I had no inheritance and have performed no feats of legerdemain. Whatever accomplishments I may have achieved have been founded in community needs and have been based on a few simple rules for success.

For example, our parent company, the Booker T. Washington Insurance Company, was started in 1923 as the Booker T. Washington Burial Society. It grew out of a need for a way to bury our people, who had little or no funds, without contributing to the racket run by professional collectors who solicited funds on paydays from various employees in the area to bury the dead. Many times the so-called deceased was very much alive, and the funds went into the pockets of the unscrupulous.

My father-in-law, A. L. (Dad) Smith, gave up his carpentry business in Meridian, Mississippi, and came to Birmingham to join me in visiting churches, making speeches, and soliciting the cooperation of the preachers. It wasn't long before the burial society had grown to the point where we were able to purchase a funeral home, which we operated under the name of Smith and Gaston Funeral Directors, Inc.

We had our ups and downs, but the insurance company continued to grow over the years and, through merger, purchased a number of smaller burial societies and insurance companies throughout the state of Alabama. We now give employment to more than four hundred people, with salaries and commissions of approximately one and a half million dollars per year, and we have more than eighty million dollars' worth of insurance in force. Our Home Office in Birmingham is housed in the new A. G. Gaston Building, which was completed in 1960 at a cost of one and a half million dollars, and paid for in cash. The Smith and Gaston Funeral Directors, Inc. is also housed in a new and modern edifice, completed in 1962 at a cost of $350,000. Our modern fleet of automotive equipment is valued at $300,000.

Because of a need for clerical help, the Booker T. Washington Business College was started solely for the purpose of training clerks and stenographers for the insurance company and funeral home. Soon there was an outside demand for pupils from the business college, and the school was expanded to serve the general public. Today the business college is operated by Mrs. Gaston, with twenty-one instructors and 329 students. All of the members of the last graduating class are gainfully employed. They serve abroad as well as at home, and there is a constant demand for graduates of the school. In fact, many companies hire our students before they actually graduate.

In another area, I saw the need for a motel and restaurant for our people, where they would truly be able to receive first-class accommodations and service. Thus were born the A. G. Gaston Motel and the A. G. Gaston Restaurant, with no thought on my part of making a profit. However, the two businesses have grown to such an extent that they now have become slightly profitable.

The Vulcan Realty and Investment Corporation was started solely for the purpose of handling real estate that had been purchased by the insurance company, and a subdivision we were developing. Outside sources then began to seek our counsel and advice, and we undertook the management of other properties besides our own. Vulcan is now beginning to show a profit.

Because of the pending scarcity and advancing prices of burial plots, the firm of Smith and Gaston Funeral Directors purchased the New Grace Hill Cemetery for the purpose of providing moderately priced burial space for its clients and for members of the Booker T. Washington Insurance Company. Through constant improvement, Grace Hill is now valued at approximately $300,000.

In 1957 I was urged by a number of my friends to organize a savings and loan association to make available more mortgage money for our people, who were unable to get sufficient mortgage money for their homes and churches. We applied for a charter from the Federal Home Loan Bank Board. Before granting a charter, the Federal Home Loan Bank Board required that the existing local savings and loan associations—all white—concur with the need for an additional association. All of them declined to support us in our application for the charter. In the appeal from the local Home Loan Bank Board to the federal agency in Washington, I appeared with Attorney Arthur D. Shores, who represented us. Attorney Shores charged no legal fees, and his expenses were borne by me personally. Because of the depth of our survey and the material presented—which clearly indicated a double-standard lending policy was being practiced by the existing associations, resulting in inferior homes for Negroes—Attorney Shores was able to convince the Federal Home Loan Bank Board of the need for the Citizens Federal Savings and Loan Association. Our charter was granted.

The Citizens Federal Savings and Loan Association has grown at the rate of nearly one million dollars per year. We currently have assets of nearly ten million dollars and have twenty people in our employ. More than $1,725,000 was paid back last year to our shareholders in dividends.

As a further contribution to community service, we have built the A. G. Gaston Home for Senior Citizens, a modern, well-equipped nursing home, where fifty-one residents are skillfully cared for. It has been constructed in the peaceful, residential area of the A.G. Gaston Sub-division, and is a source of pride for the community. It is also the source of great personal pride for me to know that we are providing comfort and security for many of our old friends and acquaintances, several of whom are former employees of our companies.

I went into none of these businesses with the thought of getting rich per se, but merely saw a need and made a sincere effort to fill that need. I recall only one business I went into for which there was not a particular need, but for which there was a desire on my part solely to profit. That was the bottling business, manufacturing soft drinks as the Brown Belle Bottling Company. After I lost $60,000 in this venture, I decided that I had made a mistake. Brown Belle was a corporation which I had organized and whose stock I had distributed to several of my friends. Therefore, when the venture failed, I took the total loss rather than have the other stockholders lose their money.

In the conduct of the various businesses there are a few rules which I have found to be very profitable to me. While they have cost me dearly in experience and in sacrifice, I am happy to pass my own home-made rules on for whatever value they may have for others:

1. Keep a part of your income. Every person should pay himself something of whatever he earns.

2. Establish a reputation at a bank or savings and loan association in order to make and achieve a productive place in society. A banker is a good person to know. The kind of reputation established at a bank can mean success or failure.

3. Don't take chances with your money. A man who has no money to lose has no business gambling; and the man who can afford to lose does not gamble because he is too smart.

4. Never borrow anything that you can't afford to pay back. Many of us borrow above our ability to pay, and at the first minor difficulty we are in serious trouble.

5. Don't get "big-headed" with the "little fellows." They have the numbers and the buying power. They are the ones you must respect if you wish to succeed in business. Should you fail to do so, you may find yourself coming down the ladder facing the very same "little fellows" you ignored while going up the ladder.

6. Don't have so much pride that you cannot wear the same suit or dress a little longer in order to reach your objective. The ultimate goal is more important than immediate desires.

7. Find a need and fulfill it. I never made any money trying to make money as such.

8. Stay in your own class and do not associate in business ventures with people with whom you cannot compete. If you can't compete with the mink class or Cadillac class, limit your competition to those on your own level. Attempting to "keep up with the Joneses" may well lead to disaster.

9. Acquire the reputation of having money, and the auto-

mobile you ride in or the type of apparel you wear will be incidental. Everyone wants to help the man on top.

Above all you should keep your sense of values no matter how high you climb. I have not had the opportunity that many have had in this age of being exposed to a sympathetic government, making it possible for every qualified person to get an education and prepare himself to serve society constructively. However, I am sure if one would observe my few rules and would take advantage of the wealth of educational opportunities and subsidies now available, success should be inevitable.

H. NAYLOR FITZHUGH

H. Naylor Fitzhugh is Vice-President for Special Markets of the Pepsi-Cola Company. In this capacity he is responsible for coordinating all phases of the Company's Special Markets Program with Pepsi-Cola bottlers throughout the United States and for passing final judgment on advertising and marketing programs designed for ethnic markets.

Born in Washington, D.C., on October 31, 1909, he holds the B.S. and M.B.A. degrees from Harvard University and has done advanced work in the field of marketing at Columbia and American Universities.

Before joining the Pepsi-Cola Company in 1965 as Vice-President, he served for thirty-two years on the faculty of Howard University in the Department of Business Administration. He has also served as a part-time faculty member at American University and as a lecturer at the Washington International Center.

Scholar, educator, and frequent lecturer before professional, civic, academic, and business groups, Mr. Fitzhugh has engaged in a number of research studies and has written extensively in the areas of the Negro market, the Negro in business, the role of public relations in business, and small-business activities in general—particulary with respect to manufacturer-retailer relations and business-government relations. As Research Associate of the Citizens' Housing and Planning Council of New York, he conducted a Study of the Medium-Rental Housing Market in West Harlem; and for the National Business Study Project, he directed a complete census of Negro firms in the nation's capital, including depth interviews with selected samples and an examination of the organizational structure of the Negro business community. He has also directed and conducted research studies and surveys for several of the leading business concerns and agencies in the country, including the Humble Oil and Refining Company, the Carnation Company, the

Gulf Oil Corporation, American Airlines, and the Area Redevelopment Administration.

H. Naylor Fitzhugh has held responsible positions in a number of national business organizations. In the National Association of Market Developers he has been the Executive Director, the Editor of *NAMD MEMO*, and National President. He has also served as National President of the National Business Education League. His service with national organizations includes membership on the Board of Directors of the American Marketing Association, the Inter-Racial Council for Business Opportunity, the National Association of Market Developers, and on the Advisory Board of the National Association of Radio Announcers. He is also a member of the National Advisory Committee to the Secretary, U.S. Department of Commerce; Chairman, Inter-Organizational Task Force, National Business League; and the Coordinator, Advertising Council, National Advertising Program, American National Red Cross.

His awards include the Certificate of Merit in Marketing Research from the Market Research Council and the Distinguished Service Award from the D.C. Chamber of Commerce.

A CHALLENGE TO BUSINESS

by H. Naylor Fitzhugh

TELEVISION portrayals of an increasingly affluent United States would lead most of us to believe that business conditions are changing for the better. This belief, I think, is essentially true, but—and this is a very big BUT—only for a limited number of minority group members. The progress we witness has not yet begun to catch up with eighty percent or more of these persons. Indeed, their relative educational, economic, and social positions have actually retrogressed in many respects during the past fifteen years. Daniel P. Moynihan pointed out in an article entitled "Employment, Income, and the Negro Family," published in the fall issue of *Daedalus*, 1965, that in terms of employment, income, and occupational status the two Negro communities—professional and blue collar—are possibly moving in opposite directions. In recent years there has been an increase of over 100 percent in the number of Negroes in professional, technical, and other white-collar jobs, and an increase in the blue-collar category, by contrast, of less than five percent. Thus, along with the noteworthy progress in the white-collar and professional categories, there still remains a need for massive short-range and long-range programs to motivate, recruit, employ, and upgrade large numbers of workers in the more ordinary occupations. This challenge jointly confronts business, organized labor, government, and the schools.

The disparity in growth between white-collar and blue-collar jobs helps to explain why many Negroes who have moved to higher levels of economic opportunity still intuitively identify with "the Negro problem." In a speech at Kent State University, for example, Carl Rowan, former Ambassador to Finland, who later became Director of the United States Information Agency and is currently a high-salaried syndicated columnist, said that the Negro slum dwellers and the Stokely Carmichaels were not the only angry black men around, and that he and every other Negro with sensitivity and pride could be counted among the ranks of the frustrated and disgusted. I must agree with Mr. Rowan's view. Regardless of station or attainment, all Negroes want what their white American counterparts want. And we certainly place high on this "want" list genuine respect for our basic human dignity, for our God-given talents and abilities. The so-called hypersensitivity of Negroes derives largely from the fact that so many whites either studiously or subconsciously refuse or fail to deal with them in ways that demonstrate respect for human dignity.

This issue of human dignity has business management implications for all ethnic minorities, and particularly for the Negro. There is little doubt that dignity is a basic issue, if not the basic issue, in current pressures from Negroes for equal opportunity in employment, in education, in citizenship, in housing, and in the courts. It is an equally basic issue in the business world.

Company communications and other business interrelationships with Negro consumers must function both on a marketing level—dealing with Negro consumers merely as consumers—and on a public relations level, dealing with them as an ethnic group with its own heritage, its own pride, and its own problems. Many companies would like to deal with Negroes solely as consumers, leaving their problems, and even their potentialities, for someone else to deal with. These companies want an ever increasing share of an estimated thirty-billion-dollar Negro market without concerning themselves with the sources of the supporting incomes or ways of appreciably expanding the per capita purchasing power of this market. This is a short-sighted view, for a market exists only as long as there is "green" power in the hands of the consumers who constitute that market. And the Negro minority market can only grow to the extent that industry and business provide jobs and job-training opportunities.

In offering employment and training opportunities, employers should consider the abilities and potential contributions of individuals to company programs and disregard those characteristics which set people apart. This policy should be carried out despite any apprehension on the part of management regarding possible effects on customers and co-workers. The present general acceptance by the public of integration throughout the business world has proved such apprehensions to be groundless.

Fair treatment has never worked to the detriment of any company. In fact, the reverse has been true, that companies have only benefited from such a policy. In the area of marketing, for example, progressive companies today know that there is a definite correlation between the spending habits of minority group consumers and the degree of fair and dignified treatment they are accorded. These consumers are demanding more and more recognition, for recognition is a significant manifestation of a business concern for human dignity. For years, many advertisers and their agencies followed a segregated policy in using advertising models, fearing that the inclusion of Negroes, even in familiar everyday settings, might be offensive to their white clientele. This policy, fortunately, has changed. My own company, for example, has developed TV sequences involving "realistic" situations, and business has actually increased.

Another of our programs to encourage self-esteem among Negro consumers is entitled "Adventures in Negro History." This program has resulted in two long-playing record albums which tell a story, authenticated by reputable historians, of noteworthy achievements of black men and women before, during, and after slavery. Among those dealt with are Pedro Alonzo Niño, who piloted one of Christopher Columbus' ships; Crispus Attucks, an escaped slave and the first American patriot to lose his life in the Boston Massacre; Prince Whipple, who crossed the Delaware River with George Washington and distinguished himself in battle against the British; John B. Russwurm, the first Negro college graduate in America and founder of the first Negro newspaper, *Freedom's Journal*; Harriet Tubman, known for her daring work with the Underground Railroad; and Booker T. Washington, founder of Tuskegee Institute. These albums have been distributed throughout the country to public and private school systems, libraries, radio networks, and other agencies, and reports we have received indicate that they have been a source not only of information but also of inspiration to thousands of young people.

A number of other companies have been active along similar marketing and public relations lines, and, as big business continues to recognize both the dollar value and the human value involved, the trend will continue. The increasing awareness of minority group consumers has special relevance to the Negro market, inasmuch as there is today a greater interest among black Americans in their Afro-American heritage than there has been at any other time in history. And this greater interest will definitely affect the kinds of portrayals of Afro-Americans that will be acceptable in mass communication media.

In addition to the concern for proper recognition in the business world at large, there is much talk today about "black business," "thinking black," and "building black." This is another manifestation of the desire for human dignity—not only at the consumer level —but at the managerial and ownership levels as well.

These latter levels, with very few exceptions, have been beyond the reach of Negroes because lending institutions, through discriminatory practices, have made it difficult for them to own businesses, and white business organizations, through similar practices, have made it practically impossible for them to advance to higher levels. Black Americans, however, have demonstrated their ability and readiness to assume the risks and to meet the personal and managerial requirements for success, on a competitive basis, in the challenging and exciting field of business, even though their numbers have been woefully small. Organized programs to encourage, support, and significantly expand such efforts, in fact, date back at least to 1900. They include the pioneering activities of Booker T. Washington and the National Business League which he founded.

Over the years, some encouragement and assistance have also come from a number of predominantly Negro colleges and universities, from a few government bureaus, and from one or two foundations. The past six or seven years have witnessed a further proliferation and expansion of programs—both governmental and private —directed specifically toward a wider participation of Negroes in the nation's business life—as self-employed entrepreneurs, as officers and managers in small and medium-sized corporate enterprises, and as holders of middle-management and junior-executive positions with major corporations and government agencies.

Many Americans—black and white—see some very wholesome outcomes from these developments. They see, for one thing, a black community increasingly able to negotiate its demands from a position of strength, power, dignity, self-respect, and responsibility. This, they feel, will compel dominant white America to consider the alternatives more seriously and more creatively. Moreover, since the historic demands of minority group citizens are in line with the best American tradition, many believe that what is good for the minority community is good for the entire nation—indeed, for the whole world.

There is a growing recognition, too, that business, which has so long benefited from the public, must assume in today's world new responsibilities to the public—responsibilities in areas of social concern heretofore considered to be the exclusive province of government. In the soul-searching that must inevitably accompany this recognition, we, in business, must expand our thinking to recognize the differences between a merely unfortunate circumstance, situation, or condition, and a problem. The former is a fact. You cannot solve it; you can only recognize, measure, or otherwise describe it. Similarly, a distinction must be made between a project and a program. When a circumstance, situation, or condition is hastily or incorrectly viewed as a problem, any step that follows is simply an activity, or at best a project. It cannot be a program in the sense of a carefully and realistically planned, coordinated, and executed set of developments deliberately directed toward the solution of a real problem.

Once a problem has been identified, expanded thinking is required in order to solve it. We need to measure, describe, and assess the various resources that are realistically available to help bring about change, or the resources that can be made available or developed for this purpose. We need to weigh alternative methods of utilizing the resources. We need to set time goals and priorities. Expanded thinking may cause us to realize that the solving of one problem is often contingent upon the identification and solution of related problems.

All of this points up one of the serious limitations of so many approaches to pressing social situations. Too many studies of what some people call the "problem" never get beyond measurement and description of the "situation." Thus, we talk about the so-called problems of unemployment, delinquency, school dropouts, and housing when, too often, we are merely listing facts about an undesirable existing situation. Such enumerations, in themselves, will not lead to change. This must have been what Whitney Young had in mind when he expressed in *Time* a New Year's wish that there would be no more studies of the Negro. Mr. Young no doubt is convinced that any such restudies of the Negro "situation," conducted in the name of a study of the "problem," would simply provide updated statistics describing already too familiar circumstances.

Business, as I have pointed out, must certainly involve itself in this question of problem-solving insofar as the racial "problem" is concerned. *The Wall Street Journal*, describing events in racially troubled Cincinnati, recently stated: "Though the [Negroes'] ostensible 'downtown' target . . . is city hall, the politicians are regarded as mere 'messengers' of the people who wield the real power—the business community."

Today's crises in urban centers throughout the land are appalling reminders of the need for human dignity at every level. How business contributes to the solution of the genuine problems that confront us will to a large extent affect the destiny of our "land of the free, and home of the brave."

FLAXIE M. PINKETT

President and Chairman of the Board of John R. Pinkett, Inc., Flaxie M. Pinkett is a well-known businesswoman who is active in civic affairs in the nation's capital. Born in St. Louis, Missouri, on November 30, 1917, Miss Pinkett completed her elementary and secondary schooling in the public schools of the District of Columbia. She attended Howard University, where she received the B.A. degree in 1936.

Employed by John R. Pinkett, Inc. after her graduation from college, she was elected Secretary of the Corporation in 1942, and was subsequently elected President and Chairman of the Board in 1958.

Among the offices she has held in various organizations are the following: President, D.C. Citizens for Better Public Education; Chairman, Trustees for the Stay-in-School Fund; Vice Chairman and Chairman, Advisory Council to the Superintendent of Schools of Washington, D.C.; Co-Chairman, United Negro College Fund; and Chairman, D.C. Council of the Health and Welfare Council. Her affiliations have included membership on the Education Committee, Washington Urban League; the National Committee for the Support of Public Schools; the Advisory Council, Department of Vocational Education, D.C. Schools; the Board of Directors, WETA-TV; the Health and Welfare Council for the Metropolitan Area; and the Board of Directors, United Givers Fund.

The numerous awards given to Flaxie M. Pinkett in recognition of her services to the community include the Merit Award from the District of Columbia Chamber of Commerce for "vision, courage, and dependability in business leadership, and untiring devotion to civic responsibility"; a citation from the Washington Council of the National Council of Negro Women for "outstanding contribution to the development of community life in the field of business"; and the Howard University Alumni Achievement Award for "outstanding service in the fields of business and community participation."

Miss Pinkett is a member of the Washington Board of Realtors, the Metropolitan Washington Board of Trade, the Washington Real Estate Brokers Association, the D.C. Chamber of Commerce, and the Cosmopolitan Business and Professional Women's Club.

HOW TO SUCCEED IN BUSINESS

BY REALLY TRYING

by Flaxie M. Pinkett

I AM the president of a real estate firm which was founded thirty-five years ago—in the depths of the Great Depression—by a man who had three strikes against him: he was out of a job, he had a wife and six children to support, and he was a Negro.

Today that firm is of substantial size. Its annual sales frequently exceed a million and half dollars. The company's physical plant, its personnel, and its business activities have a reputation for quality throughout the Washington community. The story of its growth and success is the story of Negro achievement and a very simple formula which has had much to do with making that success possible: "We are not a 'Negro Business.' We are a *business firm* which happens to be owned by people who happen to be Negroes."

My father, who founded the firm thirty-five years ago against such odds, repeated this statement many times. It epitomized his business philosophy. I agree with it completely, and my associates in the firm regard it as essential to our continuing, successful growth. What it comprehends is simply this: the first consideration of our business enterprise must be to render the best service our clients can get anywhere—regardless of the color of skin of the clients or the owners.

This formula also reflected my father's personal philosophy. For in his view, whatever achievement he might make as an individual and as a Negro would result from competence, from integrity, and from excellence. Further, this achievement would have to be made in open competition in an open market, where Negroes must compete with other Negroes and with whites.

As we all have, my father had seen, operating in the ghetto far too many "Negro businesses" which could not survive in open competition in a world where no ghettos existed. He had seen too many Negro professionals exploiting their captive clientele. (Perhaps they would have had no clientele at all in a truly free society.) He did not countenance this peculiar business philosophy of many members of his race of offering customers and clients the indignity of third-rate service in fourth-rate surroundings, secure in the knowledge that their ghettoized clientele could not go anywhere else and be accepted.

What was wrong from this business point of view was equally wrong from a moral point of view. From the standpoint of dollars and cents, the time was bound to come when large white firms would recognize the economic value of the "Negro market" and move in to offer goods, services, surroundings, and atmosphere superior to those which Negro-owned firms had been providing. At that point inefficient Negro-owned business enterprises would quickly and justifiably from an economic standpoint, lose their captive audience. From a moral point of view, Negroes who offered inferior business services to other Negroes not only were countenancing segregation but also were perpetuating the myth of Negro inferiority and dulling the ambition of the race.

My father's philosophy of competence and excellence in open competition has perhaps been our most valuable asset. It has been good for the enterprise; it has been good for the individuals associated with it; it has been beneficial for our clients; and I like to think its dividends have flowed out into the broad community.

For when the barriers of segregation began to crumble, we could record many significant "firsts": the first Negro-owned firm in the world to secure agency contracts with old-line stock insurance companies and to maintain its own underwriting department; to number among its executives the first Negro with the designation C.P.C.U.—Chartered Property Casualty Underwriter—hitherto reserved for whites only; to have as vice-president the first Negro with the M.A.I. designation, indicating membership in the American Institute of Real Estate Appraisers, hitherto a white-only organization; the first Negro-owned firm in the District of Columbia to be voted into the important, but hitherto all-white, Washington Board of Realtors; and one of the first to hold membership on the powerful Metropolitan Washington Board of Trade.

The important thing about these "firsts" is that as Negroes we were competing successfully in the open market. In making these forward moves, we were justifying the spirit of courage and citizenship that characterized the founder of this business.

In the process of achieving some measure of success, I believe we have proven some things about the role that Negroes can and should play in American society—and, equally important, we have disproved a good many false theories about what Negroes should not do or cannot do.

We have found that economic achievement is basic to acceptance. Nothing opens doors more quickly than the recognition that we are competent, successful businessmen. I do not mean that *all* doors are open, but daily we find more are opening. Whereas in the past we found few lending institutions willing to finance our clients' real estate transactions, today there are substantially more. Whereas thirty-five years ago we could not get an agency contract for insurance, today we are approached regularly by outstanding national companies in the field who are aware of our record and wish us to represent them. Whereas in the past our property management activity was restricted largely to smaller buildings in ghetto areas, now we manage large, modern, multi-unit apartments in all areas of the city.

We have found that old-fashioned integrity has a value of its own. At the risk of preaching, I can say that a reputation for business integrity has done as much for our business as any management skills we have been able to apply. The permissive climate in which Negro businessmen are often able to cut corners and engage in questionable but profitable practices would defeat us in the long run, as it has others. These questionable practices are another manifestation of the myth of Negro inferiority. The Negro businessman who indulges in them perpetuates the myth, regardless of how he benefits. We should never forget that the particular type of permissive climate with which Negroes are familiar exists only to keep us "in our place." We recognize that the myth still exists, but we must also recognize that to be accepted in the business community we have to offset the myth by our own exemplary behavior.

We have found that education and training are critical. Over the years we have had a hard time finding qualified people to work for us. A good part of the problem was due to the educational system itself and to private industry, which systematically excluded Negroes from training for the types of skills our business requires. As a result, we trained most of our personnel and in some cases provided scholarships to send them back to school to get the education required. Many of the people we have trained have moved on to professional careers or to businesses of their own. We feel their loss, of course, but we recognize that if the pattern continues to repeat itself, more and more Negroes will move from the "unskilled" to the "managerial" category. With educational opportunities so much greater than they have ever been before, we are committed to several programs here in Washington to see that our Negro youths get full access to these opportunities.

We have found that business enterprise itself solves many racial problems. Some years ago my father began to write the history of our business. His opening words were, "I decided to organize a business which would draw upon my experience in real estate and insurance to the end that I could support my family and build a business which would give employment to others as it had opportunities to serve more and more people." Certainly the purpose of supporting his family has been fulfilled in the intervening years, and it is no secret that the present employees of the firm include three daughters, a son, and a granddaughter full time, another daughter and two other grandchildren part time. His premise that it would give employment to others has also been fulfilled in that there are numerous other employees who are not members of his family, including the senior vice-president and the vice-presidents of insurance sales and real estate sales. Indeed, the time is not so long past when many of us would have had difficulty in finding comparable jobs—they existed only in the white community, behind doors that were closed to us. So, our experience has shown that the economic problems which are so closely tied to discrimination can sometimes be solved when we recognize that if we cannot get a job working for somebody else perhaps we should start working for ourselves!

We believe the businessman has a responsibility to the total community. It is not enough that businessmen make annual contributions to "united giving programs" or to their favorite local charities. As community leaders equipped with special know-how, they have the responsibility of giving man-hours and leadership in addition to financial contributions. They should volunteer service and direction in programs designed to eliminate the social ills that beset the less fortunate in their community. Their efforts should be directed to preventive measures that will raise the standard of living for all people. Likewise, they should encourage their staffs to become involved. This philosophy must be permeated with a desire to give back to the total community an "extra measure."

We have found that community responsibility goes hand in hand with economic achievement. The members of our firm have traditionally participated in a long list of community activities, including social-action groups and political parties. Our company policy supports this participation, not only because we believe in community responsibility, but because it makes good sense to work to improve the environment and the economic and the educational status of the members of the community we serve. It is a simple fact that you cannot sell real estate or insurance, or rent living quarters, to people who do not have the money to pay for them. They will not have the money to pay for them until they have the training, skills, and social conditions to encourage them to set worthwhile economic goals with the knowledge that they have a chance of achieving them. This, again, is a lesson for our race; economic goals do not stand by themselves, but must be nurtured no matter how dismal the surroundings or how depressing the work. This is more than so-called "social responsibility"; it is a practical matter of economic survival and progress.

We must never forget human dignity. In a business which deals daily with hundreds of fellow Negroes of limited education from poor surroundings, it is easy to recognize the caricatures and stereotypes that many whites still apply to us. It would be almost as easy to tear away their few shreds of dignity as many whites still do, both in our attitude while dealing with them and in offering inferior service and surroundings. This is wrong from both a moral and a business standpoint. Even if you do not believe in talking about morality in business, the fact remains that few businesses long survive on a policy of mistreating their customers; their failure to recognize human dignity is just a manifestation of an even larger ignorance about business enterprises. For years Negroes, as a race, have been fighting to obtain human dignity. If those of us who have achieved some measure of social and economic status deny dignity to others of our race (or of any race, for that matter), we will merely prove that we have not achieved status for ourselves after all. We should remember that the concept of noblesse oblige knows no color barriers.

We have learned that it is important to live in the world with all the people in the world. This is another way of saying that Negro racism is no better than white racism. Participation in either is based on an accident of birth. If we support Negro racism, we almost automatically support white racism because we accept the untenable theory that one race must be "better" than another. At that point we lose the values of morality and of science, and it just becomes a question of which race will win the battle—with probable defeat for Negro and white alike. In the course of building our business, we have dealt with people of many nationalities and many races. We do not "owe" our success to permissive support from the white community, nor to "racial" support from the Negro community. We have gotten—and given—fair value, dollar for dollar. And that is the way it should be. We prefer an economic society in which human values are good business.

We must never overlook the need for changing the image of the Negro in business. We must strive at every level to inspire, motivate, and set an example for the young black American who does believe that a good future for him lies ahead in the business world. We must invite young people into our businesses for guided tours, we must give them employment opportunities in the summer months, and we must participate in career clinics that are sponsored by local groups and schools. Yes, we must be ambassadors who prove through competent training, quality service, and civic participation that the Negro citizen of tomorrow can take advantage of a golden opportunity to participate in the mainstream of American life. We must demonstrate to young Negroes that there is available to them a financially profitable and spiritually satisfying life of service in the business world.

We have a long way to go before equality exists between the races. Those of us who have achieved to the point where we are invited to write down our thoughts in a book for others to read and follow are already in danger of being separated from the mainstream; and even those who read our thoughts are removed by several steps from the core of the problem. There are many things I could say on this score, but the most compelling argument for continuing to identify ourselves with the problems of our race, no matter how far removed from them we may be as individuals, is simply that we'll never be so far away from those problems that they no longer exist.

In the interim we have an obligation to ourselves to prepare for a better future. Today, we witness an increasing number of Negro-owned and operated businesses, with high regard for economic and ethical principles in their dealings with their clients as well as with their competitors. This is a heartening development. Pioneers, like my father, would be proud if they could witness this exciting new phenomenon.

Sports

JACKIE ROBINSON

Jack Roosevelt Robinson, former major league baseball star, was born in Cairo, Georgia, on January 31, 1919. At an early age he moved with his family to Southern California, where he received his formal academic training. He was an athletic standout at Muir Technical High School and added considerably to his stature as an amateur athlete at Pasadena Junior College, where he starred in four sports. In 1938 he led the school to eleven straight football victories and the Junior College Championship, scoring personally one hundred and thirty-one points and gaining one thousand yards from scrimmage. A top scorer in basketball, he was named "the most valuable player" in Southern California. In track he set a new world record for the broad jump by a junior college athlete. Subsequently, at U.C.L.A. he was also a four-letter man and was labeled by many sports writers and coaches at the time, "the best all-around athlete in America."

After serving in the Army for three years, he began his professional career in baseball as a shortstop for the Kansas City Monarchs in the Negro American League. In 1946 he joined the Montreal Royals, led the International League in batting, and was the best fielding second baseman. He also tied for most runs scored, and was second in stolen bases.

Moving in 1947 to the parent club, the Brooklyn Dodgers, he was the first Negro player in the major leagues, and became the National League's "Rookie of the Year."

During his ten-year stay with the Dodgers, he set fielding records, led the league in batting, and won recognition as the National League All-Star second baseman. In 1949, with a batting average of .342 he was named the National League's Most Valuable Player, and in 1962 he was elected to baseball's Hall of Fame.

Jackie Robinson left baseball in 1957 and became Vice-President and Member of the Board of Chock Full O' Nuts, a coffee and restaurant chain. At the same time he began campaigning for the

Civil Rights movement, raising funds for the NAACP and the Southern Christian Leadership Conference. In 1964 he resigned from Chock Full O' Nuts to serve as Vice Chairman of the Rockefeller for President National Committee. Two years later he was appointed by the Governor of New York as Special Assistant for Community Affairs.

Mr. Robinson is chairman of the Board of the Freedom National Bank and of the National Negro Republican Assembly, and National Vice-President of the NAACP.

In addition to the many awards he has received as a sports figure, Jackie Robinson has been the recipient, in the field of race relations, of such honors as the Carver Memorial Institute Gold Medal, the Benny Leonard Good Sportsmanship Trophy for "courage, fair play, and interest in humanity," honorary degrees, and the Spingarn Medal.

AN OCCASION FOR IMPATIENCE

by Jackie Robinson

SHORTLY after I was awarded the Spingarn Medal in 1956—an honor that I shall always cherish—I had the privilege of speaking at an NAACP Fund Rally in Los Angeles. I remember stating that our group's fight for real equality of opportunity had just begun, and that if I could choose between being named to baseball's Hall of Fame and seeing the Negro gain first-class citizenship, I would not hesitate a second to make the latter choice.

Unfortunately, there is no one formula that can guarantee how this first-class citizenship can be attained. There are views that range from violence as the only solution, to passive acceptance of the belief that time alone will effect results. Wanton violence, of course, cannot be condoned under any circumstances. On the other hand, I am convinced that merely doing nothing and waiting for time to solve the problem is also not the answer. It was, I believe, the great English poet John Milton who advocated patience and said in one of his sonnets, "They also serve who only stand and wait." But I do not think at all that patience is a virtue to be cultivated when man's fundamental rights are at stake. I believe that every legal means should be pursued to secure and maintain these rights and that one should constantly speak out against injustice, bigotry, and the like wherever and whenever they appear.

Those who feel that progress in human relations can only be made through a tedious and painful step-by-step course of gradualism, and who advocate forbearance and patience in this process, are entitled to their views. I do not share these views; and that is one reason, I suppose, why I have at times been labeled an impatient man.

Frankly, I am tired of waiting despite the fact that many of us have known opportunity and have enjoyed success. I believe that Negroes in the long run are fighting for a lost cause as long as they are content with individual opportunities and personal gains. I cannot say too loudly or too often that I think we *all* should be weary and tired of waiting, and until we *all* speak out frankly and do what we can to improve the fortunes of the underprivileged masses, there is not much chance of realizing our dream of a genuine democracy. Those fortunately situated cannot be satisfied with their own success and ignore their less fortunate fellow-men. All of us need to spend more time eliminating the remaining inequities that abound. We need to step up the fight against the forces denying complete freedom to all people and spend much less time gloating, as it were, over the gains we have made in the past.

I feel this way so strongly that I know I may have rubbed others the wrong way by things I've said; and many have called me a controversial figure. Certainly it is a fact that I have "sounded off" on issues when I might well have kept silent and avoided the labels "aggressive," "impatient," and "troublemaker." Epithets have not changed my convictions, however. When I see examples of injustice, persecution, intolerance, or other violations of basic ethics, I have to speak out. And I am convinced that it is only by speaking out and by acting through every legitimate means available that we can bring about desired change.

We simply cannot sit idly by and hope that things will "work out." I once said to President Eisenhower in a letter which I wrote after sitting in an audience at a meeting of Negro leaders that I felt like standing up and saying, "Oh, no! Not again!" when he advised his listeners to be patient. I pointed out that we had been the most patient of all people, and I wondered how we could preserve self-respect and remain patient considering the treatment accorded us throughout the years. Seventeen million Negroes could not wait hopefully forever for the hearts of men to change. They wanted to enjoy without further delay the rights they were entitled to as Americans. This they could not do unless they pursued aggressively the goals already achieved by other Americans. And I added respectfully that he unwittingly crushed the spirit of freedom in Negroes by constantly urging forbearance.

The Negro is part of the fabric of American society and must contribute his share to the national welfare. America is a pattern of thousands of communities housing people of all types who live, work, and play together. Our country was founded on a spirit of togetherness. For even before landing at Plymouth Rock, the Pilgrims had signed the Mayflower Compact, insuring the general welfare of all; and we have been growing as a nation, with laws enacted for the common good, as our boundaries expanded, ever since. Now that our nation has spread even beyond the continent, with literally thousands of cities, towns, and hamlets dotting the countryside, the greater accord for the common good that people living together can achieve, the stronger our nation will be. The important factor is the spirit in which we meet and work with people around us. If some groups are excluded from America's bounty, whether they are Japanense, or Jews, or Mexicans, or Negroes, or any other segment of the population, there can be genuine democracy for none.

Where the Negro is concerned, we have made gains; but the pace has been too slow. Even in baseball, which has come a long way since I first put on a major league uniform, there is much to be desired. Although Negro players have proved their ability in every area primarily related to the diamond—hitting, base running, pitching, and fielding—they are not yet in the ranks of field managers, general managers, and key front-office personnel. I think frankly that owners are still under the nineteenth-century illusion that a white ball player will not work for a Negro manager. This has certainly been disproved in the case of Bill Russell of the world-champion Boston Celtics basketball team. To further disprove this theory, I can cite from personal experiences with my former Dodger teammates, who ultimately showed that they cared nothing whatever about the color of a player's skin. There were difficulties at first, but even the Southerners came around. Individuals on the team would say, "Watch me, and if you see what I'm doing wrong, tell me." Or they would go to Campanella or Don Newcombe, or to anyone else who could make helpful suggestions.

The basic thing is that association permits communication to develop. The early difficulties I experienced in baseball resulted, at least in part, from a lack of communication. The white players really knew little or nothing about Negroes; they had heard that Negroes were "different" and that "things would happen" if they joined the team. But once they had an opportunity to see that we were basically no different—that skin color was the only difference—they changed their attitudes to a remarkable degree. Oddly, I think the

Southerners on the ball club were the first to give me and other Negroes assistance in time of need. They were much more cooperative than many Northerners who professed to be liberal. Dixie Walker, who had vehemently opposed my coming into baseball, changed greatly; and Eddie Stanky from Alabama was the first player to speak up for the "Rickey Experiment." Of course, personal views are never absent in human relationships, but my point is that skin color was ruled out as a factor when communication was established.

Certainly, things should be easier now for athletes than they were when I played baseball. One noticeable change is the courage displayed by Negro athletes in all sports today. They are not only willing to participate, but they are also forthright enough to speak out when conditions are not what they should be.

And conditions should become and must become better in all areas of American life. There has been progress in some respects, but not enough to boast of. In many other respects the gap between Negroes and whites is widening, and the core of resistance appears to be hardening. Unless there is a change—an almost immediate one—there may well develop a confrontation far more serious than the disturbances we have already known—a confrontation that this nation cannot afford if it hopes to survive. All of us of every race, of every conviction, and of every station must work together—with impatience if you will—to make America a true model of democracy for all the world.

JERSEY JOE WALCOTT

Arnold R. Cream, the Assistant Director of Public Safety in Camden, New Jersey, was born in Merchantville, New Jersey, on January 31, 1914. He received his early education in the public schools of his native city, and assumed as a youth the responsibilities of a wage earner to assist his parents with the upbringing of a family of nine children. At the same time, he cultivated his interest in athletics and spent long hours in developing his skill as an amateur boxer before finally becoming a professional.

Inspired by the career of Joe Walcott, a boxer who held the welterweight championship at the turn of the century, Arnold Cream adopted the ring name "Jersey Joe Walcott," which he retained throughout a lengthy boxing career and by which he is familiarly known today. During the 1930's and early 1940's Jersey Joe built up an impressive professional record. In the earlier years of his ring career he fought in several divisions, winning successively the Lightweight Championship, the Welterweight Championship, and the Light Heavyweight Championship of New Jersey. Eventually he became a heavyweight and an outstanding title contender. On July 18, 1951, he won the World Heavyweight Title from Ezzard Charles in Pittsburgh, Pennsylvania, by a knockout in the seventh round.

Approximately a year later, he defended his title successfully in a return bout against Charles, defeating him in a fifteen-round decision, but lost it to Rocky Marciano on September 23, 1952, in Philadelphia by a knockout in the thirteenth round.

After an unsuccessful attempt to regain the championship from Marciano in a return fight, Jersey Joe retired from the ring. He became a boxing referee and later began a new career as a parole officer in Camden.

Since his retirement as a fighter, Jersey Joe Walcott has been active in local civic affairs, concerning himself particularly with boys' clubs and various other programs involving juvenile activities and the welfare of youth, and has been honored on numerous occasions in recognition of his contribution to youth and his leadership qualities.

BORN A MILLIONAIRE

by Jersey Joe Walcott

Joe, would you comment on your background, early childhood, and other influences that you feel have been important in your life?

WELL, as a young fellow I always admired fighters and dreamed about becoming one. In Merchantville, N.J., where I was born and raised, there was a training center for all the old great fighters such as Jack Johnson, Sam Langford, Joe Gans, Joe Jeanette, and many others. These fighters made quite an impression on me, and I felt that with the type of physique I had and the little know-how I had acquired in boxing, I might perhaps develop into a fairly good fighter myself. I had always had a boyhood dream of becoming a world champion.

At fourteen years of age, I started going to the gymnasium to train. When I was fifteen, I had my first professional fight in New Jersey, and fortunately was able to win it in the first round. All in all, I boxed for twenty-three years. It took me twenty-one years before I became world champion.

After fifteen years of boxing, my highest purse was only three hundred dollars. Throughout the years, I had many ups and downs and many heartaches. There were many times when things looked so black and so dreary that I wondered if I could keep going. But coming from the type of family and home life that I had enjoyed, I had faith and a determination to succeed. I knew that if I wanted to succeed, I'd have to keep on trying no matter how tough the odds were.

Joe, would you comment on some of the important fights that you've had—perhaps talk about some of the highlights of your boxing career?

Yes, I've had so many important fights, particularly in the latter part of my career! I boxed most of the great fighters of my time: fellows like Jimmy Bivins, Curtis Sheppard, Joey Maxim, Lee Oma, Joe Baksi, Elmer Ray—to mention only a few of the truly outstanding fighters of my day. Any one of them at any given time could have been a world champion. Then, of course, I fought Joe Louis twice, Ezzard Charles four times, and Rocky Marciano twice.

But I suppose the real highlights of my boxing career came in my fights with Joe Louis and in winning the heavyweight title from Ezzard Charles in 1951. If I could talk for a week, it would be impossible for me to describe the true feeling I had on that night in Pittsburgh when I knocked Charles out in the seventh round and won the championship. After twenty-one years of ups and downs and disappointments, waiting for that dream day to come true, I simply can't express what I felt. You look up to the heavens and ask God's help. And then you find that God is there to answer your prayer. Well, you just can't believe what a great accomplishment it is and what an obligation you feel that you owe to God and to mankind for the opportunity you have in this great country of ours to win success. That's why I made a promise to God that if I ever became champion—even if only for a day—I would give my life to serving my community and my nation in trying to help young people.

Joe, there have been many changes in boxing over the years. What do you think about the present situation in boxing? How do you compare today's fighters with the old-timers?

Well, comparing boxing today with boxing a few years ago, the chief difference that I can see lies in the fact that there aren't as many good fighters today as there were in the past. Perhaps the fighters today don't take boxing as seriously as the fighters did when I was active. Most fighters now seem to consider boxing more of a business than a profession. In my opinion, some of the fighters today—that is, the few of them that are around—are just as good, if not a little better (more skillful, better boxers, better equipped) than some fighters in past years.

But, on the whole, the fighters of my era were much more determined. They were hungry fighters. Because opportunities were so limited, we had to go into boxing in order to lift ourselves above the conditions we were forced to live under. But now, the young men of today have so many opportunities open to them for success in other fields that very few of them turn to boxing, which, after all, offers no guarantee or assurance of success. In spite of this, though, I still believe that young men, and especially young men of minority groups, will have a difficult time choosing a profession that will give them the opportunity for greater success, wealth, and glory than prize-fighting does.

Joe, I'm sure there are some specific suggestions you can give to the young boxer just starting his career. Would you say something about this point?

I think the most important thing I could say to any young man who wants to enter boxing—or any profession for that matter—is that he must first be true to himself. He must have the firm realization that if he is true to himself, he'll be able to do the things he must do in order to give his best to whatever profession he has in mind.

So far as the young boxer specifically is concerned, I'd have to say that he must learn first of all to train sincerely. No fighter should expect to perform at his best half-conditioned. Over and above practically everything else, a fighter must train faithfully. He must be obedient to his trainers and must listen to his manager, and must avoid any type of dissipation that would be injurious to his body.

But above all these things, I found in my own career the need for depending and leaning on Someone who is far greater than I am. And so I would say: look up to the hills and have faith in Almighty God because I've found in my life that my ability and my determination have played only a secondary part in my success. The principal thing is not to have any doubts; just continue with tremendous faith, and you'll rest assured that in His time and in His way, He'll answer your prayer.

Joe, what about some of the obstacles or difficulties that stood in your way before you finally reached the championship?

That's a difficult question to answer; I've had to overcome so many obstacles in my long career! I suppose, though, if I had to single out any one disadvantage, it would be that in the early part of my career I was never fortunate enough to have a manager who was able to give me the necessary support or who had the financial backing to handle my career so that I would be relieved of financial worries and responsibilities. You know, I got married when I was only eighteen years old, and I started right out in raising a family. It took a lot of money then, as it does now, to support a family. Consequently, I wasn't able to devote my full time to boxing but had to work while I was in training. Many times I had to take a fight on a week's notice, or even on three or four days' notice. In my early career I was never really in proper condition; and when you've not trained properly, you can't perform properly. In those days, if a fight went beyond six rounds, I was in trouble because of lack of conditioning. I believe that was the chief reason that I had such a tough struggle, such a long climb before I was in position to compete against top-flight fighters.

Joe, I wonder if we could go back to your early years. Did you come from a large family? And, if so, how was it living with a large number of brothers and sisters? Do you have any special memories of your childhood? Was there any one person who meant a great deal to you, who inspired you even as a child?

You know, I think that I'm one of the most fortunate fellows in the world. I did come from a large family—four boys and five girls— a family of great love, great understanding, great friendship, and a family with wonderful guidance. It was a family of poor financial means—yet, I can't help believing that we children were born millionaires because of the type of parents we had.

I don't think—and I say this in the humblest fashion and the most respectful way—I don't think that I've ever met a man that I could compare with my father. A plain, hard-working man, he dedicated his whole life to the welfare of his family. I believe that he was truly the greatest guy that ever lived! The good life demonstrated by the everyday acts and deeds of the kind of father and mother I had played the greatest role in my early years. Their guidance, their help, their encouragement, and their example were an inspiration to me. I only wish that every child in the world had parents like mine!

So many of our boys and girls today are the victims of broken homes, or live in families that seem to place more importance on things than on human relations. Parents—the right kind—can and do make a difference!

Joe, you mentioned the work that you're doing now. Would you care to comment on the very responsible position that you hold today?

I consider myself very fortunate to live in a city like Camden that has a liberal-minded man as mayor. He's a man who serves all the people—the minority as well as the majority. And he feels that if a man can do a job, he should be given the opportunity to do it in a responsible way. When the mayor came into office, he saw the things that some of us were trying to do to improve the community; and he felt that placing me in a job with official responsibility would give me a greater advantage and more possibility of success.

This is how I—a fellow with an eighth-grade education—eventually became the Assistant Director of Public Safety after I had retired from the ring. It's a new job; it's a job that the mayor created. I'm between the chief of police and the director, and now have the opportunity to do, on a larger scale, some of the things that need to be done. Actually, I'm in charge of the Juvenile Division, which comprises eleven men—a lieutenant, a sergeant, and nine detectives—and the Community Relations Unit, which comprises six men and a sergeant. The Juvenile Division takes care of our youth problems, and the Community Relations Unit works to keep the lines of communication open between our community— all the citizens—and the Police Department, making people aware of the job of the policeman. We have to convince the public that the police officer is not just a man with a badge who comes to make an arrest; he's a man who serves the public whenever there's a problem of any kind. His job is to serve and help the community.

Joe, would you care to comment on some of the honors that have come to you as the result either of your boxing fame or your civic contributions?

When a fellow has enjoyed the great success and the great pleasure and happiness that I have gained from my boxing career, it would be difficult to ask for anything more. But rewards far beyond those associated with my boxing career have come to me in connection with the work I'm doing here in my community with the Police Department, and especially with young people. I don't think there's anything more rewarding than having the opportunity to serve your community, helping young people to find their way in life. In spite of all the money and honors I've received in my boxing career, I don't believe that I could have ever chosen anything that would give me more personal satisfaction and happiness than I get from the work that I'm doing now. You know, I said before that I was born a millionaire because of my parents and my wonderful home life. Well, that still holds true now. I wouldn't want any greater reward than the appreciation shown me by the community for the help I've been able to give to my fellow citizens in our fine city of Camden.

Joe, you probably know better than most people about social unrest and the problems we're having—particularly the racial problems of today. What's your opinion about these matters?

I believe that many things need to be done by both races. Our major problems, it seems to me, come from a lack of understanding. I don't believe that the white community understands the black community, or that the black community understands the white community. Until we have some understanding of each other's problems, it will be difficult to solve the situation.

As far as our race is concerned, I believe that we, as Negroes, have a great obligation to ourselves and to our country. If we want something out of life, we've got to realize that we must give something of ourselves. If we expect to get good jobs, we have to accept the fact that we must first qualify for them. We shouldn't expect to be given an opportunity, or a job, or a position merely because we're Negroes. The most important thing that I try to stress in my work is that we must qualify ourselves for the opportunities that exist or that will come. If we're qualified and then are turned down in any respect, we may be disturbed or feel disgusted, but we shouldn't let the way we feel change our outlook on life. You know, I said earlier that regardless of what profession a person might choose—or whether he's white or black—if he believes in himself, if he knows he has the ability, and if he has faith, no one can stop him. The whole world can't stop a determined man!

Other Professions

WILLIAM H. HASTIE

The present Chief Judge of the United States Court of Appeals for the Third Circuit in Philadelphia, Pennsylvania, William H. Hastie was born on November 17, 1904, in Knoxville, Tennessee. He was graduated from Dunbar High School in Washington, D.C., and from Amherst College, and completed his advanced studies in law at Harvard University, from which he received the Bachelor of Laws and Doctor of Juridical Science degrees.

Judge Hastie taught at the Manual Training School in Bordentown, New Jersey for two years immediately upon completing his undergraduate work. Admitted to the District of Columbia bar in 1931, Judge Hastie began to practice law in Washington, D.C., with the firm of Houston and Houston. From 1930–37 he was a faculty member of the School of Law at Howard University, where he served later as Dean from 1939 to 1946. His tenure at Howard was interrupted by a number of important assignments. From 1933–37 he was Assistant Solicitor with the United States Department of Interior; from 1937–39 he was Judge of the District Court of the Virgin Islands; and from 1940–42 he served as Civilian Aide to the Secretary of War. He was Governor of the Virgin Islands from 1946–49 and served also as a member of the Caribbean Commission from 1947–50. He resigned his post as Governor of the Virgin Islands following his appointment by President Truman to the United States Circuit Court of Appeals, Third Circuit.

During the past twenty years he has been awarded honorary degrees from numerous colleges and universities, including the Doctor of Laws degree from Hampton Institute, Rutgers University, Howard University, Yale University, Amherst College, Temple University, University of Pennsylvania, Atlanta University, Dropsie College, Central State College, Virginia State College, Lincoln University, Ohio Wesleyan University, Knoxville College, and Allegheny College. He has also received the honorary degree of Doctor of Humane Letters from Bates College.

Judge Hastie has been the subject of a number of articles published in national magazines. Throughout the years he has served as a member of numerous professional, civic, and social organizations, and has been the recipient of many honors and awards, including the coveted Spingarn Medal, which he received for distinguished service as a jurist.

Judge Hastie is a Fellow of the American Academy of Arts and Sciences and Chairman of the President's Commission on White House Fellows.

NO ROYAL ROAD

by William H. Hastie

A PHILOSOPHER once told a petulant and impatient king that there is no royal road to learning. More generally, there is no simplistic approach to worthwhile achievement in human affairs. And this is doubly so in its application to the disadvantaged individual or group identified as American Negro. Yet, difficulty need not foreshadow despair or defeat. Rather, achievement can be all the more satisfying because of obstacles surmounted.

I was reminded of this very recently. On June 12, 1967, the United States Supreme Court decided that state laws prohibiting and punishing interracial marriages violate the constitutional guarantee of equal protection of the laws. Punsters chuckle that this landmark decision is entitled *Loving against Virginia*. Otherwise, the American community seems to be accepting the Supreme Court's sanctioning of intermarriage in Loving's case with remarkable equanimity. Apparently, that decision is not evoking the widespread fulminations and defiant denunciations which followed the invalidation of racially segregated schools in the middle 1950's and earlier proscriptions of government-sanctioned racism in areas regarded as far less sensitive than intermarriage.

This may reflect the existence of rather widespread anticipation that the decision *would* be as it *proved* to be. For in the course of Supreme Court decisions over the last twenty-five years every directly challenged racist law or governmental practice has been found invalid under our Constitution. More important, the acceptance of this latest decision reflects the development of such public tolerance of an equalitarian legal order as was almost unimaginable a few years ago.

The twenty-five year contrast is remarkable. In 1942 government-imposed racial segregation and state sanction of invidious racist practices were commonplace. This discriminatory pattern covered

the franchise, public education, access to places of public accommodation, public employment, and government-owned or financed
housing. It pervaded the major areas of publicly regulated conduct.
Even our national government was stubbornly maintaining the
most offensive and inexcusable racial segregation and discrimination in the armed services, in federal employment, and in public
housing.

Moreover, widely respected leaders, generally characterized as
"liberals," were warning that government sanction of much of this
racism would persist for the calculable future. For example, the
well-known Southern editor, John Temple Graves, in one of the
most discussed articles of the period, expressed the widely held
view that the prevailing pattern of state-supported segregation "is
not going to be eliminated . . . but it does not preclude a constant
improvement in the Negro's side of Jim Crow."

Yet, in striking down the so-called "miscegenation laws," the
Supreme Court now has invalidated the last remaining major governmental imposition of invidious racial distinction in the legal
order.

Perhaps only one who was an adult Negro in America during the
period of World War II can fully appreciate that change. Gross
and unjustifiable as the indignity and injury of government-imposed
racism were, it seemed almost hopeless even to struggle against
discrimination and segregation when the law of the land sanc-
tioned or even required them in so many blatant forms. Yet, today
the American legal order is equalitarian. Organized society, at the
federal, state, or local level, cannot lawfully discriminate among
men on the basis of race, though much of individual human behavior still does not comport with that standard.

This comprehensive reshaping of the legal order constitutes one
of the most extraordinary achievements of society in our time, or
in any other. It has been the result of planned and organized effort
spearheaded by small groups of people, most of them Negroes and
most of them lawyers, functioning for a generation principally
under the aegis of the National Association for the Advancement
of Colored People. My own association with that effort during its
earlier years and my observation of its entire course embolden me
to attempt to identify the ingredients and characteristics that have

made it so outstanding and so significantly successful. I think they have significance broader than the particular enterprise.

Here was a major testing ground of the potential and efficacy of the science of law applied to American constitutionalism in the unending task of progressively ordering society. What was required was no less than the redirection of the entire course of authoritative construction and interpretation of the equal protection and due process clauses of the Constitution so that general constitutional commands that the state be essentially fair and equalitarian in its impositions would protect the members of the Negro minority in their many and varied relations with public institutions and the organized community. In area after area this required the determination, systematic elaboration, and persuasive articulation of the impact of racist rules and practices upon human beings and their society. The social presuppositions and factual assumptions which distorted the concept of equality in earlier judicial precedents had to be reexamined, and their fallacies and sophistries exposed in the light of subsequent experience, greater knowledge, and the increased human sensitivity and sophistication which characterize such a developing society as ours.

Those whose task was to persuade the courts, and the American community as a whole, that particular racial proscriptions were constitutional wrongs had first to deepen their own insight into the functioning of the legal and social order and then to translate that understanding into coherent legal analysis and sophisticated professional and popular presentations calculated to persuade courts and communities that former modes of reasoning had been faulty and now must be corrected. This process was made noteworthy and unusual by the extensive and effective use of research and learning provided by other social sciences as an integrated part of legal analysis and argument.

This meant that the architects of the contemplated changes had to bring to bear upon their problems a very high order of intelligence, professional skill, and social understanding. Bold and resourceful departures from traditional modes of proof and legal analysis were needed to establish a demonstrably better case for new views of constitutional equality than highly skilled opponents could marshal in support of theretofore accepted narrower notions. Strategically, it was necessary to calculate and plan the course of attack upon the old legal structures so that the ancient walls would first be assailed at their weakest and most vulnerable points, where the likelihood of making breaches was greatest. Thus, discriminatory voting laws were the first to be attacked, and miscegenation laws the last.

Men and women capable of engineering this reshaping of the legal order had to be first-rate in several respects. Obviously, they had to be excellent lawyers. Their minds had to be trained and disciplined for successful combat with the ablest competitors at the bar and for the persuasive presentation of highly controversial cases from the trial level to the Supreme Court of the United States. Their knowledge of a major area of law had to be cyclopaedic and systematic. In the struggle, no allowances would be made for the deficient background of any advocate, or for inferior early training, or for inadequate grasp of subject matter. Only those whose mentality, determination, and persistence had enabled them to achieve mastery of difficult subject matter and who had the ability to use knowledge creatively could succeed. For the accomplishment of such a task as this, there could be no substitute for outstanding ability and resourcefulness and years of rigorous preparation.

When Negro players were admitted to major league baseball, their success depended upon major league knowledge, ability, and drive. This is equally true of social engineering through law and of every other demanding field of human endeavor.

An enlightened and optimistic philosophy of social struggle in this country was no less essential to effective work for an equalitarian legal order. The cornerstone of this philosophy had to be a wholesome concept of the intrinsic merit of American society and the fundamental institutions of the Republic. For the effort to reform the legal order could succeed only if our national commitment to the ideal of a fair and equalitarian society, and the disposition of contemporary leadership to implement that ideal, were genuine and strong enough to motivate official action and win adequate popular support for constitutional reinterpretation.

It is often difficult for Negroes to believe that our fundamental institutions are thus sound and adapted to drastic social change, and that our nation is committed to significant movement toward a fairer and more equalitarian order. Yet, this we had to believe in order to make it seem worthwhile to undertake and unremittingly continue the struggle to reshape the legal order. Those who deny or despair of the will of the American community and its capacity through our fundamental institutions to make society more decent and more rewarding for the disadvantaged can disrupt the community, or even destroy it. Only those who are convinced of the organic soundness of the nation and its will to improve can reform it.

Beyond this optimistic view of our nation and its fundamental institutions, it is necessary that we distinguish between a battle and a campaign, and that we relate the planning and execution of each battle to the winning of the larger campaign. Obviously, it is not possible for any person, or small group of persons, to fight effectively against social injustice on all fronts at one time. And even on a single front, a particular engagement has major significance only as it helps toward the larger objectives of the campaign. Only within the framework of this concept of effective social struggle can those who plan and lead avoid the dissipation of effort and the exhaustion of their forces in the pursuit of relatively inconsequential victories.

Civilized man has to believe in the power of trained intelligence, systematically and persistently applied in accordance with sound concepts and planning, to influence and redirect the course of human events. Success achieved in the elimination of racism from the American legal order during the last thirty years has vindicated that belief. It will find further vindication as individual Negroes and Negro groups increasingly bring trained and creative intelligence to bear in persistent, carefully calculated effort, whether addressed to individual concerns or the problems of the group. There is no easier road to worthwhile achievement in human affairs.

MYLES A. PAIGE

Until his recent retirement, Myles A. Paige was Judge of the Family Court of the State of New York.

Born in Montgomery, Alabama, on July 18, 1898, he completed his elementary and secondary school training in that city, and, after graduating from Alabama State Teachers College, he attended Howard University, receiving the A.B. degree. His legal training was obtained at Columbia University, which awarded him the LL.B. degree.

Judge Paige has had a long career of public service in the field of law. A former Assistant Attorney General of the State of New York, he was appointed in 1936 as the first Negro City Magistrate of the City of New York. In 1940 he was promoted to the position of Associate Justice of the Court of Special Sessions and received in 1950 a second ten-year appointment to that post. Before the expiration of his second term, he was made, in 1958, a Justice of the Court of Domestic Relations. The tenure of his last position, that of Judge of the Family Court of the State of New York, ran from 1962 to 1966, the year of his retirement.

His extra-legal activities have ranged over a wide area. In community work, he has been a President of the Brook-Boro Club of New York, the Community Association of Brooklyn, and the Comus Club. He has also held the offices of Chairman of the Board of the Brooklyn NAACP, Co-Chairman of the Brooklyn National Conference of Christians and Jews, Vice Chairman of the Greater New York Fund, and Secretary of the National Urban League Board. In addition, he has served as a member of the Advisory Committee of the New York City Youth Board, the Hospital Council of Greater New York, the Executive Committee of the Boy Scouts of America, the Schaeffer Award Committee, the Board of the Industrial Home for the Blind, the National Catholic Interracial Council, the National Catholic Committee on Aging, the Board of the Woodward Community College, and the Board of Trustees of

Howard University. He has also been active in a number of fraternal organizations and, as a Colonel in the Army Reserve, in several military groups.

In the course of his career, Judge Paige has received numerous honors, including the honorary degree of Doctor of Laws from Howard University and Doctor of Humanities from Wilberforce University. He is an Honorary Life Member of the Bedford Stuyvesant Real Estate Board and holds honorary memberships in the Vulcan Society of the New York City Fire Department and the Cerberean Society of the New York City Transit Police Department.

REMINISCENCES OF THIRTY

YEARS ON THE BENCH

by Myles A. Paige

MY appointment as City Magistrate of the City of New York on September 2, 1936, marked the first time that a Negro had been appointed to such a position in this great metropolis. I accepted the appointment as a challenge and determined to prove false the general impression that a Negro could not be as good a judge of all people as anyone else. I dedicated all my efforts to this task in the firm conviction that the day would come when a Negro jurist would be granted full recognition.

Approximately three years after my appointment, I was called one day to Mayor Fiorella LaGuardia's office. I found the Mayor in conference with the Corporation Counsel, who was of Southern extraction. The Mayor asked if I had met the chief city law officer. I responded that I had met the gentleman a few years earlier when I was seeking a position and had been referred to his office—the largest law office in the world—by the Mayor himself. The only opening offered me then by the Corporation Counsel was a menial job, which I refused to take. Following this disclosure, Mayor LaGuardia turned to his visitor and said, "That was your loss. Judge Paige is now one of the best magistrates in this city."

This may seem small praise today, but things must be weighed on the scales of the times in which they occur. Not only was a Negro magistrate a rarity to a Southern Corporation Counsel, he was a rarity to his own people.

When I was first appointed I was assigned to a Harlem court. Among the cases to be heard while I was presiding one Sunday morning was one in which a white police officer had arrested an old Negro woman who had been in jail all Saturday night before being brought to the court. When this case was called, the officer stepped up before the bench with the old lady. As I looked at the policeman and the poor old lady, he, knowing already my attitude in such cases, spoke up immediately: "Judge, I did not want to arrest this woman, and I told her to put down the small article which she was alleged to have stolen from the 125th Street department store. I asked her to leave the store and warned her not to do that again. Whereupon she told me that she wanted to be arrested and that if I did not arrest her for this, she would take something else, so I had no choice." Then I turned to the old lady and asked, "Why did you insist on being arrested?" She stepped up closer to the bench and said, "Judge, as you can see I'm an old woman, over seventy-five years of age, and I have been waiting and hoping all these years to see a judge of my race on the bench, and I wanted to get arrested just to see you." Of course I told her that she did not have to get arrested for that purpose, as she could walk into the courtroom at any time and see me. She said, "Well, I didn't know that." I had the police officer withdraw the charge and sent her home happy.

It has always been my belief that a judge must do more than sit in a court and pronounce guilt or innocence. The cold, impartial meting out of sentences to the guilty or terse dismissal of complaints against the innocent is an essential part of our judicial system—but it is not enough by far. To be worth his salt, a magistrate must take an interest in his fellow-man, must try to understand the springs that motivate human conduct, and must do whatever he can to prevent the occurrence of crime and to persuade people to the right.

Success in law enforcement and in the total legal and educative process should be measured not only by the efficiency of the trial process, but also by the fewness of the cases for which trial is necessary. Ultimate success will be achieved when the need for trial has disappeared entirely.

In the conviction that crime should be prevented as well as punished, I have always felt that each of us in his own way should do what he could to divert others—particularly the young—from a life of potential crime or from making mistakes which might have serious aftereffects.

Ignorance of the consequences and sheer thoughtlessness have started many young people in the wrong direction. In my early days on the bench, there were many cases involving school boys, who, more for the fun of it than anything else, would go under the turnstiles or through the gate to the subway train without paying the few cents' fare. These boys were frequently arrested by transit policemen, and, when taken to court, were finger-printed and branded with criminal records if later convicted.

The serious consequences of these juvenile pranks caused me considerable concern, and I took the matter up with the mayor of the city. He agreed that I should arrange to speak at as many school assemblies as possible to advise young people that this kind of action, which seemed frivolous to them then, could be quite serious. Their records would face them in later years when they applied for jobs. Should they decide upon a career in law, a conviction might prevent them from being admitted to practice in spite of the fact that they passed all the examinations required. A desire to enter other fields might well meet with similar obstacles.

My having spent even a small amount of time in guidance—and crime prevention if you will—has paid, I believe, some handsome dividends. Many a young man in later years has thanked me for having pointed out to him the dangers in what he had considered at the time a bit of boyish fun.

In a day when individual rights, and minority rights in particular, are in the forefront of our nation's discussions and our court's decisions, it is difficult to realize how lightly these rights were taken a generation ago. It is particularly difficult for the young, who are clamoring for so-called equal rights on every front, to realize that there was a time when the indigent, the ignorant, and the oppressed had but few "rights" at all. It is difficult to realize that there was a time when there were no organizations prepared and willing to carry the fight for human rights to the highest court in the land, if need be.

I remember when there was a general practice by police detectives, particularly in Negro communities, to force their entrance into private homes where they claimed to suspect gambling or use of narcotics. Though the law required the detectives first to secure a search warrant, they usually considered this too much trouble in such neighborhoods. Even without a warrant they generally obtained convictions where card playing was found and when they alleged that they had discovered some narcotics. In many cases there had been no real gambling, and often the owner of the house claimed that the narcotics had been "planted" or brought in by the police.

In such instances, when there had been no warrant, I would dismiss the case. In similar cases, however, other judges held that the evidence was admissable, although they must have realized that the aggrieved defendant could sue the police. Even the state's highest court had upheld convictions under such circumstances. My contention was that this type of treatment was a violation of the United States Constitution, which superseded the decision of the courts. I hoped fervently that someone would have the courage and the means to carry the fight further, and thus establish once and for all the concept of equal protection under the law regardless of station in life. Yet no lawyer or defendant would appeal the conviction, since such a process was too expensive or too troublesome, particularly when the sentence given was a light one. However, after many years, a defendant in such a case in the state of Ohio did appeal to the United States Supreme Court (Mapp vs. State of Ohio), and that court held and decided just as I had done during all the preceding years.

Not all cases appearing before a magistrate are of a serious character; hence, a judge should have a sense of humor to appreciate fully the foibles of human nature. There are occasionally cases which offer comic relief to the serious and often tedious routine of dealing in unfortunate misunderstandings and human depravity.

Throughout my years on the bench, there have been many instances that I can still recall with a quiet chuckle. In one case in the traffic court section of the Magistrate's Court, there appeared before me the driver of a coal truck who was charged with failure to give a hand-signal when he was about to make a right turn. The driver, when asked to plead, said: "Judge, it was like this, I was driving this ten-foot-high-great-big-black coal truck, and it was just about near dark and the other man ran square into the rear of that big truck. Now, Judge, if he couldn't see that big black coal truck, how could he see my little black arm?"

Similarly, in the Court of Special Sessions there were many amusing cases. This court conducted hearings on charges of paternity involving support for children born out of wedlock. In one case twins were born, and the respondent was asked if he admitted or denied being the father of the twins, and he answered: "Judge, I admit I'm the father of one of the twins but, Judge, I ain't the father of that ugly one."

On another occasion in the same court, a Negro was charged with violating the law against the manufacture of alcohol without a license. When one of my white associate Justices noted that the name of the defendant was Joshua, he commented to him in jest, "Oh, you are the man who made the sun stand still." The Negro replied, "No Sir, Judge, I'se the guy who made the moon-shine."

On still another occasion a case was called for trial, and the court officer stepped up to the bench and whispered to the presiding Justice that the lawyer, who was known to be quite a drinker, was too intoxicated to try the case. When the lawyer, who happened to be white, staggered into the courtroom and insisted upon proceeding with the case, the Justice announced that the case was being postponed. The lawyer contended that he was "ready" to proceed. Though the Justice, noticing his condition, told him the case would not be tried at that time, the lawyer continued vociferously to object to a postponement. The Justice ordered the court officer to escort the lawyer out of the courtroom, but the lawyer resisted, insisting that he wanted to try the case immediately. The Justice then told him to leave the courtroom before he was held in contempt of court for being drunk. The lawyer staggered around, turned to the bench, and said: "Judge, I've known you for nearly twenty years and that is the first correct decision I ever heard you make." With that remark he stumbled out of the court.

In my thirty years on the bench, there were many such amusing instances; but the great majority of the cases were of a serious nature, and dealt with matters of considerable importance. Throughout those years I saw lawyers come and go—good ones, indifferent ones, and even bad ones. I cannot help but think of the marvelous opportunities all lawyers have today for service. This is especially true of the young Negro lawyer. It is a sad commentary on the history of jurisprudence in the enlightened state of New York that it was only thirty years ago that the first Negro was appointed a magistrate and that until today I have been the only Negro judge ever to be appointed to the Court of Special Sessions.

But the doors are open now—open all the way to the Supreme Court. The young, aspiring lawyer need only apply himself and take advantage of the opportunities that exist. In so doing, he must build a reputation for studiousness, dependability, and honesty. He must learn how to prepare his cases well and to give his very best in his clients' interests. While he must, of course, have money for immediate office or home expenses, he should avoid the "quick dollar" and over-involvement in trivial, inconsequential matters which dissipate his energies and spread his efforts over so wide a field that he cannot concentrate upon matters of greater import. Thorough dedication to "solid" cases is what, in the long run, makes the "solid" lawyer.

SCOVEL RICHARDSON

Scovel Richardson, who became, on October 1, 1966, Presiding Judge of the Third Division of the United States Customs Court, was born in Nashville, Tennessee, on February 4, 1912. He is a graduate of the University of Illinois with bachelor's and master's degrees, and of the School of Law of Howard University. He formerly practiced law in Chicago and in St. Louis, where he was an Associate Professor of Law and later a Professor and Dean of the School of Law at Lincoln University.

His government service includes a period in the 1940's as Senior Attorney of the Office of Price Administration. In 1953 President Dwight D. Eisenhower appointed him to the United States Board of Parole in the Department of Justice at Washington, D.C., and reappointed him later for a six-year term. In 1954 Attorney General Herbert Brownell, Jr. appointed him Chairman of the Board of Parole. He served in this capacity until President Eisenhower appointed him as a Judge of the United States Customs Court in New York in 1957.

Judge Richardson has been admitted to practice before the Illinois Bar, the Missouri Bar, and the United States Supreme Court Bar. His legal articles, comments, and book reviews have appeared in the *National Bar Journal*; and his articles and speeches on aspects of parole, in *Federal Probation, Vital Speeches,* and the *National Probate and Parole Association Journal.*

He has served as Secretary and as President of the National Bar Association. His broad interest in the application of law has led him to serve as chairman and member of many law association committees of such organizations as the Association of American Law Schools, the National Bar Association, and the Missouri Bar Association.

He is Chairman of the Board of Trustees of Howard University in Washington, D.C., and a trustee of the National Council on Crime and Delinquency in New York. His public service also includes membership on the Advisory Board of the National Survey Service of New York, N.Y., the Board of the Urban League of Westchester County, N.Y., and the Board of Governors of New Rochelle Hospital, N.Y.

The community has recognized Judge Richardson's contributions to society by awarding him such honors as the Congressional Selective Service Medal in 1945, the Urban League Citation for Progress in Human Relations and Civic Achievement in 1953, the Howard University Alumni Award for Distinguished Post-Graduate Achievement in Law in 1958, two awards from Kappa Alpha Psi for outstanding community service in 1959 and 1961, and the Cook County Bar Association Merit Award in 1961.

LAW AS A CAREER

by Scovel Richardson

IN the late 1930's, lawyers who agreed to handle complaints arising from acts of discrimination considered themselves fortunate if they secured for their clients an apology or, in rare instances, a settlement of as much as twenty-five dollars. Such complaints had, for the most part, only nuisance value insofar as owners of the offending establishments were concerned, since there was little or nothing to fear by way of legal redress.

Accordingly, when the Windermere Hotel Company of Chicago refused to serve sandwiches to five black women, it was considered a victory of sorts when two prominent law firms resolved the matter for three of the women for a settlement of forty dollars each. Instead of asking one of the more established legal firms to handle their complaints in the incident described, the remaining two women sought the advice of my associate, Attorney George W. Lawrence, and me.

Filled with the idealism instilled by former professors that the law was the one instrumentality through which justice for all could be obtained, and spurred, perhaps, by the brashness of youth, we decided upon a stategy that would force court action in separate trials for the two complainants. This procedure we followed, trying the one case without a jury and the other with a jury. We were successful in winning favorable action in both instances. In the first case, the court entered a judgment of $150; and in the second, we received the maximum available under the Illinois Civil Rights law—$500—the first time this had been accomplished in that state.

These two victories may appear small today, but they represented at the time a significant step forward in the struggle for equal rights. From that time on, we, together with other attorneys, were called upon to appear before the courts and other official bodies of Illinois in actions designed to remove remaining barriers to equality.

Many of us were compelled to engage in the battle for Civil Rights as a matter of sheer personal survival as well as for the sake of principle. When I moved to St. Louis, for example, and bought my first home there in 1941, there was on the property a restrictive covenant against "junk shops, pig stys, slaughter houses, and Negroes." My family and I moved into our new home on a Friday, were stench-bombed on Saturday night, and received a summons on Monday morning to appear in court to answer a suit filed by the St. Louis Real Estate Exchange, which was determined to have us evicted. The defense against this suit occupied a major portion of my time, but it was time well spent, for after an extended period of litigation, the restrictive covenants of the Exchange, which covered much of the property in the city, were negated by law, marking another step forward in the direction of equal rights.

Thereafter, I found myself increasingly involved in the preparation of pleadings and briefs and in appearances before judicial bodies on behalf of individuals and groups seeking to abolish unfair discriminatory practices in recreation, housing, public accommodation, and employment. In many instances the verdict was in our favor; in others we met with initial defeat or frustrating delays. But even in those cases in which there was no instant success, a useful purpose was served in the initiation of the action itself, in the raising of constitutional questions which laid the foundation for later victories over bigotry and prejudice.

Incidents similar to those described have been experienced by many other attorneys in various parts of the country. The impact of our isolated victories may seem slight, but the cumulative effect in making the law applicable to all citizens has brought our race a long way on the road toward full equality. Demonstrations and protests play their part in effectively dramatizing the inequities that yet exist in our society. But the law is still the most potent force that can be used by blacks in their quest for full citizenship. Since the beginning of civilization, it has been the law which has effected change or which has given authority to change when brought about by other causes.

Our own nation has been indebted to persons with legal training from its inception. Of the twenty-four men who attended the Albany Congress in 1754, thirteen were lawyers. In the first Continental Congress, which launched the Revolution, twenty-four of the forty-five delegates also were lawyers. In the second Congress, which declared the young nation's independence from Great Britain, twenty-six of the fifty-six delegates were men of legal training; and in the Constitutional Convention of 1787, thirty-three of the fifty-five members had similar backgrounds.

Moreover, approximately two-thirds of the Presidents of the United States have been lawyers. In addition, the legal profession has provided most of the state governors and a high percentage of state legislators. The same pattern prevails in Congress, for approximately seventy percent of the members of the Senate and sixty percent of those in the House of Representatives are lawyers.

Law is a type of economic and social expression in the forms of rules and regulations governing human conduct. It is a living thing responsive to progress and the growth in moral stature of our society. The capacity of our law to develop through the years in the America it serves has assured us of an enduring constitutional system. The constant striving for improvement in the administration of justice by our judiciary, executive, and legislative branches of government, and the concern and interest in public affairs on the part of civic-minded citizens are the primary vehicles through which we may keep the law viable.

To the public our lawyers represent a form of social insurance, and through them we become articulate in the courts in protesting against those practices that deny citizens equal protection under the law as guaranteed in the Constitution of the United States.

In affording social insurance and in the struggle for the recognition of human rights, the black lawyer has been particularly effective. Devoting long hours of preparation for his appearances in court, his behind-the-scene activity—often tedious, always demanding—goes largely unnoticed by the public. It is a popular fallacy that one must be a brilliant orator to become a successful lawyer. Being a forceful speaker is generally an asset, but it is not the *sine qua non* of success at the bar. The outcome of a lawsuit today does not depend upon rhetoric alone. The efforts of a lawyer in court represent but a small part of his work on a given case.

Important as his work in the area of Civil Rights has been, it is time now for the black lawyer to specialize to a greater degree in other branches of the law. There will be a need for Civil Rights lawyers for a long time to come, but the complexities of today's society require that lawyers protect the interests of blacks in many other areas as well. Black lawyers will be needed increasingly not only in the traditional fields of civil law (wills and estates, accidents, private relationships, and the like) and criminal law (larceny, tax evasion, murder, and other such offenses against the state), but also in the comparatively new field of administrative law, which relates to service on or before quasi-judicial bodies such as commissions, boards, and bureaus.

A few impressive figures at this point may help to emphasize the current need for additional lawyers in our race. Black people comprise more than ten percent of the nation's population of 200,000,000 Americans, but of the approximately 269,000 lawyers in the United States fewer than one percent are black. Americans of African descent certainly have as many legal rights which need protection as do their white countrymen. In fact, their need for legal protection is greater, since they are frequently denied legal rights which others enjoy as a matter of course and without challenge.

In earlier years, black lawyers had to be content with relatively small fees or a mere "thank you" for services rendered. Now, financial rewards are substantial, but the greatest reward for the young person entering the field today still will be the satisfaction gained from helping in the struggle for racial justice on all fronts. Black lawyers who have sincerity of purpose and integrity of character are leaders to whom we can turn to see that our liberties are respected and our equality observed. They can insure that we are afforded an equal opportunity to give to America and to the world the best and richest within our power to give.

PAUL R. WILLIAMS

Paul R. Williams, a Fellow in the American Institute of Architects, has earned renown as a designer of private residences and of a wide variety of public buildings, including hotels, stores, schools, office buildings, banks, educational institutions, and a number of civic structures.

Born in Los Angeles, California, where he still resides, he received his architectural training at the University of Southern California, at the Beaux Art Institute of Design, and at two other art schools. His first professional experience came in the design of private homes. Altogether he has designed more than three thousand residences ranging in cost from $10,000 to $600,000. These residences are located in various sections of the United States and in South America, and include the homes of such celebrities as Frank Sinatra, Tyrone Power, Danny Thomas, Desi Arnaz, Cary Grant, Julie London, and the late Bill "Bojangles" Robinson.

Buildings he has designed stand in South America, Jamaica, and Puerto Rico, as well as in various states of our nation. Some of his outstanding commissions include the Music Corporation of America's office building in Beverly Hills, the Beverly Hills store of Saks Fifth Avenue, the Los Angeles Court House, and three buildings of the University of California at Los Angeles. He has also designed ten buildings for the Bank of America and was recently named Consulting Architect for the Southern California Division of this bank. He is Associate Architect for the $27,000,000 Federal Customs Building in Los Angeles, and for the $50,000,000 Los Angeles International Airport. Two of his most recent commissions are the headquarters building of Litton Industries, to be erected in Beverly Hills, and Los Angeles' first high-rise educational building, Wilson High School. He has just completed a redesigning commission for the Mammoth Life and Accident Insurance Company in Louisville, Kentucky.

Among the many awards Paul R. Williams has received are the

Spingarn Medal in 1953, the Los Angeles Chamber of Commerce's Award for Creative Planning in 1955, and the University of Southern California's Alumni Merit Award in 1966. He has also been the recipient of four honorary doctoral degrees: two in architecture, one in science, and one in art. He was appointed by President Eisenhower to the President's Advisory Committee on Housing; by Governor Earl Warren to the State Redevelopment Commission; by Governor Goodwin Knight to the State Housing Commission; by Governor Patrick Brown to the California Beautiful Commission; and by Mayor Norris Poulson and Mayor Sam Yorty to the Los Angeles Art Commission.

Despite his numerous architectural commissions and appointments, Mr. Williams has found time to publish two books: *Small Homes of Tomorrow* and *New Homes of Today*.

TOMORROW

by Paul R. Williams

ON my first day in high school I was handed a list of subjects from which to select the course I wanted to study. When I marked *architecture*, the counselor smiled and said, "How can you make a living as an architect? I have never heard of a Negro architect and your people do not have enough money to build large homes or expensive buildings. Why don't you study to be a doctor; everybody gets sick."

My answer was if I could be a creative architect, I was sure I could make my way as an architect in America.

With this challenge, I knew I had to blaze a different approach; so after my architectural training at the University of Southern California, I attended three private art schools at night and later worked in different architects' offices, each selected because of some unusual design criteria or business technique. As a gimmick, I learned to sketch a house upside down, including the interior of the furnished living room, so that the client sitting opposite me could see the plan develop without my having to turn the sketch around. The first client to experience this upside-down demonstration became one of my best boosters.

When I was a youngster I sold newspapers on a downtown street corner in Los Angeles. My most important customer was Frank P. Flint, an attorney, in whose office I sold six papers every day to the various employees. Mr. Flint was later elected United States senator from Califorina, which meant that I did not see him very often; but many years afterwards when he retired, he formed a company which purchased several hundred acres of foothills in Pasadena, and he wanted a young architect to make sketches for a suburban-type home to be built in this new development. This was about the time I had just won first prize in three competitions for the design of a small country home. He had recently seen reproductions of the competition winners, and asked me to meet with him. Imagine his surprise to learn that now—twelve years later—the winning architect he now wanted to employ to design his houses was his former news-boy! I have since designed thirty-two homes in Flintridge alone costing from twenty to forty thousand dollars each.

In each home that I design, regardless of size or price, I try to include an unusual conversation piece, which might be a specially planned kitchen with a glass wall overlooking an outdoor patio or garden, or a kitchen located at the front of the house convenient to the front door where the housewife would have a view of the passing street parade as she prepared dinner. A well-planned home today has no yesterday's "backyard." We now call it a garden area, which invariably has a small screened-off service yard, a play lawn, and fruit trees or berry bushes around the border.

Several years ago I designed a small French cottage for a very charming elderly lady using this theory of casual but friendly living. About two years later I received a telephone call from a gentleman who said his wife had seen this small house which I had designed for her aunt and that he wished me to design his new home. This is how I became the architect for the thirty-two-room mansion for Mr. Cord, the automobile manufacturer. Great oaks from little acorns grow!

On one occasion I was designing a very important home in Beverly Hills and, when the home was nearing completion, the owner telephoned and mentioned that she was expecting a distinguished house guest when the home was finally finished. She wanted to know what could be done at this stage to the guest suite to make it different and outstanding. Since the home was almost completed, I discussed the problem with my color consultant, who incidentally is my daughter, Norma Williams Harvey. This was her suggestion: "I would not recommend any changes in the structure—I would design and furnish the suite in 'twenty-one' shades of white." Her idea sounded fantastic, but the final results produced a most restful and delightful room. Here again was that "conversation piece," but color problems are not always so readily solved. I had for example another client who liked green; but when my consultant mentioned that there were over one thousand shades of green, my client decided that the use of green might require too many decisions. As a matter of fact, every tree or bush is a different shade of green; thus, a thousand shades might be a gross understatement.

There is that old cliché that a decorator, in order to get the best artistic effects out of his paint, mixes good taste with his color. A simple way of testing good taste is to examine five or six home magazines of earlier periods and to note how many of the older home styles and interiors—including colors—are appealing today. Lasting appeal is certainly one of the most important criteria in this indefinable thing we call "good taste."

Color is the fourth dimension in architecture, a dimension by means of which one can make a room look larger or smaller, depending upon the sunlight or the depth of color of the walls or ceiling. Color can also create a sunny or depressing influence upon one's attitude. Color, moreover, is an essential ingredient of good taste.

In the practice of architecture, one learns many practical things which are not a part of his academic training. For example, if you want to build a commercial building, you must be sure to buy enough property to provide for necessary and convenient parking or you will have difficulty obtaining a construction loan. Before most lending institutions will grant a construction loan, their executives require a feasibility report which indicates the buying power of the neighborhood, the competition of neighboring stores, and the amount that should be spent on improvements. This information can usually be obtained from a real estate appraiser for a relatively small fee. After the site has been selected, you should have your architect prepare sketches of the exterior, together with detailed sketches indicating the conveniences and innovations of the interior plan. Then you must get commitments for tenants, for it usually takes sixty percent lease occupancy to justify a construction loan.

In the acquisition of land for any type of construction, there are always questions of availability and price. Many people who have recently arrived in Florida or California marvel at the population expansion and the high prices of land; and when they compare today's prices with those of raw land twenty years ago, they frequently ask the old-timers, "Why didn't you buy a hundred acres of swamp or desert land when it was twenty dollars an acre?" Hindsight, of course, is far easier than foresight! There are still swamps and desert land available—they are only farther out. Who knows what the next generation will say to us about lost opportunities.

There is usually a reason why a city expands either to the north or south, east or west. A prospective land purchaser should study the existing trends, read chamber of commerce reports, ask questions, and use his imagination. If he plans to buy raw land, he should try to buy up to a section line; for if the county builds a public road, it is usually built on the section line, and access to roads is of the utmost importance in the purchase of land.

In America today there is a strong revival in our cities in the creation of cultural centers. This is a great idea, but we should ask ourselves whether we are not really building music palaces and sports arenas only for the already cultured. Our cities primarily need "skill" centers where teenagers can express themselves and participate in the humanities and various branches of the arts in an environment at the community level. With the right kind of program, financial assistance can be secured from the federal government to help discover and sustain creative talent and leadership in our cities.

Science tells us that the world population will double every thirty-two years and, by 1982, another billion people will have been added to our planet. In this short time many of us will see this change as it affects America. Where will this great expansion of people live? Who will produce food to feed them? These problems existed thirty-two years ago; they were solved then, but a solution will be more difficult tomorrow. The point is made that the solution lies, at least in part, in the creation of new cities. The formula for a new city is a good water supply, transportation, climate, and jobs. Maybe we should turn the entire old city into a new concept of job centers, tearing down slums and every existing building that does not conform, and creating a parklike atmosphere in which to work; and around the outside periphery of this high-rise work area, develop a new greenbelt area of homes, apartments, hotels, and shops grouped in clusters, creating a pleasing aesthetic environment. This would simplify our city transportation problem and tend to give a new value to the property in the old town.

We must give our attention to the more efficient use of land and to better methods of processing and storing food. Future scientific developments will certainly have a bearing both on architecture and on engineering. The government, for example, has just authorized the spending of $14,000,000 to develop a new protein concentrate called FPC, which will provide all of the protein a child needs at a cost of a penny a day. This protein is a sea food which is odorless and tasteless—a product that will represent a tremendous breakthrough in the war on hunger. This is just a start in the discovery of marine resources. It would be difficult to predict what new trends architecture will follow in the light of new storage and processing requirements.

Frank Lloyd Wright was asked what should be done with our old cities. His answer was that old cities should be abandoned. However, this is just one man's idea for an easy way to get rid of the slums. There is no question in my mind that our cities have a brighter future, and that America will spend billions to improve the sociological environment of our people. This revitalizing of the cities will create jobs and investment opportunities. All of us should look forward to playing a role in this revitalization process.

The construction industry is one of the largest industries in America, and until the last few years it has been controlled by the unions. Today, to a great extent, and we hope tomorrow without exception, the construction trades will accept all qualified men. To be qualified, one must first get a general education and then trade school experience in carpentry, electrical work, plumbing, plastering, or bricklaying. One should talk to trade union officials, ask about special training classes, learn to read blueprints—then try to be the best apprentice in town. The wages are good, and there is a great feeling of pride in saying, "I helped build that building."

To be a successful architect, inventor, or writer, one must have imagination. Imagination cannot be acquired in school, but I think one can develop this faculty. Developing the imagination begins with small things—small solutions to small problems—such as devising a means of distinguishing one key on a key ring from another. Even such a simple problem as this could have degrees of complexity, depending on the number of keys involved, the lighting situation, and so on. One develops his imagination when he learns to apply to intricate problems the principles used in the solving of simple ones.

We have all heard the saying, "Strive to get to the top—it is not so crowded up there." At graduation time, the engineering schools of the nation are besieged with representatives of various firms seeking to recruit graduates with a bachelor's degree. One need only look at the want-ad sections of the daily newspapers to realize the large number of jobs available for trained persons. I remember when only three kinds of engineers were listed. Today we have electronics, space, industrial, air conditioning, structural design, computer, nuclear, and about twenty additional classifications of engineers. I remember also when an architect concerned himself solely with the design of a house or building. Today architects are involved with housing developments, large shopping centers, industrial complexes, and, in fact, with urban and suburban planning in general. Architects today are in great demand and short supply. There is a new breed of architect as there is a new breed of engineer; and in the years to come, there is no doubt that additional avenues will develop. In fact, some analysts say that within the next twenty years, forty-five percent of the population will be engaged in jobs which do not even exist today.

I have often said when a member of a minority race *wins* in a highly competitive field, whether it is in baseball, basketball, engineering, or architecture, he wins the special applause of the Nation. This signifies the greatness of life in America—*the land of opportunity*.

MAL GOODE

A highly respected correspondent and news broadcaster with ABC News, which he joined as a United Nations correspondent in 1962, Malvin R. Goode has covered a variety of assignments both at home and abroad.

He was born on February 13, 1908, in White Plains, Virginia, but moved at an early age to Homestead, Pennsylvania, where he attended the public schools. He completed his formal education as a graduate of the University of Pittsburgh, and later became Boys' Work Director of the Central Avenue Y.M.C.A., where he led the fight to eliminate discrimination in the Pittsburgh branches of the "Y."

After leaving the Y.M.C.A., he served with the Pittsburgh Housing Authority for six years until 1948, and then joined the staff of the *Pittsburgh Courier*. In the following year he began a career in radio with Station KQV in Pittsburgh, and subsequently was named News Director of Station WHOD in nearby Homestead. For a period of six years, he and his sister, the late Mary Dee, were a well-known brother-sister team in radio.

After his assignment as an ABC UN Correspondent, he came to national attention during the Cuban missile crisis, carrying a major responsibility for the coverage of UN activities in the course of those critical days. Another aspect of his UN work involved joining with three colleagues, in 1963, in conducting journalism seminars for African students in Lagos, Nigeria, in Addis Ababa, Ethiopia, and in Dar es Salaam, Tanzania. In addition to his UN activities, he has worked with the ABC News Election Unit on special assignment for various Presidential primary elections and for the Republican and Democratic national conventions. He has also served the news department of WABC-TV, an ABC affiliated station.

Among the many organizations to which he belongs are the Association of Radio-TV Analysts and the National Association of Radio and TV News Directors. He is a member of the President's

Plan For Progress Committee, a group comprising representatives of large corporations in America. This committee has accepted the responsibility of visiting high schools and colleges to urge Negro students to continue their education with the assurance of federal government support in opening doors of opportunity once closed.

Mal Goode himself is in constant demand as a speaker before educational, church, and civic organizations.

ALL GOD'S CHILDREN

by Mal Goode

"I WANT you children to remember two things: one, you are no better than anyone else; and two, no one else is any better than you." The emphasis was on the second point, and the statement came from my mother, the daughter of slaves who served their masters in Augusta County, Virginia—slaveholders who at the time of the Emancipation Proclamation gave their slaves a little more than the stipulated "40 acres and a mule." They provided them with some funds to purchase seed and plows and equipment to till the soil and prepare eventually to be independent. My mother was educated at West Virginia Collegiate Institute (now West Virginia State College) with some of those funds set aside before she was born.

There were eventually six of us in the family, four boys and two girls; but in the early years of the century from 1908 to 1916 I remember best when there were only James, the oldest, William, myself, and Mary. Our frame house on Twelfth Avenue in the steel town of Homestead, Pennsylvania, had only five rooms and an outhouse on the back of the lot; but when Allan, the fourth son, was born, my father contracted to have another bedroom added and a glorious bathroom with hot and cold running water—an innovation which added immensely to our social status in the community. For days afterward mother had no problem getting us to take a bath. Previously, we had used the galvanized tub in the center of the bedroom floor and had lugged hot water from the kitchen.

Ours was one of two Negro families in the block, and the Fifth Ward elementary school, just half a block away, seldom had more than two Negro children in each of the classrooms for the six grades taught. We were generally accepted as part of the community, visiting with our neighbors, sharing gifts at Christmas time, building "swimming holes," picking elderberries, sleighriding, and kite-flying in season together. I recall a fight or two between Negro children and white children about name-calling, but generally good will prevailed, and race was never a neighborhood issue. Our Fifth Ward teachers were persons in my childhood I will never forget. Their teaching and training methods were fair, and equality was a watchword with them.

We had no PTA in those days, but Mom was a frequent visitor to the school, not to quarrel, but mainly to assure the principal and our teachers that they could count on cooperation at our home. We knew that if chastisement was necessary, there might be additional punishment waiting for us at home. "We send you to school to learn," Mom used to say, "and remember you carry our name and represent this home when you are away from it whether at school, at church, on the playground, or in the street." This attitude was a fetish with my mother. "There's nothing like a good name," she used to say. Frankly, without harping back to the old days, I wish there were more of this type of parental counsel today. It did two things: It served to inspire us to accomplishment in our school work, and it strengthened our confidence in being "as good as anybody else."

I've said little about my father up to now, but he was a remarkable man, who had only three weeks of formal schooling in his life. At eight years of age he entered the first grade of a rural school in Brunswick County, Virginia, where his parents had been slaves less than two decades before. This was in September, 1878. When harvest time came, however, his father took him out of school, contending, "You are too big a boy to be wasting your time in school." After that Father never returned to the classroom. I'm certain that without the counsel and conviction of my mother about the need for an education, we might have suffered the same fate. My father believed children should go to work early, earn some money, and add to the family coffers; but mother was determined that we should all get an education, the best possible. She had implicit faith that someday the doors of opportunity would open wider for Negro children. On one occasion she had heard Mary McLeod Bethune make a speech and say, "It is better for 1,000 to be qualified when the door opens than none to be ready when opportunity comes."

Father was a steelworker for the old Carnegie Steel Company at its Homestead, Pennsylvania works. He eventually reached the top grade for a Negro in the Open Hearth—a First Helper, and during World War I helped to establish a steel production record on old furnace No. 60 in O.H. 4. One of his principal gripes was his responsibility to train young white boys in the Open Hearth and to teach them how to tell when a heat was ready for "tapping," only to have many of them eventually become his boss melter, the really well-paying job in the Open Hearth. Many mornings at the breakfast table, after a fourteen-hour shift at night, we heard Father complain to Mother about the unfairness of the mill's policy. This is what led him to establish a Fish and Poultry business in 1917. Of course, he also hoped to found a business that would flourish for the children to take over. This was not to occur as planned, although the business expanded. Limited knowledge of business methods and the inclination to grant too much credit to friends led to our selling the store some nine years later.

While in high school I was employed in the same plant where my father had worked for almost thirty years. The foreman arranged for me to work at night and continue my education in high school. I graduated in 1926 and, because there were already two brothers in college, James at Howard University and William in Pharmacy School at Pitt, I could not enter the University of Pittsburgh until the Fall of 1927. The mill job was a lifesaver, for it helped pay my tuition at college and allowed something extra toward the family mortgage.

College commencement in 1931 was the "commencing" of a rough time. The nation was mired in the worst depression of its history: plants were shut down all over the country; men sold apples and candy bars in the streets; there were "Boweries" in every town and hamlet; thousands of once-affluent business people took their own lives by jumping from bridges or high buildings, or by shooting themselves. In 1932 a porter's job at Richman Brothers' Clothing company opened, and I took it at a starting wage of eight dollars per week and continued there until 1936, when I was appointed a probation officer in the Allegheny County Juvenile Court at the fabulous salary of $125 a month, a position nineteen other young Negroes were seeking. After two years, the Centre Avenue Y.M.C.A. needed a Boys' Work Director, and because of my record at Juvenile Court, I was selected. Those five years were the most fruitful of my life. The salary never exceeded $175 a month, but there were other rewards which no amount of money could buy. Today there are middle-aged business and professional men in Pittsburgh and in many other cities who were boys under my jurisdiction during those fruitful five years.

As rewarding as those five years were, I nevertheless found myself constantly at loggerheads with the officials of the Y.M.C.A., who wanted to deny my boys participation in city-wide conferences and athletic contests, and the touchiest situation was the "Y's" summer camp. Because of a strong laymen's committee we won that fight in 1941, and Negro boys have been admitted regularly since then without incident. The die was cast for my future with the Y.M.C.A. when the executive secretaryship, which meant a salary increase of $1,200 a year, became vacant, and officials made it clear I would not be considered. My chairman, who was also my friend, made it possible for me to be appointed an assistant manager at a local Housing Project on July 1, 1942. Six weeks later I was named Manager of the Bedford Dwellings Development, one of the few interracial projects in the nation, with 420 families. Now my salary was $300 per month, and for my growing family I could reasonably see the light of day financially. After three years at Bedford, I was transferred to an 888-family project in Terrace Village. In my third year there I suffered a heart attack and did not work for almost six months. My doctor urged me not to work for a year, but this was a virtual impossibility, as I then had five children, ranging in age from one year to eleven years. I accepted an offer with the *Pittsburgh Courier* to work in Circulation, principally with the newsboys, and I was assured that I would not have to exert myself physically. It was a golden opportunity which later led to the career in which I am now engaged.

After less than a year I began traveling to strengthen circulation in a number of cities, most notably Chicago, then Memphis, Nashville, Roanoke, and many other cities of the South. One trip covered eleven weeks in 1950. It was one of my life's richest experiences, giving me an opportunity to meet mayors, governors, and outstanding Negro business and civic leaders. On this trip I learned of the great respect the *Courier* commanded, even from whites in the South, who hated the publication because of its policy of demanding equality for Negroes. One mayor in Tennessee, in his slow Southern drawl told me, "I don't like your paper but this is America and you have a right to print what you want. However, if you have any trouble with our police while you are here just call me, night or day, because I want you to give us a good press when you leave here." He then gave me both his private telephone numbers. In Tupelo, Mississippi, the chief of police urged me to call him or Dr. Zuber, a popular Negro physician, because, "You know Dr. Zuber's just like the mayor in this town."

During my travels I encountered many paradoxes. In Clarksdale, Mississippi, I first met Dr. Aaron Henry just two weeks after his property had been set on fire by whites who resented his criticism of the Negro schools there. Yet in this atmosphere, the white editor of the Clarksdale paper told me to let him know if there was any help he could give me in my work. I met whites in the vicinity of Bayou, Mississippi, who had great respect for Dr. T. R. M. Howard, another Negro leader, who had to leave his hospital, home, and practice the following year because of the many threats on his life. In Memphis, I spent an hour with Attorney Lucious Burch, a good friend of Negroes, who was powerful enough politically and financially to speak out against the wrongs in his city.

On the other hand, I found Negroes, particularly those in schools and so-called Negro businesses, who felt it was wrong to advocate equality. After I addressed the students at Booker T. Washington High School in Memphis and told them, "Someday I may come back to Memphis and find you going to school like other American children," one Negro teacher asked me, "What about our jobs?" My answer, of course, was, "Individually, you really don't count in the scheme of things." I'm not gloating, but in 1966, sixteen years later, I saw Negro and white children attending a public school in Memphis. It's not a fully integrated situation, but full integration must eventually come.

Just prior to my Southern tour in 1949, I had started a radio program on Station KQV in Pittsburgh. Early in 1950 we moved to Station WHOD, in nearby Homestead where my sister, the late Mary Dee, had a disc jockey program. After six months I was involved in three news programs each day.

Following my Southern tour, I returned to Pittsburgh and resumed news broadcasting, and by the end of 1951 had four newscasts and a ten-minute sportscast. On the latter appeared many of the top stars in baseball: Jackie Robinson, Monte Irvin, Hank

Thompson, and Willie Mays, among others. In 1952 I was named News Director of WHOD and joined the National Association of Radio-TV News Directors, an organization in which I met some of the finest young men in the trade from all over the country, who went out of their way to make me feel at home. I still hold membership in this organization, which has grown tremendously in the past decade.

I continued my work with the *Pittsburgh Courier* as a troubleshooter, public relations representative, advertising salesman, and general utility person. Needless to say, my connection with the *Courier* was a valuable one, although it did not pay very handsomely. But in spite of my success in newspaper work, the road became rocky.

In 1956 my sister, the late Mary Dee, and I were given thirty-day notices when Station WHOD was sold to new owners. Mary went to Baltimore for a year at WSID, then to WHAT in Philadelphia, where she died in 1964. I went to WMCK in McKeesport, Pennsylvania, for less than a year, and left because of friction with a manager who feared I wanted his job. I started banging on the doors of Pittsburgh's major radio and television stations, always getting the same answers, "Keep in touch," or "Don't call me, I'll call you."

Discouraged, disillusioned, and frustrated because of the "closed-door" policy of local stations, I finally decided to go to the top. In 1961 I visited Leroy Collins, then President of the National Association of Broadcasters, when he was in Pittsburgh on a speaking assignment. He suggested that I go to New York to talk with top network people. I did this, but found it almost impossible to see them. Finally, in March of 1962, Jackie Robinson was in Pittsburgh to speak for a B'nai B'rith lodge. I met him at the airport. He had breakfast with my family that Sunday morning and I took him to his assignment. On the way to the airport he told me of his talk with Jim Hagerty of the American Broadcasting Company the week before. ABC had decided to employ a Negro correspondent, and Jackie suggested that I contact Mr. Hagerty. This I did, and subsequently visited him in New York. Mr. Hagerty told me he had to interview a number of other candidates and urged me to contact him in May, but no decision was made until July, when eight of thirty candidates were selected for on-the-screen auditions. My wealth of experience served me to good advantage, and God must have had His eye on me. After a tense wait of almost three weeks, I was notified that I had been selected.

I started with ABC on September 10, 1962, and was assigned to the United Nations. My first interview was with the Ambassador of Iran, Dr. Mehdi Vakil, and turned out to be a really nerve-wracking experience. The network scheduled it nevertheless, feeling, I suppose, that it was necessary to expose me to the viewers. The next occasion involved one of the world's most serious crises—the Cuban Missile Crisis, and the worst time was the weekend of October 27-28. On Sunday, October 28, I was alone at the United Nations, but because of a series of meetings between the Russian and United States representatives and the then Acting Secretary-General U Thant, I was privileged to do seventeen radio and television reports that one day—a crucial day in history. On the previous Thursday, October 25, I was within a few feet of the late Ambassador Stevenson in the Security Council when he challenged Soviet Representative Zorin on the Cuban missiles, declaring, "Don't wait for the translation—answer me! Are these your missiles? I'm prepared to wait until Hell freezes over for your answer."

My next break came in June, 1963, when Mr. Hagerty selected me to join a team of instructors to conduct workshops in journalism in Africa for a ten-week period that summer. Those experiences represent a book in themselves. For the grandson of slaves, an American Negro, it was in many ways a heartwarming and rewarding set of experiences, since the African students made me their idol; and I cherish today the many friendships made in Dar es Salaam, Addis Ababa, Kenya, and Lagos, Nigeria. This trip was quickly followed by the awful four days of the Kennedy assassination when few of us got to bed for we were busy reporting the events before, during, and after the funeral. My most striking recollection in this terrible period was hearing the trembling words of tribute from an African ambassador, "A great oak has fallen in the forest of men."

Since that tragic event I have continued a busy schedule at the UN and have from time to time taken on a number of other assignments. These have included interviews of celebrities in the field of sports and in other walks of life, and speaking engagements throughout the country.

As a result of this accumulation of personal experiences over the years, I am convinced that we are today coming into a tremendous era, particularly where the Negro is concerned—an era of opportunity which our predecessors could not have dreamed of just five to ten years ago. Looking back, for example, to the twenties, the thirties, and the early forties, one remembers Martin Dihigo, Wee Willie Wells, Cool Papa Bell, and Josh Gibson in baseball; Fats Jenkins, Eyre Saitch, Willie Smith, and John Isaacs in basketball; Duke Slater, Bill Bell, Ozzie Simmons, and Buddy Young in football. If one compares their financial opportunities with those of present-day athletes, one comes to realize that young athletes today are part of a great new day in sports. They are the beneficiaries of unlimited opportunities, mainly because no other area of life—government, business, or even the church—has done more to bring about equality than has the world of sports. This is not to say that all is well even in sports; but the situation for the Negro has improved more rapidly in this field than it has in most other areas of life. I can recall Lennie Moore at Penn State and his early exploits with the Colts; Jackie Robinson stealing home at Forbes Field; Willie Mays catching that fly ball of Vic Wertz; the National Collegiate basketball championship game of 1964, when at one point nine of the ten players of Loyola and Cincinnati University were Negroes; and major league baseball games with a predominance of Negro players. My network once sent me to Baltimore to do a story with Barbara Robinson, the wife of superstar Frank Robinson; and after a final game which Frank won with a home run—after the party in the dressing room—it took ten policemen to get him through the admiring crowd into his car. And who can forget that back in 1953 the fans of Jacksonville held a DAY for Hank Aaron at the end of the season in the very park where six years before officials had put a padlock on the gate because Jackie Robinson was scheduled to play there with the Brooklyn Dodgers. I cite all these instances—and there are hundreds more—only to point out the challenge of the times for young men today.

However, there are greater challenges in this life than hitting a home run to win a game in the bottom of the ninth, or running back a punt ninety-five yards for the winning touchdown with twenty seconds to play, or stuffing the ball in the basket to win a game by two points just before the clock runs out, or streaking down the track to break the tape with a new world speed record. Robert Frost once said that we have promises to keep and miles to go before we sleep. Young Negro men must realize their responsibility to use their athletic talents in helping to tear down every single barrier still existing, to open every long-closed door of opportunity for their children and the children of others; and to accept every single challenge that comes their way—both while they are playing and long after the shouting of the fans has ended.

Many of our young athletes competing today come from poor, humble homes, but I urge them not to forget those homes. Some of their fathers worked on two jobs to send them to college, and some of their mothers left home early in the morning, washed clothes, scrubbed floors, and minded babies until late hours at night to keep them in school. Those fathers and mothers are worthy of the highest love, praise, and honor. One of the reasons why I've grown to respect Jackie Robinson, Jimmy Brown, Monte Irvin, Hank Aaron, Ernie Banks, Willie Mays, and others with the same attitude is that they never forgot where they came from, nor the people they knew as lads in their humble homes. No matter how humble a person's background or heritage is, he should never be ashamed of it.

Negro youth has a heritage of which it can rightfully be proud. Unfortunately, most of us are not aware of this heritage. Generally, we don't know that Negroes were responsible for the traffic light, electrically operated shoe-repair machinery, the first successful open-heart surgery; nor do we generally know about Dr. Charles Drew and blood plasma. We are not very knowledgeable about the highly significant role that Negroes have played in our wars: the Revolutionary War, the War of 1812, the Civil War, the Spanish-American War, World Wars I and II, the Korean War; nor are we generally aware that approximately one-fourth of the boys fighting in Vietnam are Negroes, despite the fact that we approximately constitute only one-tenth of the total population.

Important as a knowledge of this heritage is, it is just as important for Negroes as it is for members of other groups to feel that they are somebody, purely as Americans. Everyone needs to be somebody!

In my early years with the Y.M.C.A. I saw this need clearly demonstrated by youngsters in their efforts to rise above mediocrity or anonymity. In my travels throughout the land in former years as a journalist and later ones as a correspondent and speaker, I've seen it among adults in their understandable desire for recognition. It has been apparent among the many sports figures I've interviewed in their fierce determination to excel. And in my work with the UN this need is daily evident in the struggles of the young, emerging nations to win respect before the world. This need to be SOME-BODY is universal.

Americans—black and white—are blessed to be part of a nation of almost unlimited opportunity and potential. This potential will never be realized, however, until a conscious effort is made by us all—black and white—to solve, in a spirit of total understanding and brotherhood, the remaining problems that beset us.

Every sign of material and spiritual illness points clearly to the need for ALL of us to become involved in lives of dedication to the love and service of our fellow-men. In such lives there must be the realization that all men are the children of God. The story is told of a little girl traveling with her parents on an ocean trip. Standing on the ship's deck one afternoon she suddenly asked her mother, "How big is God?" The mother answered, "As high as the sky, as deep as the ocean, as far as you can see." The child replied, "Gee, then we're right in the middle of Him aren't we?" If this is true and if we recognize His presence among us, we must understand that we are brothers—that the world is just a neighborhood, and as President Johnson has said, "We must make it a brotherhood." To bring about this brotherhood, each of us must determine to make some contribution to the elimination of those problems that generate war, hatred, and divisiveness. We should remember the words of Justice Oliver Wendell Holmes, who said that we should so conduct ourselves that history will record that we have lived.

JOHN BONNER DUNCAN

Until the appointment of John B. Duncan as Commissioner of the District of Columbia in 1961 by the late President John F. Kennedy and his subsequent reappointment in 1964 by President Lyndon B. Johnson, no Negro had held this highest post in the government of the nation's capital. After the expiration of his second three-year term in 1967, he was asked by President Johnson to continue in office for several months until the District of Columbia government was reorganized. Subsequently, he was appointed by the President to the post of Special Assistant to the Secretary of the Interior.

John B. Duncan was born in Springfield, Kentucky, on February 6, 1910, and at the age of seven, moved with his parents to Salisbury, North Carolina, where he attended public school. In 1934 he graduated with an A.B. degree from Howard University, and in 1938 with a law degree from the Terrell Law School in Washington, D.C. In 1963, Livingstone College conferred upon him the honorary degree of Doctor of Laws.

After being admitted to the practice of law, Mr. Duncan held a number of government positions. He served as Attorney for the Bituminous Coal Commission (1942–43) and as Senior Attorney for the Solid Fuels Branch of the Office of Price Administration (1943–46), for the U.S. Office of the Housing Expediter (1947–49), and for the Research Section, Law Division, U.S. Housing and Home Finance Agency (1949–52). During the nine years preceding his appointment as Commissioner, he served as Recorder of Deeds for the District of Columbia.

Mr. Duncan's broad and continuing interest in civic affairs is reflected in the many and varied positions he has held on committees or boards of local and national organizations. In recent years he has been active in approximately fifty organizations representing a wide range of interests. He has served as an officer or director of such groups as the Federation of Civic Associations, the Urban League, the NAACP, the Washington Federation of Churches, Big

Brothers, Inc., the Community Chest Federation, the American Cancer Society, the Federal City Council, the United Negro College Fund, the Arthritis and Rheumatism Association, the Health and Welfare Council, the National Negro Opera Foundation, and the National Conference of Christians and Jews.

In recognition of his extraordinary performance in these many roles, he has been presented with approximately seventy citations and awards. To mention but a few, he has received the Washington Urban League Award, the Brotherhood Award of the National Conference of Christians and Jews, the Big Brother of the Year Award, the Annual Layman's Award of the Council of Churches, the American Legion Award for Community Service, the National Business League Award, and the United Cerebral Palsy Humanitarian Service Award.

A NEED FOR BROTHERHOOD

by John B. Duncan

WHEN, approximately forty years ago, a young Negro came for the first time to the nation's capital from his home in the Deep South, he was filled with enthusiasm for the new life he anticipated in what had long been, as the symbol of freedom and the seat of democracy, the city of his dreams.

In a very brief period he was to learn from humiliating experience that his "dreamland" had segregated schools and that there were separate theaters, hotels, recreational facilities, hospitals, and churches. Eating establishments permitted Negroes to handle their food, cook it, and serve it; but Negroes could not enjoy the privilege of sitting at tables or counters except in a few, small, segregated restaurants. Discrimination, he was to learn, was the prevailing pattern even in government.

Since he had lost his father and needed to earn money for his education at Howard University, he obtained all the political recommendations and character references considered necessary for a governmental position and went to call upon the senator from his state.

When he presented his credentials, he was advised that the only jobs available to Negroes were those paying $1,200 a year or less. Despite his clerical skills and previous experience, he was compelled to face the sober fact that Negroes were denied typing, stenographic, and clerical positions throughout both the federal and District of Columbia governments, although white applicants with much less training and far fewer substantial recommendations and references found no difficulty in securing employment along these lines.

When it became obvious that he could not obtain a clerical position, he sought employment as a guard in a storage facility of the government. Denied even this, he was compelled to accept a messenger's job in the United States Department of Interior at wages of $1,080 a year.

Upon completion of his undergraduate training, the young man received a scholarship to do graduate work in philosophy. Faced with the necessity of changing from day to evening work in order to pursue his educational program, he sought a job as a guard in the Department of Interior garage. He was offered, instead, a job—at no increase in salary—washing cars from three o'clock in the morning until one o'clock in the afternoon. His duties consisted of caring for nearly forty automobiles, but permitted him to attend graduate courses in the afternoon and early evening hours.

Shortly before completing his graduate studies, the youth was offered a three-year tuition scholarship to take up the study of law. When he subsequently matriculated in law school, he was obliged to seek another assignment which would not conflict with his new class schedule. He was offered, and accepted, a job mopping floors of the Department of Interior—five city blocks of hallways, from twelve o'clock midnight until eight o'clock in the morning at the now familiar salary of $1,080 a year. Since his first class began at eight o'clock in the morning, the youth was compelled to use part of his meager salary for taxicab fare, arriving for class a few minutes late with the permission of the instructor.

After graduating from law school with the equivalent of three degrees, he again attempted to secure a clerical position, but such opportunities were still not open to Negro youth. He did, however, manage to obtain a job as a "mail clerk" in the basement of the Interior Department—a job which consisted of receiving and forwarding heavy, dirty mail bags to various divisions.

The unfortunate plight of this Negro youth continued until his and other cases of outright discrimination were brought to the attention of a new agency of government, the Fair Employment Practices Commission. After an investigation by that Commission, he experienced few difficulties in securing positions commensurate with his training and abilities.

Obviously, serving as a messenger, washing cars, mopping floors, and handling dirty mail bags fell short of the real ambitions of that Negro youth. Equally obvious was his belief that he should be fully prepared when, and if, equal opportunity should come; and though he suffered hardships and discrimination, he was never influenced by those who questioned the wisdom of pursuing an education for a life of doubtful opportunity.

The experiences I have related are still vivid in my memory because *I was that Negro youth!* My story—by no means unique—illustrates the racial climate that existed a generation ago. The situation today with respect to employment in government is vastly changed. Negroes are scattered throughout various government agencies at practically every level. I, myself, have recently returned in an executive capacity responsible only to the Secretary of Interior, to the agency—to the very building—where I once mopped floors.

Despite the fact that conditions have improved appreciably for some Negroes, not only in employment but in other areas as well, there has been so little improvement for the Negro masses that the question of Civil Rights has become the nation's most explosive domestic issue. It is an issue that is being fought on many fronts: education, housing, employment, and the courts. But a lasting solution will depend upon a fundamental change of attitude resulting in a true feeling of brotherhood among men. It has been said that "underlying the fundamental problems of our times is the fateful fact that science and technology have narrowed the world to a neighborhood before man has broadened it to a brotherhood."

Though man has come to understand in large measure the complexities of the atom, he is still far from understanding his fellow-man. Though he has learned to perform near-miracles with electronic equipment, his mind, on the other hand, has been unable to cross the narrow boundaries of prejudice. Though he has made impressive strides toward the conquest of outer space, he still has much to learn about the intricacies of *inner* space, about man himself and his aspirations for friendship and justice.

In the pursuit of these aspirations there is as much need for brotherhood within the Negro minority as there is between the races. We must not slip into the error of divisiveness among our own people, for though the approach and efforts of one group may be different from those of other groups, all are working toward the goal of American democracy. We must recognize that it is the sum total of all such efforts that will lead our nation to the realization of this aim. This is not the time to bicker among ourselves, nor to be critical of others, whether they advocate legal action, passive resistance, or pressure tactics. No single group can win the battle alone.

No ultimate victory can be won without the sober cooperation of all, and wisdom dictates the necessity for such cooperative effort.

We have the dual responsibility to end divisiveness within our own ranks and to cultivate a deeper sense of brotherhood with white America. We cannot live *in* this nation and *apart* from its culture at the same time. The Negro's stake is here, and even in the face of crushing odds—as in my own case—he should prepare himself thoroughly to make as meaningful a contribution to American culture as possible. Bitterness on the part of some Negroes is understandable in the light of nearly two centuries of enslavement, but such bitterness is folly. We would do better to adopt the philosophy that it is the obligation of the former slave to set his master free—free of ignorance, bigotry, hate, and un-Americanism.

But the responsibility for brotherhood is not the Negro's alone. It is the obligation of *all* Americans. *All* must start today by treating rich and poor, Christian and Jew, black and white in a way that will clearly reflect our belief in this basic ideal.

White Americans can no longer stand on the sidelines as mere spectators while the struggle involving the century's greatest domestic crisis takes place before their eyes. The outcome will affect everyone—white and black, without exception—for in this struggle there can be no stalemate. If chaos is to be avoided, men of good will must speak out, and speak out now.

There must be on the part of each of us a rededication to the principle of brotherhood, a principle which runs like a golden thread through the rich tapestry of our history. It is a principle enshrined in the Declaration of Independence by Washington, Jefferson, and the other founding fathers; a principle captured in prose by Tom Paine and turned into living verse by Walt Whitman; a principle which over the years has fired men's imaginations and kindled their hopes for a better world.

PAUL P. COOKE

Dr. Paul P. Cooke is the President of the District of Columbia Teachers College, where he has been a member of the faculty since 1944. In addition to serving as Professor of English and Dean of the College, Dr. Cooke has been visiting professorial lecturer at Howard University and also at Trinity College. He has been a teacher in various public and private secondary schools, and in the United States Army. He has also served as Director of the Inner City Target Area Program and as Director of the Model School Division of the Public Schools of the District of Columbia.

Born on June 29, 1917, in New York City, he received his schooling in the nation's capital. After graduating from Miner Teachers College, Washington, D.C., Dr. Cooke went on to receive a Master of Arts degree, concentrating in the field of higher education, at New York University. He also earned an M.A. degree in English at the Catholic University of America and a doctorate in education at Columbia University. His postdoctoral work in public administration was done at American University.

Dr. Cooke is a regular lecturer on the subject of minority group relations at the Washington International Center, the Foreign Service Division of the U.S. Department of State, and at the International Trade Union Exchange of the U.S. Department of Labor. He also lectures for the United States Information Agency. He has served as consultant to the U.S. Office of Education, the U.S. Department of Commerce, and the American Council on Human Rights.

Dr. Cooke's articles, papers, and book reviews have appeared in numerous general and educational periodicals, and deal with such varied subjects as race relations, education, the English language, and the disadvantaged. One of his most recent publications is a booklet entitled *Civil Rights in the United States.*

He has been a member of the Ford Foundation's Great Cities Research Council Task Force, the Commissioner's Advisory Council on Higher Education in the District of Columbia, the Commission on Human Resources of the Washington Center for Metropolitan Studies, and the Committee on the Model Cities Program of the D.C. Health and Welfare Council. He is an active member of the American Veterans Committee and has held in this organization the offices of National Vice Chairman and National Chairman. He has been a delegate to the United States Committee on UNESCO, and has served abroad as a delegate to the World Veterans Federation in Holland, Switzerland, and Denmark.

Dr. Cooke is also a member of the National Association of Intergroup Relations Officials, the Board of the National Capitol Area Civil Liberties Union, the John Carroll Society, and the Urban League. He is a life member of the NAACP. He has served, too, as Executive Secretary of the Catholic Interracial Council of Washington, D.C.; and in 1967 received the "Personal Commitment to Civil Rights Award," from that organization.

MOTIVATION:

A PROBLEM FOR SOCIETY

by Paul P. Cooke

WHEN children do not measure up to national educational norms, there is a common tendency to blame the schools. The failure of pupils to achieve at acceptable levels frequently brings forth angry demands that the superintendent of schools resign. Often indignant citizens criticize teaching methods and question the quality and the dedication of faculties and staffs. Many of these well-intentioned persons petition for smaller classes and more competent instructors and insist upon the introduction of innovative and imaginative programs to raise the level of what they consider to be inferior education.

Admittedly, a change in superintendent may result in new aims and revitalization of existing programs. Improvement in teaching methods and quality of faculty as well as smaller classes and better facilities are, of course, always desirable and remain the goals of every progressive educational system. Innovative programs and special projects all have their place and can help to enrich curricular offerings. Similarly, the introduction of broad-based community schools, the decentralization of school districts, and the sharing of policy-making power with faculty and parents can increase community participation in the educational process.

The problem for the ghetto child, however, particularly one from a low income Negro or other minority group family, is not principally that of crowded classrooms, incompetent instructors, or other such factors. His problem is an almost total lack of motivation, and without this essential force he will continue to perform poorly despite any and all educational experiments and programs designed to help him.

The real cause of the problem for the unmotivated child does not lie in the schools. It is not the fault of the educational process, and education alone cannot furnish the solution. The roots of the problem lie in social and economic conditions, and the solution rests ultimately with society.

The lack of motivation found generally in children of low income families stems from an inability to grasp the meaning of education and to understand the desirability and often the necessity of obtaining formal training. The Negro child has the additional handicap of feeling that society does not really intend for him to succeed. Hence, he believes that his efforts in school are futile. His model, for the most part, is a father out of work, or employed in a menial job at a low wage. His background is that of a family which has been on welfare for several generations. Consequently, the Negro youngster has no compelling reason to believe that going to school will affect the conditions he faces daily—unemployment, poor health, unstable family life, and unsatisfactory living conditions.

The children of educated, higher income families take for granted that there is an association between education and income, between education and success, between education and a better standard of living, for most of them have tangible evidence that such correlations do exist. Their parents and many others they know are examples of the relationship between education and the "good life."

Ghetto Negro youth, with no parental models to emulate, with no close friends who have demonstrated their abilities to achieve a better way of life through education, and with no neighbors any better off than they are, cannot see the need of going to school and striving to perform well. In fact, in their low income communities, the most successful model may be the "numbers man" in a pink Cadillac, himself a school dropout. For these millions of deprived young Americans there is little hope for a good job and a decent home, and therefore no apparent relationship between acquiring an education and obtaining a higher standard of living. Many of them will swell the ranks of the unemployed; and for others, the ultimate hope is any type of job that will afford them mere subsistence.

Speaking recently at the Higher Education Seminar in Washington, D.C., Seymour Wolfbein (formerly Director of the Bureau of Labor Statistics and now Dean of the School of Education at

Temple University) discussed "disaggregated" unemployment figures, that is, figures analyzed by categories. A national unemployment rate in 1968 of 3.5 percent ceases to look reassuring when we disaggregate this "gross statistic" and find unemployment at a rate of (a) 14 percent for Negro high school dropouts and (b) 13 percent for Negro high school graduates. Negro youth may not know these figures, but they know the situation they face and sense the relevant meaninglessness of high school education. They know that society has no work for them, or if it does have work, it is, because of white racism, limited to lower level jobs even in government. Thus, unfortunately, they are caught on the one hand between an economy that fails to produce enough jobs and, on the other, continuing discrimination.

There are Negroes in large numbers, of course, whose backgrounds, whose home life, and whose economic status are similar to those of many successful white Americans. Yet, according to a U.S. Labor Department statistical report issued a few months ago, many more remain "trapped in the poverty of the slums, their living conditions either unchanged or deteriorating."

The gap between black and white is actually widening in many instances, and a gap between black and black is emerging. The successful Negro does exist and does move up the economic ladder. Negroes are holding jobs today never held by members of their race before, and many are receiving salaries they never dreamed possible for them. But in areas like Watts the incidence of poverty and the proportion of broken homes have increased, and the rate of unemployment has remained virtually unchanged. It is useless to condemn the schools in Watts because pupil performance there does not rival that in Beverly Hills where there are models to motivate children to achieve.

Schools cannot solve the problem of motivation. Education per se is not the answer because social and economic weaknesses in American life have established conditions that schools cannot and are not intended to remedy.

Millions of dollars that will eventually total billions now flow into inner city, low income schools for the express purpose of raising the level of achievement. Various projects—Head Start, Upward Bound, and others—are being funded throughout the nation. To promote racial integration, Negro children are bussed to white schools and in some instances the process is reversed. Some cities have built "educational parks," mammoth complexes of several schools accessible both to black and white children. None of these strategies, however, provide the means of enabling underprivileged Negro children to relate education to decent jobs.

It is not enough to say that excellent employment opportunities exist for those who finish school and are "qualified." That there are at the moment six thousand skill-type jobs available in the nation's capital alone is a meaningless abstraction to the Negro youth who is faced each day of his life with countless examples of unemployment.

For the underprivileged Negro youth, motivation to learn and to achieve in school derives from an economy that promises a job and decent living conditions. Reasonably full employment—which will affect his own family and community—will come only when the executive and legislative departments of the federal and state governments join with business and industry to develop a new mode of thinking about people and employment, to create more jobs, to plan and develop "new careers" (especially in human services), and to provide on-the-job-training as a standard practice.

We must make real our philosophy that "all men are created equal" and thus are entitled to equal opportunities. Only when this ideal has been reached will we see stability in the Negro family and improvement in its health and general living standards. The Negro child will then have models to stimuate his self-respect and motivate him to achieve acceptably in school, and society will have remedied the ills for which education is now too often blamed.

LESTER B. GRANGER

A practitioner and administrator of community organization for forty years, from the close of World War I to the end of the Eisenhower administration, Lester B. Granger is a retired Executive Director of the Urban League who served in that capacity for twenty years.

Born in Newport News, Virginia, on September 16, 1896, he graduated from Dartmouth College in 1918 and subsequently pursued graduate studies at New York University and professional studies at the New York School of Social Work.

He began his professional career as Extension Worker at the New Jersey State Manual Training School in Bordentown in 1922 and remained in that post until 1934. From 1934 to 1938 he was Educational Secretary of the National Urban League, and from 1938 to 1940 he was Secretary on Negro Welfare for the Welfare Council of New York City. His affiliation with the National Urban League began in 1940 when he was appointed Assistant Executive Secretary. In the following year he was named Executive Director of the League and served in that position until his retirement in 1961. He then became Professor of Sociology at Dillard University where he taught until his "second retirement" in 1966.

A member of numerous organizations, he has held the following significant positions in the field of social work: Vice-President of the American Association of Social Workers (1942); President of the National Conference of Social Welfare (1951–52); Chairman of the U.S. Committee of the International Conference of Social Work—now the International Conference on Social Welfare— (1952–61); and President of the International Conference on Social Welfare—a federation of national committees representing more than three-score nations—(1960–64).

Lester Granger has served the community and the nation in many other notable capacities. He has been Chairman of the Federal Advisory Council on Employment Security. Appointed by

President Truman, he served as a member of the President's Committee on Equality in the Armed Forces. He has served also as a Trustee of the State University of New York, St. Paul's College, and Brandeis University Graduate School for Advanced Studies in Social Welfare.

Among the honors he has received are the Distinguished Civilian Service Medal, awarded by the Secretary of the Navy in 1946, and the President's Medal For Merit, awarded by President Truman in 1947, for advisory services to the Navy resulting in the ending of racial segregation after the close of World War II.

He has been the recipient of the honorary degree of Doctor of Humane Letters from Dartmouth College in 1946, Wilberforce University in 1948, and Columbia University in 1954; and the honorary degree of Doctor of Laws from Oberlin College in 1951, Morris Brown College in 1952, and Virginia State College in 1953.

THE VANISHING

SOCIAL SCIENTIST

by Lester B. Granger

EARLY in 1961 I began preparations for closing up my twenty-year stint as Executive Director of the National Urban League, an event which would take place formally with the arrival of my sixty-fifth birthday in September. After forty years in community affairs— thirty of them with the Urban League movement—I looked forward to turning over the leadership of the organization to Whitney Young, who had been designated as my successor.

Upon my retirement, *Ebony* magazine was generous in featuring an article evaluating my career with the League. "The End of An Era" was the title, but the title, catchy as it was, really missed the point. The end of an era both in the Urban League and in racial affairs throughout the country could not be marked by any event in my own life or that of a quasi-public agency. The era's end had occurred much earlier, after it had become apparent that the Supreme Court ruling of 1954 outlawing racial discrimination and segregation in public education had not brought about any appreciable change. It was then that passive measures and redress by law gave way to more militant tactics. Long pent-up forces, generated in the emotions of the masses, launched a flow of social developments that no single individual or organization could possibly have initiated or controlled. These developments took the form of demonstrations of one type or another and marked the beginning of a new period in the struggle for human rights.

This new era, the Era of Negro Protest, is a social phenomenon without precedent in national history with regard to its intensity, persistency, and widespread nature. When it began with group demonstrations of young people, there were few who would guess, and none who could predict with confidence how long that protest would continue and how effective it would become. Not even the boldest commentators surmised that the Negro Protest would result in a nationwide social revolution and set its mark indelibly on the strategies and objectives of present-day social reform.

Faced with retirement and the desuetude of age, I found myself unwilling to close the door on the arena of public affairs at the very moment when the big acts of "the show of the century" were moving into the center ring. Consequently, I welcomed two developments that kept me busy for six years after retirement. I was elected at Rome, early in 1961, to the presidency of the International Conference of Social Work—since renamed the International Council on Social Welfare—a world-wide federation of national welfare interests linking threescore countries across the globe. A few months later President Albert W. Dent of Dillard University invited me to come to New Orleans as his college's first Edgar B. Stern Distinguished Visiting Professor. Though I was uncertain about my ability to adapt to campus life after an absence of forty years of involvement in community organization, I hesitated only momentarily. I accepted for one semester only—and stayed five years, labeled by my colleagues as "The Professor Who Came To Visit."

I would not have missed a single minute of these experiences. The presidency involved four years of traveling throughout the world; the professorship established my base on a beautiful campus among nearly a thousand students and a friendly faculty. Thus, I was immersed in welfare needs and programs of countries on five continents in the half-decade when new nations were a-borning and old ones were changing form and policy. I talked with goverment heads and their ministers, with educators and welfare officials, with urbanites and villagers. And I did all of this from the vantage point of forty years of experience with national social welfare programs in my own country.

The Dillard experience probably left the deeper mark on me. Overseas I had looked, listened, talked, and learned; but in teaching I had the opportunity to serve as confidant and advisor to interested students, and to share with them the philosophy derived from my own observations and conclusions. From young minds, pliant enough to accept fresh ideas, yet mature enough to test, criticize, and reject that which should not be accepted with automatic, unthinking obedience, I benefited in return.

These activities kept me in the midstream of those developments which had been of prime concern throughout my adult life. Through the dual contact I came to understand better why the politics of protest, more than any other combination of factors, will determine the direction and extent of the social development of American Negroes, especially those at lower income levels, during the next decade.

This last statement will seem commonplace to some; yet it is ironic that those who set up mass protests are least apt—unless they are professionals—to understand the full potential of the masses with which they work. And the Negro Protest has resulted almost unvaryingly from the efforts of amateurs who have learned as they worked (or failed to learn and therefore misused their responsibility) and who are still in the process of learning. But despite the dismaying frequency of inexperienced and sometimes incompetent leadership, the formidable weight of mass action, actuated frequently by blind emotionalism and marred at times by unguided violence, has produced during the past eight years deep and broad changes in the economic structure and social patterns affecting Negro life.

There are those—generally cynics or the uninformed—who would argue that mass protest accompanied by the threat or actuality of violence has produced, and therefore can continue to produce, more solid change than all the formally established organizations which have worked on the national scene for more than fifty years. The premise would provide for an interesting debate, were the proposition offered for ordered discussion, but such a debate would be a sterile time investment. For who can tell what is solidly and what is weakly based immediately after change has been effected or while it is still in the process of being effected? Is the "white backlash" only a figment of news commentators' imagination? Is change always growth? Is all movement progress? It takes years to make an intelligent assessment.

Meanwhile the crowd is in control—the crowd and its exhorters, who are sometimes leaders, sometimes only instigators, and at other times merely acrobatic flip-floppers who are ready to change pace and direction when threatened with the loss of their following. As objectionable as the notion of crowd action may be to some, we must face the fact that it exists. What cannot be ended must be endured, the philosophers tell us. What must be endured can often be utilized, community organization experience advises. This is one reason why the older, more stable organizations attacking racial problems have done more than merely survive for half a century. They have produced solid gains which sometimes have been the conventional product of regular, ongoing programs and at other times the result of skillful improvisation making use of the atmosphere of emergency.

Today's emergency is, in a sense, tailored to the leadership potentials of the Negro social scientist; however, there are few indeed on the national scene who are meeting current crises in the forthright manner that characterized earlier Negro social scientists. Charles S. Johnson, Ira De A. Reid, Carter G. Woodson, Charles Wesley, and others spoke out against the ambiguous policies of the New Deal, the costly racism of World War II, and the failure to eliminate racist practices when this nation "reconverted" to a peacetime economy. These earlier Negro social scientists were among the most vigorous —and persuasive—critics of patterns and policies which tended to impair further the already desperate condition of Negro working masses. Their standing as scholars inspired respect for their opinions as they exploded racial myths, unraveled sick fancy from solid fact, and battled stereotypes that tended to dehumanize Negro citizens.

The almost total disappearance of this kind of authoritative spokesmanship from the academic scene has coincided with the appearance of "instant authorities" on the race question, such as erudite but inexperienced Ph.D.'s and opportunists only recently interested in the Negro question.

Not all of the newcomers, of course, are to be regarded lightly. There is much serious and solid work done in this field, but it is not done by the "instant authority" type. Unfortunately, however, there have appeared in recent years a number of mediocre—or worse —publications capitalizing on the reading public's fascination with the race question and "what Negroes will do next, and why."

These publications, to a great extent, have gone unchallenged, and we have come bitterly to realize how badly we can be hurt— and never realize the hurt until long afterward—by the open license to be an "authority" on the race question given to those with absolutely no qualifications for such a rating. A doctor's dissertation on the Black Muslim movement several years ago—subsequently published as a "first" on the subject—was so poor as to reflect discredit more on the faculty members who approved it than on the successful doctoral candidate. Yet this work will stand as the "authoritative" history of a significant religious and social deviation of a body of American Negroes, unless it is discredited and replaced by a work of higher standard; it will be the recommended reference work for generations of students seeking information on the mounting rejection of American norms by citizens of African descent. Negro sociologists and historians were derelict when they did not challenge this study.

Sociologists were similarly derelict when, during a full decade, E. Franklin Frazier's *The Negro Family in the United States* was being cemented into place as the university bible on Negro family life. It did not seem to matter that Frazier obtruded into a serious sociological discussion that could have set a high-water mark in social research on the subject, airy and undocumented theories of the nature of Negro family life. Too few noted that *The Negro Family* was creating a new stereotype, one especially harmful because it would affect professional social welfare training and policymaking. That stereotype has jelled into a concept of *the* Negro family as a matriarchate in which the father is absent or in which he is a nonentity. It is a family structure derived directly from slavery days of a century ago—a stereotype that does not take into account changes in the family resulting from the ending of chattel slavery and movement from farm to city. Similarly, it does not take into account the shift from hoe to machine, from illiteracy to schooling, from votelessness to bloc voting. Only in a discussion of Negro life would social science in reputable universities accept as bible truth theories affecting the treatment of a mammoth social problem merely because the theorizer was a scholar of reputation.

When Daniel P. Moynihan's study of the Negro appeared, angry protest backed by sober authority came only from a limited number of Negro social scientists. Moynihan will be with us for generations as a "noted family-life sociologist"—product, at least in part, of the muteness of Negro scholars.

It is not surprising that such success should have inspired other "instant authorities" on the race question, including even those of already enviable prestige in academic circles. The teaming up of Harvard professor David Riesman, author of *The Lonely Crowd*, with Christopher Jencks, a contributing editor of the *New Republic*, resulted in a widely circulated treatise on Negro education in the South. Professor Riesman has belatedly joined the ranks of those "liberals" of both races who immediately called for closing Negro colleges after the 1954 decision of the Supreme Court, on the ground that to support them would be contributing financially to "continuance of segregation." This attitude still persists in some areas despite the fact that more than a decade after the Court's decision the end of all barriers against Negroes in state and municipal colleges of the South cannot be announced.

Until all barriers of racial discrimination are removed, there will be a continuing need for the Negro college, which represents the only hope for thousands of young Negroes to begin careers above the level of errand-running, stoop-and-polish, and mind-the-baby jobs characterizing mere subsistence living.

Moreover, it is the responsibility of the Negro college to help supply, to a large extent, the effective leaders that we vitally need today, especially in the area of race relations. Negro colleges, however, should not attempt to develop "instant authorities" of their own, for this could discredit their spokesmanship entirely. There is another way of beginning to repair losses of years of attrition in leadership ranks; it is to effect a consortium of scholarship strength in Negro universities and colleges throughout the country, with special emphasis at this time in the social sciences—sociology, psychology, economics, and history.

Ten years ago this idea would have been a proposal to be dismissed as "impractical." Today there is dismay on many campuses over what has happened as a result of the brain drain to larger, richer, and more prestigious institutions. It is right that Negro scholars should have their chance to join in the draining process as drainees, if they wish. It is not right that those institutions that still carry the principal burden of higher education for Southern young people of color are unable to offer such scholars some constructive alternative to "leaving-and-eating or staying-and-starving," as one prospective drainee put it.

A consortium such as proposed could be this alternative. Professorial exchanges, refresher seminars, consultant participation in regular seminars by such leaders as Allison Davis, Hylan Lewis, Kenneth Clark, and John Hope Franklin are examples of arrangements which would stimulate academic concern, stir student interest, and attract the financial support of certain foundations that have long desired to see more cooperative enterprises carried on by Negro higher educational institutions.

Such programs would by no means solve the problem of the "vanishing social scientist." They could lead the way to such a solution, however, and in the meantime would be certain to improve the use and heighten the morale of the talent now on faculties. There is no more pressing need in academic circles than to increase the ranks of the social scientist, for there is no single member of a college faculty today who has a greater opportunity to make a constructive contribution in the milling and moiling of racial tumult.

Regardless of the approach, here is a problem which Negro higher education must solve. In such fluid, scalding periods of social change as the present, there is a role for the Negro intellectual—the social scientist in the immediate present—which cannot be played by "imported talent," whatever its motivation, training, or experience. For this is a period when Negro scholarship must enlighten the people—black and white.

Foreign Affairs

GEORGE L-P WEAVER

George L-P Weaver was born in Pittsburgh, Pennsylvania, on May 18, 1912. He received his elementary and secondary schooling in Dayton, Ohio, and attended the Y.M.C.A. School in Chicago (now Roosevelt University) and Howard University Law School in Washington, D.C. He has spent almost his entire working life in the labor movement, gaining extensive experience as an administrator in the field of Civil Rights and international labor.

Mr. Weaver began working for the Congress of Industrial Organizations in 1941 as a member of the War Relief Committee. In 1942 he was named Assistant to the CIO's Secretary-Treasurer and Director of the CIO Civil Rights Committee, serving in both capacities until the AFL-CIO merger in 1955. After the merger he was appointed Executive Secretary of the AFL-CIO Civil Rights Committee. In 1958 he became Assistant to the President of the International Union of Electrical, Radio and Machine Workers from which post he directed the IUE's political education program and International Labor Affairs program.

Mr. Weaver took several leaves of absence for special assignments in the U.S. Government and the International Confederation of Free Trade Unions. In October, 1950, he was named Special Assistant to the Chairman of the National Security Resources Board, and in 1951 he joined the Reconstruction Finance Corporation.

During the mid 1950's, he served on several missions to the Far East and to Southeast Asia to work on labor problems for the ICFTU. He also attended the 1957 and 1958 Conferences of the International Labor Organization in Geneva, Switzerland, as an American worker-adviser.

On July 21, 1961, the late President Kennedy appointed George L-P Weaver Assistant Secretary of Labor for International Affairs. Immediately prior to this appointment, he had served as Special Assistant to the then Secretary of Labor Arthur J. Goldberg.

As Assistant Secretary of Labor for International Affairs, Mr.

Weaver is the U.S. Government representative on the Governing Body of the International Labor Organization, and is chairman of the U.S. delegation to the annual ILO Conference at Geneva. He played a leading role in the Kennedy Round of tariff negotiations in 1967.

In 1961 Mr. Weaver was awarded the Eleanor Roosevelt Key for outstanding service to the world community, the highest award given to alumni of Roosevelt University in Chicago. He received in 1962 an honorary degree of Doctor of Laws from Howard University in Washington, D.C. In 1963 he was the first American to be presented with the Malayan honorary award of the Panglima Mangku Megara which he received personally from the Malayan Head of State at a special investiture ceremony in Kuala Lumpur. In 1968, he was elected Chairman of the ILO Governing Body, and was the recipient of a Malaysian award and two medals from the Government of South Vietnam.

THE SKY IS THE LIMIT

by George L-P Weaver

TO have been a Negro in the segregated America of the thirties was to think of the future in terms of what one would be *permitted* to do, not what one would *like* to do or was *capable* of doing. The color of one's skin was a primary factor in whether one would be able to utilize his skills and abilities toward achieving a decent standard of living for himself and his family.

The young Negro of today finds himself in a world which, though far from perfect, is at least more color-blind on the subject of race than it has ever previously been. The opportunity for a minority member of our society to be accorded a measure of dignity and respect for his professional achievements is now being translated from promise to reality. But my generation is conscious of the days of Jim Crow when the question was whether racial justice and human rights, with all the meaning they carry for a fruitful life, would ever be realized in our lifetime.

I was fortunate, in 1941, to find a satisfying outlet for my efforts: while attending Howard University Law School, I was employed by the Congress of Industrial Organizations. From the following year until the AFL-CIO merger in 1955, I served as Director of the CIO Civil Rights Committee as well as Assistant to the Secretary-Treasurer of the CIO. After the merger, I was appointed Executive Secretary of the AFL-CIO Civil Rights Committee.

These were the green years, a time of seed-sowing in the field of human rights. Each year some progress could be seen. It was possible then to tell that the numerous efforts on all sides of the Civil Rights front would finally bear fruit. Of course, there were moments of discouragement. One can still recall a feeling of futility, so often present in the early days of the 1940's, an atmosphere of apathy affecting countless able young Negroes whose lives were constricted by the color of their skin.

Today, one is emboldened to advance the proposition that the limits to success for a qualified Negro are those he sets for himself. True, the heritage of slavery and a century of inequality still burden the Negro. One does not easily compensate for more than a century of denial in a few years—or even in a generation. Nevertheless, the question of success or failure for the Negro American increasingly rests on his own shoulders, and not on the birthright of the past.

Many subtle shades of discrimination have yet to be banished from the technical, managerial, governmental, and professional fields. Many more man-years of painstaking work remain if complete equality of opportunity in all fields is to be assured every individual in America. However, enormous steps have been taken to render discrimination obsolete in many important areas, not the least of which is the field of international affairs.

It is in the arena of international politics that the Negro American may now play increasingly important roles. Fortunately, one aspect of this development is that he is very much needed in this nation's foreign policy activities.

In terms of years, we are not too far away from the days when America's image abroad took the form of a very proper gentleman with striped trousers and with a background more attuned to traditional diplomatic concepts than to social needs. The American diplomat was generally a man who had gone to the right schools, who enjoyed a family and monetary background well above the average, and who, of course, was white. Thus, there was virtually a total absence of nonwhites in the old foreign service. True, occasionally a Negro would be appointed Minister to Haiti or to Liberia as a matter of political patronage; but, in reality, the representatives of the United States foreign policy around the world were people with white, not dark skins.

It may be that our country's image did not suffer unduly from this, for those were the days when colonialism was rampant, when the sun never set on British soil, and when the French, the Dutch, the Spanish, and the Germans, among others, competed with the British for colonial holdings.

The world, however, has changed radically. Colonialism is a part of history and is rapidly following slavery toward extinction. Africa is a dramatic case in point. During the past decade, the movement toward independence has swept through the greatest part of Africa like a whirlwind. This is accurately reflected in the changing membership of the United Nations. During the first decade of the UN, only four of its sixty members were Africans; and of these, only two—Ethiopia and Liberia—were from Black Africa. During the past ten years, the number of independent African nations rose from four to forty-one, nearly a third of the membership of the entire United Nations.

From the Mediterranean southward through three-quarters of the continent, political independence in Africa is nearly complete —certainly the most singular political development in modern times. The only remaining areas still suffering from colonialism, or from the oppressive rule of the small white minority over the large black majority, are in Southern Africa: the Portuguese territories, Southern Rhodesia, Southwest Africa, and the Republic of South Africa.

So, speaking in political terms, our world "constituency" has undergone a marked change, thus demanding of our country an equally marked change on the part of those responsible for communicating with other lands and other peoples. Therefore, the role of the Negro in the foreign affairs of our nation is a natural and, I believe, a crucial one.

The "winds of change" bring with them the need for a new diplomacy, and this new diplomacy demands a new kind of diplomat who must be able to function in a world caught in the throes of social, economic, and political change. He must communicate with people who, in many instances, are just emerging from centuries of oppression and colonial rule, and who are desperately seeking aid and guidance in their struggle toward a viable existence. In many instances, he must compete with other countries which, in response to their own urgent needs, seek to capitalize on the legitimate aspirations of the newly independent nations.

It was during the 1950's that an awareness developed of the great need for qualified Negroes in the international field. At that time I was active in the international labor movement, filling special assignments for the International Confederation of Free Trade Unions in the Far East and other areas. It was apparent then that there was an excellent potential for Negroes in many highly politic areas overseas, especially in places where color plays a sensitive role.

It was obvious at that time that many Negro Americans were admirably equipped to fulfill the role required in the new diplomacy.

Who better than those who have struggled for their own rights can communicate with people engaged in the many-faceted struggle for social, economic, and political survival? Who can speak more effectively from the depths of personal experience and, by example, help pave the way for others toward a richer life? Who can better convey with warmth and sympathy the essence of freedom and the democratic experience?

Increasingly, the government of the United States appreciates the fact that Negro Americans can command attention in the less developed worlds of Asia and Africa. The trend in the conduct of our foreign relations, therefore, is toward greater utilization of non-whites in key positions abroad.

The figures tell the story. In 1961, when I assumed the position of Assistant Secretary of Labor for International Affairs (and, incidentally, became a member of the Board of the Foreign Service), only forty-five persons in the entire foreign service, or less than one percent, were Negro. Today, seven years later, the total is more than three times that number—still small, to be sure, but encouraging in its promise.

The Department of State is conscious of the imbalance and is moving to correct it; thus, the future is brighter for eligible young Negroes who desire to serve their country in the nation's foreign service. It is gratifying, as a member of the Board, as well as an American concerned with the image of our country abroad, to observe the ever-growing number of Negro diplomats who are joining the foreign service at all levels. At the same time, it is important to note that they are entering the foreign service on the basis of their own skills and talents alone, with no lowering of the service's high standards.

The roll call of Negroes in high State Department positions is impressive. In 1968 there were five Negro Ambassadors representing the United States: Franklin Williams in Ghana, Hugh Smythe in Malta, Elliott P. Skinner in Upper Volta, Clinton Knox in Dahomey, and Samuel C. Adams in Niger.

Within the highest councils of the State Department in Washington, a number of Negroes are making important contributions to the conduct of U.S. foreign policy. They include Dr. Samuel Z. Westerfield, Jr., Deputy Assistant Secretary of State for African Affairs; Chester Carter, Deputy Chief of Protocol; Charlotte Hubbard, Deputy Assistant Secretary of State for Public Affairs; Barbara Watson, Administrator, Bureau of Security and Consular Affairs; and many more who escape public attention.

The distinguished President of Howard University, Dr. James M. Nabrit, Jr., recently completed a highly successful term as U.S. Representative to the UN Security Council. Another outstanding American diplomat, Mercer Cook, former Ambassador to Senegal, is currently a Senior Fellow at the State Department's Foreign Service Institute and is working on a special assignment at Howard University. Mrs. Patricia Roberts Harris recently completed an assignment in Luxembourg as the first U.S. Negro woman ambassador.

Increased opportunities for Negroes in international affairs are by no means limited to the U.S. foreign service. Qualified Negroes are constantly being recruited for both domestic and overseas positions by the United Nations and its agencies, and by such private organizations as the Ford Foundation, the African-American Institute, and the Rockefeller Brothers Fund.

Then, too, there are openings for Negroes in the international division of U.S. Government agencies such as the Department of Labor. One of the most stimulating developments in U.S. foreign policy since World War II has been the recognition by our Government that essential services in support of U.S. international activities must be performed by domestic agencies such as the Labor and Commerce Departments, the Treasury Department, etc.

In the light of this, a number of highly talented Negroes have played key roles in the international work of the Labor Department. One of the best examples is Edward C. Sylvester, who was named Special Assistant and Deputy Bureau Administrator of the International Affairs Bureau in 1961. A native of Detroit with an outstanding combat record as a World War II Army officer and later a distinguished civil engineer, Mr. Sylvester was regarded so highly by Secretary of Labor W. Willard Wirtz that in 1965 he was appointed the first Director of the Department's Office of Federal Contract Compliance with the responsibility for ensuring nondiscrimination in the implementation of U.S. Government contracts. Late in 1968, he was named by President Johnson as Assistant Secretary for Community Health Services in the Department of Health, Education and Welfare.

Of the small group of area specialists in the International Labor

Affairs Bureau—international experts for their specific areas—one of the most outstanding is William Steen. Mr. Steen performs highly important analyses of political and labor developments throughout Africa. For over two decades, before coming to the Department in 1961, he was thoroughly conversant with the African scene through study and personal visits to that continent. But, as in the case of many other Negroes then, his talents received little notice. When he was invited to join the Labor Department, he was pursuing, at the Army Map Service, an occupation scarcely suited to his abilities.

Since his appointment to the Department, Mr. Steen has proved very adept in his relationships with African officials, and has received high praise from the State Department for his service as a U.S. Delegate to the International Labor Organization Conference in Geneva.

In the Department's increasingly important role in the trade and tariff field, one of the outstanding international labor economists is Mrs. Gloria Vernon. During 1966 and most of 1967, Mrs. Vernon served in Geneva as the Department's representative on the Sixth (Kennedy) Round of GATT Tariff Negotiations. She was the only Negro as well as the highest ranking female professional among the large group of U.S. Government officials in Geneva.

One of the major activities of the Department in support of U.S. foreign policy objectives involves international technical assistance. To facilitate the Department's role in this area, the Department of Labor International Technical Assistance Corps (DOLITAC) was formed. DOLITAC is composed of labor and manpower specialists who are assigned to technical assistance missions in the developing countries for periods varying from two weeks to two years. Two of the most qualified members of this corps happen to be Negroes: George L. Jackson and Edward H. Mouzon. An expert in labor law, Mr. Jackson was given a Meritorious Achievement Award by Secretary Wirtz for outstanding work in Okinawa in a sensitive labor-management situation. Mr. Mouzon, a Wage and Hour Law specialist, is fluent in both French and Spanish and has received high praise for his work both in the United States and overseas.

The International Exhibits Branch of the Department of Labor is fortunate in having, as its second highest officer, Ike Golden, a Chicagoan who, between trips about the world to arrange exhibits depicting the American worker and his way of life, is very active in volunteer activities of the Department. Mr. Golden was elected three consecutive times as President of the Department's Federal Credit Union and is also Vice-President of the Department's Lodge of the American Federation of Government Employees, AFL-CIO.

We have taken a degree of pride in the fact that some bright young Negroes have exhibited sufficient talent to expand their horizons and go on to other responsibilities in the international field. Two of these are John Means, a native of Detroit with a Ph.D. degree from Georgetown University, who went on to a two-year assignment with the ILO as Chief of the Non-Governmental Organization Branch to supervise a world-wide survey of discrimination, and Wilbur Wright, a Johns Hopkins University graduate who was immediately engaged by the State Department and is now a foreign service officer assigned to Rome, Italy. Another is Oscar F. Morrison, formerly an international analyst with the Bureau of Labor Statistics before joining the foreign service. He is now assigned as Labor Attaché in Colombo, Ceylon.

I would say that the most serious problem we have involving Negroes in the international affairs field is not in finding *jobs* for them, but in finding *them* for the jobs. The opportunities for fruitful and meaningful service in the international field abound; it is simply a matter of being properly prepared to take advantage of them. Never has the outlook been brighter for the Negro interested in pursuing this vital field as a career.

Not so long ago, the legacy of discrimination discouraged able Negroes from serving in this demanding but rewarding work; but this is not the case today, nor will it ever be again in the future. I reiterate, therefore, that the limits to success for a qualified Negro are those he sets for himself.

JAMES H. ROBINSON

The Reverend James H. Robinson is a pastor whose creative innovations and dedicated service have benefited communities both here and abroad. Born in Knoxville, Tennessee, on January 24, 1907, he acquired an education largely on his own initiative, graduating in 1935 from Lincoln University in Pennsylvania as class valedictorian, and in 1938, as president of his class, from Union Theological Seminary in New York City. In the latter year, he was ordained to the ministry of the Presbyterian Church, and shortly thereafter founded the Church of the Master and the Morningside Community Center in Harlem. During twenty-three-and-a-half years of his leadership, these two institutions have acquired world-wide fame. The Center includes a day nursery, a youth service program, two summer camps, a credit union, and a cooperative store, and provides psychiatric counseling service. The two camps were built with the volunteer help of students from preparatory schools and colleges, enlisted by him in 1942. Since that time more than 5,000 young people have given voluntary service to the camps and to similar projects.

His first visit to Africa gave him the idea of exposing American students to that continent; out of this idea grew Operation Crossroads Africa, for which a pilot program involving sixty-two students was carried out in West Africa in the summer of 1958. Since that time, twenty-three hundred young men and women have participated in 135 projects in twenty-eight countries.

For his many volunteer services, James H. Robinson has received numerous awards and citations from community service groups and has been given several honorary doctorates in Humane Letters, Divinity, and Laws. The institutions which have conferred honorary degrees upon him include Lincoln University, the New School for Social Research, Tufts University, Wooster College, Wesleyan University, Dartmouth College, Carleton College, Howard University, Fairleigh Dickinson University, and Victoria University in Toronto, Canada. Appointed by President Lyndon B. Johnson, he has served as Special U.S. Ambassador to the Independence ceremonies of Botswana and Lesotho in Southern Africa, and as United States Representative to the World Assembly meeting of the International Secretariat for Volunteer Service in New Delhi, India.

As an author, he has been praised for his autobiography, *Road Without Turning*, published in 1950. The lectures he delivered at Yale University, as Lyman Beecher Lecturer, have been published under the title *Adventurous Preaching*. He is editor of *Love of this Land*, the story of race relations and Negro contributions in America, which has been translated into six languages by the United States Information Agency. Other significant writings include *Tomorrow is Today* and *Africa at the Crossroads*.

UNLIMITED HORIZONS

by James H. Robinson

I AM often asked how I, trained in a theological seminary, ordained as a Presbyterian clergyman, pastoring the Church of the Master in Harlem for almost a quarter of a century, and directing the Morningside Community Center for even longer, emerged into a significant role in the field of foreign affairs. I admit that I sometimes ask myself this question, particularly when I look back on the fact that I did not always *want* to be a minister. My earliest and most persistent ambition was to be a poet. I desired most of all to write a sequence of forty sonnets. To this day, I remain a frustrated poet. It was a combination of my religious background, the association with a number of outstanding religious personalities, and a burning concern to be of help to people in trouble and desperation, in want and in hunger, that combined to lead me into the ministry and eventually into international service. The compassion for others was with me from the early days of my youth as far back as I can remember. But it was a concern not just for those I was closely related to, or for the people who lived in my community or my town, or for my race, but for all people everywhere. In my early days in the bottoms of Knoxville, Tennessee, the slums of Cleveland and Youngstown, and continuing through my ministry in some of the most deprived and depraved parts of Harlem, I began to emerge from the prison of my mind, although I could not break the physical barriers of segregation, prejudice, and discrimination. My horizon was never limited to these boundaries, and when the opportunity came to go abroad on meaningful programs, I seized it.

When I was growing up I sought opportunity wherever I could, even against the wishes of my own colleagues and compatriots in the community, to become acquainted with and get to know better, people other than my immediate associates. In high school I sought out the Hungarians and the Poles, who made up the majority in the area where I lived, although they were a minority in the community just as we Negroes were. In college, university, and seminary, I sought to cultivate friendships and to explore the minds of European, African, and Asian students. At the Church of the Master I initiated an annual International Day Service: I invited two hundred foreign students to a Sunday service and arranged for families of the Harlem community to ask them to their homes for dinner for the purpose of bringing them into contact with an even larger group of people from the community. The tide of national and international opportunities and relations which began to flow from these simple efforts could not be dammed, and I found myself with a parish that was not merely in Harlem or in New York or even in America, but which was as wide as the world. Eventually foreign leaders and friends sent invitations not only to me but to my associates and church members to visit them in their countries.

In my own case, the decision to make a basic vocational change in the midstream of life came after serious and agonizing consideration of the new challenges of international affairs. Acting on advice sought from competent, experienced, and trusted individuals, I asked myself the following questions: "Is this new avenue of international service worthy of the best I have to offer?" "Can I enrich my own life as well as the lives of others while making a living?" "Can I find happiness and joy even though the task is a difficult one?" "Does international service provide opportunity for a larger ministry?" "Will it be of benefit to my fellow man and my nation?" "Will it contribute to the progress and integration of young American Negroes, and will it help them to enrich society by making possible new opportunities for the nation and the world as a result of unleashing their creative abilities?"

There was no ready answer to these questions since, in the field of international relations, the Negro traditionally had met with frustrations and difficulties at almost every turn. But I was to discover later in the foreign service that every question I had raised could be answered affirmatively.

Until a decade ago, the number of Negroes who, during any one year, had served in the foreign service of the United States government, or in overseas positions of responsibility in education, finance, business, or even the foreign missions of the churches could almost be counted on one hand. After an abbreviated roll call that would include James Weldon Johnson, Frederick Douglass, Harold Lanier, and Lester Walton—none of whom had been assigned to posts of really great importance or reached the rank of United States ambassador—the list would be almost exhausted. Historically, Negroes were not wanted by officials in high places of our governmental, educational, religious, and business institutions, and as a result were discouraged when they applied for positions and discriminated against when they persisted in their applications.

The whole process was further complicated by foreign officials, many of whom were themselves prejudiced and afraid that Negroes might too easily identify with the masses in colonial lands, influence their thought, and possibly undermine official authority. Moreover, to some extent the emerging indigenous leaders felt that if they accepted Negro foreign service personnel, they would be consigning their countries to a second-class relationship, since they did not believe that American Negroes representing the United States could get a first-class hearing when they reported back to Washington, a situation which was undoubtedly the case until recently. This discouraging state of affairs further blunted whatever little urge there was for those who wished to enter the international field.

However, a changed world situation, with newly emerging nations in Asia and Africa, the rise of the masses of colored peoples of the world into a new, important, and significant role, the necessity of the United States to relate effectively and constructively to these nations, a new political surge and importance of American Negroes, and the way that time and history are tying the ends of the earth together—all have created a situation favorable to the entrance of Negro citizens into the field of foreign affairs. Only during my lifetime have Negro Americans risen to the rank of United States ambassador: Edward Dudley to Liberia; Mercer Cook to Niger and Senegal; Elliott Skinner to Upper Volta; Franklin Williams to Ghana; Carl Rowan to Finland; Hugh Smythe to Syria and later to Malta; and Patricia Harris to Luxembourg. President Kennedy's appointment of Carl Rowan and President Johnson's appointments of Hugh Smythe and Patricia Harris may have been far more propitious appointments than either of the two Presidents knew; for the appointment of Negroes to the top posts of the United States government in Europe and the Middle East speaks not only to all

Africa with a message of the new role and importance of American Negroes, but especially to Europe, which most leaders of the United States still believe is more important in international relations than other parts of the world. These appointments in themselves would not be significant were it not for the fact that there has been a slow but persistent upgrading of Negroes to positions of importance in supporting roles in the embassies, the United States Agency for International Development (AID), the United States Information Services (USIS), and above all in the State Department itself and in the headquarters of other agencies of United States foreign affairs. All this is encouraging, and doors are opening wider every day.

While there are great opportunities, there are yet some great disadvantages and difficulties to be overcome. There are still some white people in high places who go only as far as they have to in taking Negroes into their departments; and there are some Negroes in the upper ranks who are concerned only with their own advancement and security and make no effort to be catalysts for younger Negroes. Too few Negro parents, teachers in Negro high schools and colleges where the majority of Negroes are still enrolled, and leaders of the Negro community have traveled to any extent beyond the usual tourist trip to Europe. Still fewer have had the opportunity to share with their families, schools, and communities the experiences gained from important assignments in foreign countries.

The continuing and perplexing problem of race relations, despite the new confrontations and advances, imprisons the mind of the Negro youth as it imprisons his physical life in the ghettos and demands an overwhelming proportion of his time just to fight for equality of opportunity and personal dignity and respect within the boundaries of his own country, leaving very little time for him to explore the international horizon. The dilemma is made more difficult by the economic situation in which the average Negro youth finds himself. Thus, when the opportunity comes for the young Negro to go abroad on American Field Service or with Operation Crossroads Africa, either he cannot raise the funds to support himself or, if he receives a full scholarship, he sometimes cannot go because he has to work in the summer to get enough money to continue in school in the fall. When he goes about his community asking for support, he is discouraged by such observations as the following: "Aren't you content to stay here?" "Why do you want to waste your time over there?" "You're just looking for a tourist joy-ride." "Your task is here in race relations."

Although all the difficulties I have listed have a deterrent effect on young Negroes, I believe the most crushing are the lack, at an early age, of economic resources that would enable them to begin an exploration of the international opportunities which are open to youth, and the lack of encouragement and support, on the part of Negro leaders in all professions, to those Negro youths who are adventurous. There is urgent need for all the organizations interested in enlarging the international horizons of American youth to give special attention to ways in which they can involve and encourage more Negro young people. There is an urgent need, too, for Negro leaders to give earnest consideration to ways in which they can help the young people of their institutions and communities prepare for careers in international affairs.

The demand for American Negroes in foreign service is rapidly outrunning the supply, primarily because the opportunities are opening up more rapidly than Negroes realize. Educational institutions, business and industry, the mission boards of churches, as well as foreign service agencies of the government, are earnestly seeking trained Negro personnel, as are practically all of the private international organizations and such world-related agencies as the United Nations. Negroes need not be afraid that they are running away from the race problem if their talents and abilities lead them into the field of international relations. In one sense, and a very vital one at that, playing an important role in the field of international affairs is as helpful to the improvement of race relations as becoming involved in the Civil Rights struggle at home. America now has a role of world leadership which God has never given to another nation in the history of mankind. Among the emerging nations there are many serious questions about the United States, and some of the most important revolve around the problem of America's inability to handle the race problem more intelligently, constructively, and creatively than it has done. A great deal of the racial progress we have made within this country in the last ten years owes as much to the efforts to establish friendly relations with these emerging nations as it does to the leadership of those who have fought the battle within the boundaries of our country. In the color-conscious world in which we live today, America's need to relate to *all* the nations of the world will become an increasingly valuable asset in the struggle for Civil Rights at home—not the only asset, nor indeed an overriding one, but one far more significant and important than either American Negroes or whites have yet realized.

HUGH H. SMYTHE

After serving as U.S. Ambassador to Syria from 1965 until that country broke relations with the United States, Hugh H. Smythe was appointed by President Lyndon B. Johnson as Ambassador to Malta in September, 1967, and is currently serving in that capacity.

Born in Pittsburgh, Pennsylvania, on August 19, 1913, Ambassador Smythe received his public school education in that city. He later attended Virginia State College, Atlanta University, and Northwestern University, which awarded him the B.A. degree, the M.A. degree, and the Ph.D. degree respectively. He also did graduate work in International Relations at Columbia University's East Asian Institute.

Ambassador Smythe has served as Consultant on African, Asian, and American Problems and International Affairs for the Institute of International Education, the Unitarian Service Committee, the Residential Seminars on World Affairs, and Operation Crossroads Africa. He has served also as Consultant to Industry Incorporated, Doubleday and Company, *Time* and *Life* magazines, Stanford University Press, and various other organizations.

In the area of governmental service he has been a member of the staff of the United States Mission to the United Nations as Advisor on Social and Economic Affairs, and a member of the U.S. Delegation to the 16th General Assembly of the United Nations. His world travels, extensive and intensive research, and his analyses of domestic and international affairs have resulted in numerous publications in leading professional journals. He has published more than 150 articles and 500 book reviews and is co-author of *Educating the Culturally Disadvantaged Child*; he is also co-author, with his wife, of *The New Nigerian Elite*.

Ambassador Smythe is active in several professional organizations and has served as a Board Member of the African Studies Association, the Committee for World Development and World Disarmament, the Museum of African Art, and Operations Crossroads Africa.

A Fellow of the American Anthropological Association, the African Studies Association, and the Society for Applied Anthropology, Ambassador Smythe's honors include fellowships, scholarships, and grants-in-aid from the Julius Rosenwald Fund, Atlanta University, the American Council of Learned Societies, the American Friends Service Committee, the Hattie M. Strong Foundation, Fisk University, the British Colonial Office, the Social Science Research Council, and the Ford Foundation.

REACH FOR THE STARS

by Hugh H. Smythe

LOOKING back from the vantage point of a few years past the half-century mark, I am impressed by the variety of people and events that go into developing and shaping a human being. My training in the social sciences has focused my attention on people, society, and history; I am not sure how this emphasis came about, but I am glad that it did. As I moved from a Pittsburgh, Pennsylvania, childhood, in which material poverty was ever-present, through years of adolescence, in which normal difficulties were made even worse by depression and war, into adulthood, it dawned upon me that to see everyone attain economic security and prosperity would be a most constructive goal towards which to work.

Two women had much to do with shaping my personal philosophy and in setting the basic guidelines that have directed my life. Very early in my existence my widowed mother, who worked long, hard hours as a domestic servant to support a daughter and four sons, said to me: "Always know you are no better and no worse than any other person, for people are essentially the same everywhere." As I write these lines, I realize that my experiences in teaching social science at a Japanese university; researching people, places, politics, and culture in West Africa as a Ford Foundation Fellow; serving as a United States delegate to an international conference in Europe or in the United Nations; advising a government in Southeast Asia; or representing the United States as an ambassador in a Middle Eastern country—all have confirmed the inherent truth of this observation made by a woman poor in formal education but rich in the wisdom of life.

The other woman who influenced me, my grandmother, told me when I was about six years old, "Reach for the stars; aim high and make something of yourself. As you move up, never forget those who helped you in your climb, for everybody needs help to get where he wants to go." The validity of this advice has been repeatedly demonstrated as the years have passed.

Both of these wonderful women knew that life was going to be hard for me in the years ahead, not only because they had neither position, privilege, nor purse to pass on to me, but also because as Negroes they were aware of the numerous racial barriers that had blocked their way and would hinder mine. But they also knew that society is ever changing, and they encouraged us children to work hard, to get as much education as possible so as to be ready to seize opportunities when obstacles lessened and things became better. My mother and grandmother have long since gone from this earth, but these things they etched lastingly into my character and personality, and I am the richer for their having done so.

Thus, education became a must for me as I realized how necessary learning was to those with the handicap of color, religion, creed, national origin, and sometimes sex, who would beat upon the doors of new opportunity. To get an education, like many other youngsters who belonged to underprivileged groups, I worked at any and all jobs. For a two-year period, while my mother was ill, I had to leave school and support the family, which had by then shrunk to three. In 1932, after completing high school, I left Pittsburgh for college with the blessings of mother and grandmother, forty-five dollars in savings, and a loan of twenty dollars from a railway mail clerk who lived in the Young Men's Christian Association where I was a boy of all work. Possessing some modest athletic ability and a great willingness to work, and filled with fear, all 112 pounds of me showed up at all-Negro Virginia State College in Petersburg, Virginia.

I had been aware of racial segregation and discrimination in Pittsburgh, but Virginia State was my first real experience in a completely Negro setting. It was there I became conscious of how educationally and culturally deprived were those who had been trained in a so-called "separate but equal" school system. I, who had often been the only colored pupil—and I had never had more than one or two Negro classmates—in my elementary and high school classes in one of the best school systems in the country, quickly found out how poor were the backgrounds of my fellow students. But the president of the college and a few older and several younger Negro faculty members, just starting their teaching careers after graduate study in some of the best universities in America and abroad, set the stage for four full, fascinating, formative years.

This was the era of the New Deal with its programs that led to reshaping much of America in a social revolution brought on by the greatest depression in our history. The potent need for change stimulated overdue attention to the problems of the masses and the poor. Schools on all levels responded to the efforts of President Franklin D. Roosevelt's National Youth Administration. Life was not yet easier, but the promise of better days was heartening. The idealism of some of the Negro youngbloods on the faculty, coupled with the wisdom of older heads, gave hope and direction which we youngsters of that period heeded.

After graduation I moved on to study for a master's degree at Atlanta University and had an eye-opening year of experience in the Deep South, as well as contact with Negro personalities of distinction in the scholarly world. From there I began my professional career which, broadened by further advanced study and work in both the North and the South, eventually led me in the direction of international affairs.

As I moved through the years just sketched, discrimination against color and a lack of money, as with so many others, were major handicaps. I learned soon that as regards the former there were some people in the majority population who rejected color prejudice as unworthy of an avowedly democratic society. Yet, as I continued to push against barriers on the job front, I experienced many humiliations even when I was better qualified than my white competitors. By this time, however, I was convinced that the obstacles would fall if well-prepared people kept demanding opportunity.

After World War II Army service, work for the National Association for the Advancement of Colored People gave me added insight into the techniques needed by a weak minority group. By then I was living in New York, where I found an increasing number of white fellow-citizens who were genuinely concerned, as I was, about the gap between American ideals and practices. They did and said things in my behalf when it would have been easier and more expedient to keep silent; they risked personal profit and influence because it was the right and just thing to do. This spirit helped to open new doors, and partly because of this I was able to become a diplomat.

I had been rebuffed in my efforts to join the Department of State, first when I completed my college work, and again immediately following World War II, even though by then I had earned a doctorate and had compiled a creditable professional reputation in specialties for which the Foreign Service advertised it was seeking qualified personnel. But the global conflict of the early 1940's shocked the United States out of its isolation and made integration an international asset, and as a world leader our government needed people trained and experienced in affairs overseas. Sensing opportunity and desiring to further expand my own horizons, I enrolled in Columbia University's graduate school of East Asian studies, then went to Japan to teach for two years. Later I went several times to Africa, as well as to Europe and Asia.

Eventually the State Department began to call upon me as a lecturer at its Foreign Service Institute to help prepare career officers and to brief Fulbright grantees, and invited me to serve with the United States Mission to the United Nations. Meanwhile, action on the Civil Rights front, not only in America but abroad as well, had some effect in lessening the resistance against Negroes who wished to enter the foreign affairs field. Subsequent developments concerned with the New Frontier concept of the late President John F. Kennedy and with the Great Society program of President Lyndon B. Johnson helped also. But it is still far from easy for women, and for Negroes and other minority group members to enter the State Department at the officer level, although the Department has been making a conscious effort to reduce barriers and alter its image as an exclusive club preferring male white Anglo-Saxon Protestants.

Theoretically, all posts—even that of Cabinet-level Secretary of State—are open to all. But the realities of American life make it extremely difficult, as I have already pointed out, for women, and for Negroes and other minority group members to have the kind of experience required to qualify for the top five positions in the Department. Qualifying for levels below the top is almost as difficult. In the 119 embassies and some 360 other overseas establishments employing 3500 Foreign Service officers, there are still fewer than thirty Negro career officers in the Foreign Service, and only five ambassadors. Of these latter top-ranking diplomats, only one was a career Foreign Service officer before his relatively recent elevation, and he will soon reach retirement age; the other four had established themselves elsewhere before receiving their appointments.

As disappointing as this tally is, there are signs of improvement. The Foreign Affairs Scholars Program of the Department of State —one of the most imaginative projects in government—was devised specifically to attract into the foreign service more bright young people from minority groups. Negro colleges and universities are now included in the regularly scheduled tours made by recruiters sent out from the Department.

In addition, there are other avenues to overseas work connected indirectly with the State Department in the Agency for International Development and the United States Information Agency. Also, one can work overseas as a Defense Attaché of the Armed Services, or as an Attaché for such government agencies as Agriculture; Labor; Commerce; Health, Education and Welfare; and others.

Although prejudice has not yet disappeared from the Foreign Service, current democratic trends in our society today inhibit open expression of anti-minority feelings, which can seriously harm the careers of the prejudiced in today's world. What is really important as I write this is that the Department is making a serious effort to analyze its defects as a "social system." It will be some time before the Department of State can expect to have a staff totally accustomed to dealing easily and naturally with minority group applicants; the latter, on the other hand, do not yet have, as a group, the training and background needed to take advantage of the opportunities open to their white counterparts. Under these circumstances, experience has taught me that the few opportunities that are available go to those who work harder to get ahead and who make up for more limited experiences by making the best of those they have.

The ideal preparation includes a solid grounding in the social and physical sciences, as well as in the humanities. It helps, too, to be able to read rapidly, to speak with clarity, and to write well. One should develop his sense of curiosity and should travel overseas, preferably to some part of the underdeveloped world. Along with this it is useful to acquire experience in management and administration, learn self-discipline, as well as a foreign language, and keep one's finger on the pulse of the political process and economic and social change taking place not only in America but the world over, by becoming an avid reader of the daily newspapers and the mass-circulated weekly news magazines.

Diplomacy, properly pursued, involves loyalty to country, devotion, determination, and dedication to the job, and it requires hard, demanding work. Although it is an asset to be primed in the social graces, as long as one is considerate of others he need not worry about the stereotype of the striped-pants diplomat. One must be bright, think big, look beyond the shores of the U.S.A., be himself, have drive and courage, and cultivate the knack of getting along with all types of people while remaining basically honest, unselfish, and forthright. One will need a sense of conviction, and should not be afraid to express and defend his views so long as he exercises tact in doing so.

It is also helpful in building a foundation for a career as a Foreign Service officer, although it will be difficult, to secure experience in international relations activities, such as attending or serving as a delegate to international conferences, working on special task forces overseas, attending world conferences of professional organizations, and so on—all of which are assignments that have long been denied to minorities. A Foreign Service officer must be ready to make real personal sacrifices; when the job requires it, he may need to be away from home and family or to forego customary comforts. And it is necessary that he be in excellent physical condition and ready to take on many diverse responsibilities at a moment's notice. A Foreign Service officer must train himself to be patient, must learn to conquer his frustrations, and must be prepared to accept a peripatetic way of life. Working outside of government, as well as inside, helps him, at times, to move to higher levels. This type of experience enables him to retain more objectivity and helps him view foreign affairs with broader perspective than if his experience were confined to purely Departmental activities.

In formulating United States foreign policy, Negroes have yet to be in a position to make a major contribution, since they have never occupied positions in the hierarchy where the ultimate decisions for American foreign policy are made. But just as significant positions have opened for them in other government agencies, key positions will materialize for them, too, in the Department of State. Two things encourage my hopes in this regard: first, American society is undergoing a positive reorganization in human relations, and we are finally making a real effort to bring long-proclaimed democratic principles into line with actual practice; and second, in the American milieu into which I was born and have matured, we are reared to believe that the best is none too good for *all* the people, not only for the chosen *few*. This I believe.

FRANKLIN H. WILLIAMS

The former U.S. Ambassador to Ghana, Franklin H. Williams, is now Director of the Urban Center at Columbia University. He was born in Flushing, New York, on October 22, 1917. It was here that he obtained his public school education before attending Lincoln University, where he received the A.B. degree in 1941, and the Fordham University School of Law, where he received the LL.B. degree in 1945. Following the completion of his legal training, he was admitted to the bar of the State of New York, the State of California, and the United States Supreme Court. He holds the honorary degrees of Doctor of Humanities from Windham College and Doctor of Laws from Lincoln University (Pennsylvania).

From 1945 to 1958 he was associated in various capacities with the NAACP. From 1959 to 1961 he served as Assistant Attorney General of the State of California and as chief of the Constitutional Rights Section of the California Department of Justice.

Ambassador Williams' federal service began in 1961 when he was named Special Assistant to the Director and Chief, United Nations and International Organization Division, U.S. Peace Corps, responsible for developing, coordinating, and implementing all U.S. Peace Corps relationships with the UN and other international agencies. Subsequently, he was appointed Director, Division of Private Organizations and University Relations, U.S. Peace Corps (1962), and Director, African Region, U.S. Peace Corps (1963), in which latter capacity he developed and negotiated all Peace Corps programs in Africa.

In 1964 he was named Ambassador to the UN, serving as U.S. Representative on the Economic and Social Council. In the course of the next year, President Lyndon B. Johnson selected him to serve as U.S. Ambassador to Ghana.

At present he is a member of the National Association of Intergroup Relations Officials and Vice-President of the Urban League of Greater New York and a member of the Board of Experiment in

International Living, Operation Crossroads Africa. He is also a member of the Board of Directors of Americans for Democratic Action, the Dalton School, the Verde Valley School, the College of the Virgin Islands, and Lincoln University.

I BELIEVE

by Franklin H. Williams

AS an Ambassador, representing the President of the United States, it was my task to interpret our foreign and domestic policies. At times, questions arose dealing with problems of nuclear war, Red China, and Vietnam; and, at other times, questions arose pertaining to our poverty and job opportunity programs, Medicare for the aged, education, or Civil Rights. I attempted to handle these matters as diplomatically as possible and in such a way as to reflect the preeminent world position of my country, and I hope that history will record that I performed my duties effectively.

Although I have spent the greater part of my adult life as a Civil Rights advocate, often forced, by necessity, to criticize governmental policies in helping America to fulfill her high promise, I found no contradiction in being an official and vigorous spokesman for American democracy in its finest tradition.

I believe the great strength of our democracy rests in its basic commitment to an open society which affords the individual the chance to develop his own social philosophy. *I believe* the greatness of our country lies not in her military prowess, her technological superiority, nor in her vast accumulation of wealth. The foundation stone of America's greatness is the freedom to express one's opinion. I am aware that such freedom may possibly expose our shortcomings, but there is no need to conceal our weaknesses. Exposure can result in recognition, debate, and correction, while silence may well nurture the cancer of democratic contradiction.

I believe that often there is a direct relationship between being a dedicated Civil Rights leader and a leader in American society generally. As an activist in the Civil Rights movement, I have sought self-fulfillment within the context of our society. When I was a youth, young blacks were hemmed in by social and psychological barriers which limited our aspirations mainly to positions in medicine, dentistry, law, and teaching. Few of us had ever met a black architect, stockbroker, industrial chemist, electrical engineer, or the like. The black leader then—the person looked up to with respect —followed the paradigm. There are still many depressed areas in which black youths live believing that the field of professional sports represents their only outlet for achievement. In these areas the atmosphere is filled with such social static that communication regarding new opportunities is almost unknown. But in the last several years, there have been changes; and new horizons have emerged. Identification by race is no longer the barrier it once was. And those who earlier fought so hard to bring about these changes have not been penalized by America. In fact, America has recognized and honored many of them. Dr. Robert Weaver, former Secretary of Housing and Urban Development, and Thurgood Marshall, Supreme Court Justice and former United States Solicitor General, are two such examples.

I believe it is necessary for us to take pride in our racial and cultural heritage if we want to compete and succeed in a dynamic society. Many people look upon the growing integration of blacks in American life as a means of eluding identification as blacks. This is silly! Integration does not mean the loss of racial identity. Our society can accommodate racial and cultural differences and can accord recognition and honor to all who succeed. Facing problems is inherent in the game of living, and one need not turn his back on the past in order to adjust as a person in our contemporary world.

To take pride in our past does not mean, as many people believe, that the contemporary black must embrace a "back-to-Africa movement." To me, such a movement has always represented a basic fallacy, for the truly mature black American knows that his salvation lies in his own country. It is incongruous to speak of a black American as an African. In fact, until quite recently, the mass of black Americans had little knowledge of Africa, and few had contact with Africans.

I believe further, that the emergence of African nations as independent states and the rise of distinguished African statesmen have given the black American a pride in race and self. These developments have helped him cast off the stigma of color and overcome a feeling of shame concerning his identity. Similarly, in the rise of Africa, the black American can feel justly proud, for it was he who first pressed the modern concept of freedom which gave birth to pan-Africanism. Africans saw and felt the black Americans' drive for achievement and advancement, and in their own lands they, too, became determined to set their peoples free. This cult of freedom is what joins the African and the black American. Moreover, the cross-fertilization now occurring between Africa and America is affecting not only the black but the white American as well. This is evidenced by America's ever-widening involvement in African affairs.

I believe that all young Americans, and especially young blacks, are facing a dynamic and awesome period in our world's history. To succeed they must set their values high. Black youngsters must understand and believe that their chances of employment and success will depend more than ever upon merit. True, there will be some barriers of social class in the prestige occupations of our society—a fact, unfortunately, that has been true in all societies. But these barriers, too, will be breached, now that the issue of caste is being resolved.

In training for the future, there are four attributes which I believe black youngsters must cultivate: first, they must develop the habit of listening—really listening to the views of others and retaining an open mind; second, they must strive to acquire and effectively apply essential knowledge; third, they must accept and fulfill their responsibilities to their race and to their nation; and last, they must develop pride in themselves as young black men and women.

I believe that the cultivation of these attributes will enable the young black American to face the future, confident of his ability to achieve his rightful place in America—a hesitant America perhaps, but basically one committed to justice, dignity, and equality for all men.

The Ministry

JOHN M. BURGESS

Born in Grand Rapids, Michigan, on March 11, 1909, the Right Reverend John M. Burgess is the present Suffragan Bishop of the Diocese of Massachusetts. Bishop Burgess graduated from the University of Michigan, where he did postgraduate work in sociology, receiving the M.A. degree. He was awarded the B.D. degree in 1934 by the Episcopal Theological School in Cambridge, Massachusetts.

Following his formal training, he began his ministry in Michigan and later served in Ohio. In 1946 he became a University Chaplain in Washington, D.C., where he founded Canterbury House, a Student Episcopal Center. During his stay in Washington, he also became a Canon of the Washington Cathedral. He served as Archdeacon of Boston and Superintendent of the Episcopal City Mission from 1956 until his consecration as Suffragan Bishop of Massachussets in 1962.

Bishop Burgess represented the Episcopal Church as an official delegate to the Central Committee of the World Council of Churches that met in Lucknow, India, in 1952, and as a delegate to the Third Assembly of the World Council of Churches that met in New Delhi, India, in 1961.

He is a member of the General Board of the National Council of Churches and of the General Board of the Greater Boston Y.M.C.A. He is a Vice-President of the Massachusetts Council of Churches and a member of the Massachusetts Advisory Committee for the U.S. Commission on Civil Rights.

Among the many types of recognition the Right Reverend John M. Burgess has received are honorary degrees from the University of Michigan, St. Augustine's College of Raleigh, North Carolina, the Assumption College of Worcester, Massachusetts, and the Berkeley Divinity School of New Haven, Connecticut.

THIS I BELIEVE

by John Melville Burgess

LITTLE has been written by students of society about the Negro in the ordinary town or small city of the North. It has been more popular and attractive to uncover the dismal facts of the great urban ghettos, to trace there the causes and incidents of crime and delinquency, to mark the decline and fall of family life, to describe the crushed and maimed victims of outright prejudice and exploitation. It is right, of course, that social pathology, like all forms of deterioration, elicit attention and response because, if any relief is available, it surely ought to be directed toward those concerns that cry out for immediate correction. There is a question, however, whether in dealing with any field of knowledge, attention solely on the abnormal is the only method by which we can understand the normal —whether the study of disease is the only sure way to understand health. As a matter of fact, careful analysis of what usually might pass as ordinary or commonplace often uncovers circumstances that merit further examination.

I have in mind my own upbringing in Grand Rapids, Michigan. In my youth, the city had under 100,000 citizens and a Negro community of a few hundred. Since my maternal grandparents had arrived there in the early 1870's, we considered ourselves, along with several other Negro families, among the old settlers. As a young person, I was not particularly aware of racial discrimination or even of racial identity. The town was so dominated by a Dutch majority that all other racial or ethnic groups underwent certain disabilities as "Gentiles." The two Reformed denominations in no way reflected their South African counterparts, but maintained an aloofness from the Negro as from the Italian, from the Methodist as from the Roman Catholic. Negroes seemed no better or worse than their white neighbors. Grand Rapids, living under strict Calvinism, was a clean, law-abiding Republican city. Solid citizens owned their homes and went to church; and Negroes reflected much of this atmosphere. I think we took it with a certain lightness and vivacity, however, for I recall my Dutch playmates reading our Sunday newspaper, which they were forbidden to purchase, and listening to my accounts of movies which some were not allowed to attend. One could surmise that this city, and many of its kind, had "solved" the race problem ideally by fulfilling the dream of a free and democratic community. Our living standards, our involvement in civic affairs, our participation in cultural pursuits reflected, as I have mentioned above, the standards of a healthy American town, and I cannot dismiss these advantages when assessing those things that have come to bear upon my own life. Probing a bit now under the surface, however, I see a pattern of racism which is not pleasant and which I confess with some embarrassment.

The Negro in a small Northern community is a perfect example of the man without roots or identity in American society. The tragedy is often seen in his unawareness of his predicament. In Grand Rapids Negroes lived in well-defined areas of the city, defined quietly by politicians and real estate dealers. Enough white neighbors were interspersed so that we were not really aware that we were living in a "Negro district" and that there were areas where we could not live. Employment followed a similar pattern. One or two jobs in the public schools, the post office, and the police department somehow led us to accept the fact that the rest of us were relegated to common labor, domestic service, and jobs as porters and waiters in hotels and on trains. These latter had status as white-collar jobs. Identifying closely with the tastes and customs of affluent employers, the Negro community had its own social elite. It was a tribute to their resourcefulness how well they lived on so little money! In the light of present-day employment opportunities, one can weep to recall that women among this upper stratum thought it fortunate to be employed as stock girls and elevator operators in department stores. Except for visits to Chicago and Detroit and to Idlewild, an all-Negro resort, we made little contact with the larger Negro community outside. An anemic chapter of the NAACP brought Dr. Du Bois, Dean Pickens, or an occasional African "prince" to remind us of wider interests. But I am afraid we regarded these more as missionaries reporting on conditions out in "the field."

The sterility of this superficial identification with the white community became dramatically apparent with the advent into our city of Southern Negroes after World War I. No welcome mat awaited them from either black or white groups. Shunted off into the area around the railroad tracks, they found little warmth in churches, fraternal organizations, or social groups. Parents cautioned us about "those new people"; high school students were embarrassed by the dress and behavior of their newly-arrived companions. Unaware that the white community had, for generations, classified us as Negroes and therefore "different," we were afraid that these new people would create a "problem" and we would all be the object of the white man's displeasure. It can be said that the Negro community, through its reluctance to take leadership in helping the migrants to adjust to their new surroundings, was largely responsible for the many problems that did ensue. These Southern plantation workers, bereft of the simplest implements of ordered living, contributed in the long run our most valuable asset—namely, a sense of racial identification that stemmed from a knowledge of who they were and where they wanted to go.

The discovery of my own identity as a Negro in American society came upon matriculation at the University of Michigan. At Ann Arbor I met keen, sensitive graduate students from the Southern colleges. From them I heard first-hand testimony of the lynchings and burnings perpetrated upon black people. In visits to Detroit I saw my people herded into St. Antoine and Hastings Streets. I saw the role of the Negro minister leading and dominating his people, and became convinced of the significant place of the church in the black community. I am persuaded that the Southern Christian Leadership Conference, following the guidelines established by the late Dr. Martin Luther King, represents a valid approach to the problem, for it is based on a givenness as well as an ideology that must be reckoned with by anyone who would deal realistically with the black community.

This racial identity did not come easily. I had not only to discover my own "Negritude" but prove it to my new companions. One of my roommates who had been raised in Florida accused me of trying to be "white." He used words and pronunciations I had never heard. I had never eaten grits and had had rice only occasionally, and then in a pudding. I actually knew white people whom

I regarded as my friends and had been unable to muster hatred against the whole white race. I asked him questions about the South, and he concluded that I meant them in a derogatory way. Eventually we both had our eyes opened to how *American* the Negro really is as he reflects the regional, ethnic, and class customs of this most variegated land. I believe that one of the evidences of the power of the Civil Rights movement is that it has overwhelmed the differences that have separated Negroes in Michigan and Mississippi, in New York and Georgia, in Sugar Hill and Watts, in Boston and Kingston, Jamaica. Our unity has been forged on a decisive understanding of a common exploitation, and on a common will to achieve dignity and freedom.

I paid for my college education by washing dishes in a fraternity house and was joined in this employment by dozens of other Negro students who were determined to make a place for themselves and their people. We had all worked in some menial capacity for white people and had seen "the man" in his less attractive moments; so white supremacy was a picture that held no fears for us. The contributors to Alain Locke's *The New Negro* were our spokesmen; Roland Hayes, Paul Robeson, and Ethel Waters expressed in song our inmost feelings; Ernest Just, Charles Johnson, and John Hope assured us that scholarship of the highest caliber was attainable and worth the effort to achieve. This awakening knowledge of the position of the Negro in American life led me easily to become a student of society, not only as an area of inquiry and research but also as an area of life-commitment and purpose.

This resolve was furthered by my introduction to the teachings of Charles Horton Cooley, Professor of Sociology at Michigan. It was he who opened my eyes to the nature of the social order, its wholeness and its process of change. Never content with the glibness of formulas, lifeless statistics, and impersonal mechanics, he helped me see society and the individual as inseparable components, constantly acting, reacting, and interacting in a dynamic process that opened ever new vistas and possibilities for the human race. His profound insight and simplicity of expression still stand for me in marked contrast to so much pedantic and unreal "scientific" study of man in the present day. I found that my experience at Michigan made me a man aware of myself, my roots, my possibilities, and of my place in society, with its attendant responsibilities and opportunities. When, twenty-five years later, my alma mater conferred upon me the degree of Doctor of Humanities, no award was ever more gratefully and humbly received.

My decision to enter the Christian ministry was, in fact, a coming-together of these many currents. Shocked into an awareness of the evil and perfidy of human society, I wanted to do something about it. Looking about and examining the various panaceas freely presented in place of the Gospel, I saw none that offered a way out "over the long haul." I use this phrase advisedly, for it is always tempting to try to correct an injustice by smashing a jaw, passing a resolution, winning a law suit, or even by shaking hands and having a drink. Final victory must be grounded in something more basic and permanent. The Christian Gospel is founded in history, and it is the communication of that Gospel that is the sole objective of the Christian minister.

Democratic humanism, in popular evidence among both black and white leaders in the fight for freedom, is not to be depreciated, nor is the current faith in the ultimate universalism of technocracy to be minimized. We still face the fact that it is man who is the democrat or the technologist, and man has shown no evidence that, given the choice in the use of his talents and dreams, he will choose the best rather than the worst.

I would be the first to admit the dark pages in Christian and human experience, but I must go further and say that we are driven from cynicism to utter despair if we cannot, through faith, place our ultimate loyalty in One who is above the strivings of men. The Christian goes further and says that his God has come among us in the person of Jesus Christ and in Him we catch at least a glimmer of the nature and purpose and final end of history.

To fight for justice in order to be in a position to be unjust, to put down our exploiters only to exploit, to escape degrading poverty into a dull prosperity—all would entrap us in a cycle of despair. The power, wealth, and know-how which America possesses in abundance are no guarantee of peace, security, and fulfillment. The black man's struggle for freedom must have as its aim the abolition of those very things that have served to enslave him. The definition of "Black Power" seems to depend largely upon the person who uses the term. I could say from my own point of view that I heartily endorse this concept: that the Negro, in the face of injustice, strive for the respect that will enable reconciliation to be achieved between the races, rather than seek redress through violent means. Only peers can be reconciled. As the Negro recognizes his own worth, feels his own strength, and achieves his own purposes, he will then be in a position to deal graciously with those who oppose him.

The only power that has legitimate coinage in human relations is the power of love. The Christian, looking at both his Gospel and the sordid pages of history, says to modern man, "Love or perish." The popular quip, "Christianity has not failed; it has never been tried" serves to remind us that we have, in these revolutionary days, a great opportunity to bring something new into human experience. In Jesus Christ a new dimension has been added to the moral possibility of men, and by this standard they are better—or worse.

This is the challenge that the Christian ministry presents to Negro youth today. The daring and selflessness often found in the Peace Corps and Volunteers in Service to America, and the sacrifice and excitement of the various activist groups working throughout the land are to be commended and encouraged. They stand in marked contrast to much of the bland leadership of the NAACP and the goodwill-dinner approach of too many liberals. Their enthusiasm and conviction, however, must be grounded in the purposes of Christ and given a permanence and stability that can contribute to the well-being of all humanity, regardless of color. Humanism is not destroyed only by those who seek to dehumanize. There are enemies within as well as without the Freedom movement. Fights over status, jealousies over leadership, and corruption of character defeat us as surely as bombings, lynchings, and disfranchisement. Anger and retaliation are self-defeating. To damn the stupidity of the war in Asia while engaging in a war at home is neither rational nor constructive.

I would agree that if we must die fighting for freedom, it had best be done here; but need it be done at all? Is this not the area in which Negro Americans can make their most significant contribution? Both our Christian heritage and the facts of modern history lead me to believe that the Negro is in a strategic position to enrich our common life.

The trained minister can give his people a coherent account of a conceptual interpretation of his faith, and following in the steps of countless witnesses before him, can become a courageous leader in the march toward universal freedom. His leadership does not result from a shocked recoil from lash and terror; it is not driven by vengeance and turmoil. He gives himself for his people, for he is loyal to his Master, who bestowed on him a ministry of reconciliation. Fully conscious of the terrible ways in which he and all Christians fall short of this privilege, he walks with humility and yet with assurance along this path of reparation and reconciliation, knowing that there is no other path that leads to universal peace.

My own identification with the Episcopal Church is an extension of this basic point of view. For me it has provided a sure anchor with its persistent regard for historical roots and processes. It seems to me to have combined this high regard for the past with a most adaptable view of the present, providing a large area in which the Gospel can be declared in varying ways. Its insistence on a historically rooted ministry, an ordered worship, and a trained leadership insures that its contribution to the religious life of our people will be responsible, reasonable, and aesthetically inspiring. That it, too, largely fails to bear true witness to its Gospel of love is all too evident; yet the multi-racial character of its membership and its worldwide constituency assure us that, working through the inevitable tensions of such a fellowship, whatever solutions result will be beaten out on the hard anvil of bitter and blessed human experiences.

Though I have had from birth a satisfying home in the Episcopal Church, I am grateful that in this day ecumenism has added an exciting dimension to the Christian Church. Again the Negro Christian makes his contribution. The unity that must finally be realized will be far more than the amalgamation of hierarchies and the enrichment of doctrines. It will be the coming together of all who profess the Lordship of Christ and the fellowship in Him of all men. As a Christian I have confidence in history, for it continues to be the concern of a God who cares. It is my deepest concern that men be enabled to respond to that love in daily commitment and service.

WILLIAM HOLMES BORDERS

Born on February 24, 1905, in Macon, Georgia, and representing the third generation of preachers in his family, the Reverend William Holmes Borders as a youth picked peaches in Houston County, picked cotton in Twiggs County, sold papers on the streets of Bibb County, and carried mail in Macon to earn a living and to finance his education. Since his graduation from Garrett Theological Seminary, he has forged a steady path upward in the ministry and is currently minister of the Wheat Street Baptist Church in Atlanta, Georgia.

The Reverend Mr. Borders holds a bachelor's degree from Morehouse College and a master's degree from Northwestern University. He is the recipient of the Doctor of Divinity degree from Morris Brown College, Shaw University, and Gammon Theological Seminary; of the Doctor of Humanities degree from Wilberforce University; and of the Doctor of Laws degree from Atlanta University and Howard University. These honorary doctorates are among his many awards.

He has done far more than minister to spiritual needs. Possessor of a strong business instinct, he has freed from stifling encumbrance every church and congregation he has served. Under his leadership Wheat Street Church, a two-million-dollar structure, after standing incomplete for seventeen years, was finished in nineteen months, and all indebtedness was eliminated in a little over three years. Forty-three auxiliaries were established, thirty-six hundred new members were added, surrounding property was purchased, and a $400,000 Religious Education Plant was built. Wheat Street Gardens, a housing project of 520 units, was completed and serves the community on an open-occupancy basis.

The Reverend Mr. Borders has been an active leader in the cause of Civil Rights. He is President of the "Triple L," the movement which effected the desegregation of buses in Atlanta, and Chairman of the Adult-Student Liaison Committee, which was responsible for the desegregation of lunch-counter facilities.

Writer and public speaker, he has preached and spoken throughout the nation and in many foreign lands. He is the author of six books; and many thousands of copies of his sermons, addresses, religious poems—popularized over his successful radio program of twenty-six years—have been sold. He has been called a man who "always has time to take up time with anybody who has time to take up with him."

MY BROTHER'S KEEPER

by William Holmes Borders

IMBUED with the idealism that characterizes the typical young theology graduate, I accepted, in the early 1930's, my first pastorate at the Second Baptist Church in Evanston, Illinois. Here I was fully determined to emancipate my charges from their state of spiritual lethargy by sharing with them my recently acquired intellectualism.

Although I spent hours in planning, writing, and polishing my sermons, Sunday after Sunday I sensed that I was not arousing the interest of the church members. They were polite, but I became increasingly aware, without knowing the reason, that I was failing to reach them. This lack of communication distressed me, and I wrestled with the problem but never really solved it. Fortunately for me and the congregation the problem, in the end, solved itself, for I was offered, and I accepted, a teaching position at my alma mater, Morehouse College in Atlanta, Georgia.

While at Morehouse I was invited on several occasions to serve as visiting minister at the nearby Wheat Street Baptist Church. Again I met with only polite response, experiencing the same difficulties I had known in Evanston—failure to communicate effectively with the members of the congregation.

Deeply disturbed, I took counsel with myself and concluded that the fault lay with me and not with the church members. I sought advice from my father, the pastor of a small rural church in Georgia, who had always been my source of inspiration. I turned also to my Heavenly Father in prayer.

After much soul-searching I began to sense the magnitude of my own shortcomings: that I had lost the common touch, and that self-importance had taken the place of humility. I realized that religion must be brought down to earth and related to the hopes, aspirations, and needs of the people it is intended to serve. Man, as a

343

religionist, must come to grips with reality. In this new realization, I determined to dedicate myself to the service of my fellow-man, to become not merely a preacher, but "my brother's keeper."

On my next guest appearance at Wheat Street Church, I experienced a new warmth radiating from the members of the congregation as I talked with them in terms that I felt were related to their own problems and experiences. For the first time, I knew that I had actually reached a congregation, and this strengthened my belief that spiritual rapport can exist only when religion is related to life. Shortly thereafter, I was invited to fill the vacant post of regular minister at the Church and attempted to put into practice the concept that religion, to be meaningful, must provide practical as well as spiritual benefits.

As a result of this concept, the Church, with the full cooperation of its membership, has devoted its efforts over the years to meeting the many needs of the congregation and the community. The physical plant has been expanded to include a Christian education building with a library, auditorium, classrooms, lounges, offices, and recreational areas. Through the facilities of the Church, social services are offered to the blind, a nursery school accommodating three hundred youngsters daily is maintained, religious services are provided for inmates of local penal institutions, and programs have been initiated for neighborhood indigents. These examples represent but a few of the many attempts made by the Church to fill both spiritual and practical needs.

My own involvement actually extends beyond the many projects and programs of the Church—to Civil Rights and to civic and political activity. It is the responsibility of a minister, in my judgment, to serve the needs of the "total man" and not his "Sunday needs" alone. Although his first obligation is to God, his next is to the community.

Years ago, the typical pastor was a dignified figure whose duties consisted of preaching sermons, visiting the sick, and performing marriage and funeral rites. Today, a pastor must perform these functions and many more besides.

The modern church is an inseparable part of the community; it is a force vitally involved in every aspect of man's societal life. A large share of a minister's time today must be spent in helping people to solve the problems they encounter outside the scope of their religious lives.

The difficulties that we all face as a result of the complexities and ironies of modern life are formidable. But face and overcome them we must. This has been man's challenge. John Milton completed his masterpieces in spite of blindness; Louis Pasteur, stricken with paralysis, went on to make his greatest discoveries; Helen Keller, blind, deaf, and mute, became one of the world's most distinguished women; Abraham Lincoln, Booker T. Washington, and George Washington Carver rose from humble beginnings to world acclaim. These individuals found happiness in a way of life that not only conquers but makes capital of difficulties.

It is far easier to state a problem than to solve it, and all too frequently many of us use our problems as excuses for indifference or lack of effort. We view minor frustrations and annoyances through high-powered glasses and create mountains from mole hills and giant oaks from slender twigs. But difficulties in life give true religion an opportunity to provide a sustaining faith that can see us through the most serious crises.

Faith alone, however, is not always enough. It must at times be given a helping hand. I think of a devoted church member who fourteen years ago came to me in tears with a financial problem she could not solve. Despite the fact that she held two jobs and worked nearly fifteen hours a day, she earned no more than fifty dollars a week. For more than two years she had been repaying a three-hundred-dollar loan negotiated to take care of medical expenses and other family problems, without missing a single payment. The interest charged was so high, however, that she could not measurably reduce the principal. She was more than willing to pay her debt but saw no way out of her dilemma. The immediate problem was solved by my borrowing from the Church treasury to pay her loan in full and arranging for her repayment in a way that would not strain her meager resources.

The case of this unfortunate woman caused me to wonder of what avail Sunday sermons could be to those who were distressed by personal or financial problems the remaining six days of the week. After talking with financial experts and reading several books on banking and investments, I saw clearly that Wheat Street Church needed and could support a credit union. With an initial investment of forty-five dollars such an organization was established in 1956. Today, the membership comprises more than 715 accounts and the assets exceed $250,000. Open after regular church services, the Credit Union is rapidly becoming one of our busiest facilities. It is filling another practical need of our people.

Wheat Street Gardens grew out of a similar urgent and basic need on the part of our church members and hundreds of other Atlanta residents. In an effort to help provide decent housing at reasonable rentals, Wheat Street Church acquired an adjoining twenty-two-acre site on which was constructed a 520-unit housing project. The Church's employment agency is also intended to serve a practical purpose, and we are planning now to build a shopping center to increase the Negro's economic independence in Atlanta. These cooperative efforts represent "Black Power" operating in a positive manner.

Our recreation programs, designed to help our youth develop "sound minds in sound bodies" and to provide meaningful use of leisure time for all, are further illustrations of our concern with the everyday life of the community. We know that idleness breeds trouble and crime. We know, too, that the church has traditionally frowned on certain types of commercial amusement facilities—the risqué dance emporiums and similar havens of questionable character. While such condemnation may be laudable in principle, the church has generally failed to provide adequate wholesome recreation to offset the influences of congested urban conditions and the crimes they incubate. Though we would perhaps have some degree of crime even if all its immediate causes were removed—since Adam fell from a perfect state—we must nevertheless do all within our power to direct the energies of our youth into positive and creative channels. An official of the California Penitentiary said some time ago that the finest prison is but a monument to neglected youth.

How much more important it is to direct Negro youths into positive and creative channels, for too often they are the unemployed, the generally frustrated, who see little hope of rising above the deplorable conditions under which many of them must live.

The contemporary Negro minister, alert to the dynamic changes occurring almost overnight in practically every aspect of modern society and fully aware of the vital relationship between religion and the everyday life of his people, has been instrumental—and is daily challenged to become more so—in effecting improved living conditions not only for his own constituents but also for the victims of discrimination throughout the sprawling urban areas.

This kind of modern spiritual leader, as an articulate Civil Rights advocate, has guided demonstrations and led marches that have in turn led to the integration of police forces, the hiring of Negro firemen and bus drivers, the building of better schools, and the revamping of obsolete educational programs to prepare our youth for the advanced technological society we are now entering. In short, today's Negro minister must help his fellow-man to translate assumptions, concepts, and beliefs into practicalities. He knows that a dozen rules on how to eat and how to behave mean little in themselves; that a book on etiquette does not insure good manners at the table; that a framed copy of the Constitution does not make citizenship a reality; that a cookbook on the shelf does not assure a delicious, balanced meal; that a Bible in the home does not guarantee the good life. He knows all of this, yet he does not advocate discarding books of etiquette, the Constitution, cookbooks, or the Bible. What he does is to relate idealistic concepts to the realities of life in a meaningful way, and in so doing becomes truly his brother's keeper.

JAMES S. THOMAS

The Reverend Dr. James S. Thomas, Bishop of the Iowa Area of the Methodist Church, is serving his first episcopal term as the leader of 300,000 Methodists and 916 churches—Iowa's oldest and largest denomination and the nation's second "most Methodist" state. American Methodism's youngest bishop, the Reverend Dr. Thomas, with his assignment to Iowa in July, 1964, became the second Negro Methodist bishop responsible for a predominantly white area.

Born in Orangeburg, South Carolina, on April 8, 1919, he is the son of a Methodist minister, the late Reverend James S. Thomas, Sr. Educated at Claflin College in Orangeburg, Bishop Thomas majored in sociology, receiving his B.A. degree in 1939. In 1943 he received the B.D. degree from Gammon Theological Seminary in Atlanta and went on to do graduate work in sociology and cultural anthropology, earning an M.A. degree from Drew University in 1944 and a Ph.D. degree from Cornell University in 1953, where he was a General Education Board Fellow and Crusade Scholar.

He has held positions as a rural school principal (1939–40); as Pastor—on two occasions—to the South Carolina Conference (1942–43 and 1946–47); and as Chaplain at South Carolina State College (1944–46). From 1947 to 1953 he served at Gammon Theological Seminary in such capacities as Professor of Preaching and Rural Church, Head of Practical Studies, and Acting President. He has also served as visiting professor in the Perkins School of Theology at Southern Methodist University (1958). From 1953 to 1964 he was Associate Director, Division of Higher Education of the Board of Education of the Methodist Church. Since his ordination in 1944 as an elder in the Methodist Church, Bishop Thomas has been a frequent lecturer on college campuses. In a ministry to over eighty college and university campuses, he has spoken at schools in all sections of the country.

He is the recipient of several honorary awards: among them, the

349

D.D. degree from Claflin College; the LL.D. degree from Bethune-Cookman College, Simpson College, and Morningside College; and the L.H.D. degree from Cornell College and Ohio Wesleyan University.

A TESTAMENT

OF LIFE AND FAITH

by James S. Thomas

THE late Supreme Court Justice Felix Frankfurter once said: "A man brings to the bench what he himself is and what he has learned from his life and experience." Indeed, this is what a man brings to every position which he occupies. The difficulty is that few men take the time to assess carefully who they are and what they have learned from life. When they do, they give us a mirror in which each of us can see himself more clearly and understand something of the many and complex forces which make his life what it happens to be.

I believe that my early life was decisively influenced by the place and circumstances of my birth. While this is certainly true of every person, I can remember my earliest feelings about living in the town of Orangeburg, South Carolina, as if they set the entire course of my life. First of all, it was a college town. South Carolina State and Claflin Colleges were just across the fence from each other on "our end of town." The big bell at Claflin College sounded throughout the neighborhood as if to summon all the people of the community to the rare privilege of learning. Students came from the country to board with us and our neighbors and attend the high school department of the college. Some of these boarders told me about their work and stirred within me the hunger for learning which has always been a part of my life.

It was quite natural for me to begin my first year of school on the Claflin College campus, because it was the one place nearby where one could begin in the first grade and continue through college graduation. The state of South Carolina was very slow in providing adequate schools for Negroes; and where such schools existed, they

were of such poor quality as to lead my foster parents to choose
Claflin. Earlier, they had made the decision that I got into too
much trouble just being around home; and so, in 1923, at age four,
I became a first grader.

The early twenties was a time when one could be influenced as
much by the stories one heard as by the actual facts of life. Some
of these stories were a part of the folk tradition. They were true,
apocryphal, funny or inspiring. Much depended upon the person
telling the story and his own standing in the community. Newspapers were few; books were distant; television was not imagined.
But the quiet hours of evening provided the setting for the stories
that came out before an open fireplace. One night we could hear
how many persons were converted in a camp meeting. Another
night we would hear about the horror of a lynching in a nearby
community some years ago. Still other nights were reserved for
stories of an epidemic, or a man of uncommon physical strength,
or of some hero who grew up in our state.

While all these stories were interesting, the ones that moved me
most were the true stories about members of my family whom I did
not know. It seemed to me that if I could know more about them,
the puzzle of my own life would be more complete. And so, I never
tired of hearing about my mother and father, both of whom had
died before I was two years old. I was told how far my father, who
became a Methodist minister, walked from his country home into
town to get an education. With great sacrifice, he made his way
through high school and then through college. Before the turn of
the century, he became a college graduate. It was, at that time, a
distinction shared by few of his age and generation.

My mother attended college and became the first member of
the family to receive a "normal diploma." According to the standards of the time, this qualified her for teaching. But she met my
father at Claflin and they were married not long after her graduation.

Surrounding these stories were incidents involving Dr. Mary
McLeod Bethune, whose home was near my mother's, and other
great Negro South Carolinians. As I reflect on it, these stories, possibly more than anything else, accounted for the fact that there
was never a time in my life when I questioned the great value of
higher education. The difficulties were present in great abundance,

but I found it unthinkable that I should quit school before I had finished.

Though my father died when I was very young, I nonetheless grew up in a minister's home. After my parents' death, my two sisters and I went to live with my mother's sister, who was also married to a Methodist minister. It was in this home that we heard the stories and received the stern discipline that became a philosophy of life.

One does not suddenly move into his education; it is occurring all the time and does not end. Yet there are places along the way where dramatic encounters with teachers make a decisive difference in the way life is understood and lived.

From my early start in school, there was a steady progression, grade after grade. By the time I was eight years old, we had moved from Orangeburg to Sumter, South Carolina, a distance of some sixty miles. It was there that I came in contact with some of the most remarkable teachers it has been my privilege to know.

According to the discipline of that day, it is not an overstatement to say that my elementary school was a reflection of its principal. To him and the teachers of that school, the unruly boys of my generation owe an unpayable debt. He was a striking figure, bald and one-armed, with a stern visage that tolerated no nonsense. The word was that he could whip any boy in school with that one arm, and I know only two boys who doubted it. Those who did only confirmed the story that every boy in school had heard: he could and did control his school with an iron hand.

Two incidents stand out in memory. One spring day, the boys and girls found it particularly difficult to end the recess period in the school yard. The principal came out with his bell ringing in solemn rhythm and waited for all to form the usual lines in which we marched to our classes. As the lines were forming, the noise was almost deafening. The principal slowly walked from one end of the group to the other and sternly called for silence. Those who did not respond were told to leave the line and go to his office. No one had any doubt about what would take place when the noisy ones were disciplined. Within four minutes, there was absolute quiet in a school yard where bedlam had reigned before. Three hundred students stood in respectful silence until permission was given to march inside.

It was only when we reached the principal's seventh grade class that we discovered he was not all steel. There was a reason for his being so stern. He knew how many strikes we had against us and how foolish it was for us to waste our time. He insisted on perfection in the classroom. And when it came, in any one recitation, his face brightened and he said, "Good!" Any indication of slovenly speech or procedure would receive just as sound a rebuke.

The day came when he subjected the entire class to its sternest test of reading, arithmetic, and memory work. It was a long and grueling afternoon. When it was over, only seven of us had survived. He called us into his office and gave each of us a book inscribed in his beautiful handwriting. Even though this was thirty-six years ago, I still treasure my copy of *Aesop's Fables*.

Similar stories of great teachers could be told of my high school and college years. I suppose the stern discipline of home prepared me to expect the same at school. Like any other youngster, I often rebelled against this discipline or simply forgot to heed it; but, when I did, the reminder was both swift and sure. Even more impressive was the fact that these were people who constantly wished to do the best thing for us. In a very real sense, they wanted to save us from the helplessness that ignorance would certainly impose. They knew that the segregated limitations within which we lived might not yield to character and education, but they also knew that one's best chance of having personal integrity was "to be somebody." So deep was this conviction that it became a sort of weekday religion. One simply had to be somebody and "make something of his life."

These earlier influences gained more form and substance during the high school and college years. A succession of teachers who would not let us feel sorry for ourselves had saved us from self-pity. But in high school and college we had teachers who set our minds on lofty goals. We were told that no one could take away the essential dignity which came with a good character and an informed mind. Actually, this all-too-simple formula was to receive some very rude shocks, but by the time the shocks came, we had developed enough inspirational momentum to take them.

For me, as for every Negro youngster in South Carolina, the specter of segregation hung over our finest dreams. But this constant reminder of our inferior position never overwhelmed us. It was the Big Lie, never to be really believed. In a strange sort of way, it became a part of my motivation to attain something worthwhile. I knew that if I quit, even for a moment, I would never get started again. So the best thing to do was to keep going.

Out of these and other significant experiences, a faith and a life style began to emerge. For me, they did not proceed in any orderly fashion; there were too many difficulties for that! Rather, as I came to certain points of crucial decision, the unspoken faith that I had rose up to help me. It was a faith in God, who, in older religious terms, "made a way out of no way." Even when my college-trained mind rebelled against a faith so simple, I found myself carried along by some glad surprise: the unusual generosity of friends, the steady encouragement of teachers, the fortuitous meeting of need and opportunity. This was the kind of faith that was experiential. It did not need to be intellectualized at this level because it was so living and real.

One of the crucial questions I had to resolve was what I would do with my life. This dilemma was quite different from intellectualized belief. For now I had to act, to place all that I was in the service of my generation. It was only when I asked this question seriously that I discovered within myself a strong bias. It was a bias against poverty and against the tame and unadventurous life that I had lived up to age twenty-one. For me, the ministry, though a noble profession, seemed to be synonymous with poverty. It did not count, as I thought it should count, among people who could really move the world. So I set out on a premedical course and began to visualize myself as a doctor who made a decisive difference in a community.

Life's increasing complexity included the poverty of people like myself and those all around me. Other questions came: How could these people be convinced that life had deep meaning, that difficulties could be overcome? How, indeed, could a good life be lived in spite of great difficulties? After a period of earnest prayer and searching, and talks with several wise persons, I finally determined that, for a long time, my deepest predispositions had led me to the ministry. It was not an easy choice, but it was the only one in which I thought that all of my life could be given.

Out of this kind of experience came a philosophy of life and a total world view. My decision to preach led me to the seminary.

There my world was broadened in many ways. I could now intellectualize and deepen the faith that I wanted to communicate to others. Also, it was the first time that I ever had a white teacher. Beyond that, the city of Atlanta was like the gateway to a new world. I had rarely been outside my native state, even though I was twenty-one and had served for a year as a school principal. It seemed that life was meant to be much bigger than I had ever known it. The senseless separations of men, their cruelties and prejudice, did not fit the educational or ethical standards which Americans generally professed. Moreover, this meant for me another conversion. For while I could look back on the narrow prejudices of others in my home state, I had to face my own feelings and attitudes. I had to find some way to forgive the lynchings, the indignities, and the cruelty that had been so interwoven with my boyhood experiences as to become a part of the picture.

While this latter struggle is one of a lifetime, one is forced to some definite feelings along the way. I had a deep respect for the religious life of the American Negro, even though I recognized the excesses and sometimes the abuse associated with it. Perhaps it was because I could see it in context. There were two worlds in which a Southern Negro lived his life. One was a world of almost ceaseless toil in cotton and tobacco fields. Here he was almost always vulnerable. His major preoccupation was just trying to eke out a living. But there was also the world of religion, through which life's ultimate meaning was articulated. Struggles were seen and understood in terms of the Biblical faith. And one could persist because God was in it all. The Sunday world, then, was more than a time of excessive emotional release. It was coming to terms with life where it mattered most.

Whatever limitations this point of view may have had, it possessed some qualities which a later and much better trained generation of Negro youth could well bear in mind. This is an age in which the crucial questions of American race relations are at least as fateful as they have been in any period since the Civil War. Out of several summers of widespread racial violence have come questions of great perplexity. The gains of many years—as America counts gains—are threatened by dangerous voices of the extremes. Paradoxically, what has come through a generation of reason, merit, and hard work is now subject to the emotional heat of slogans, retaliation, and violence. And, what is more, there is now enough alienation within the total social system to sustain this kind of approach. It is simply true that we are a separated people—young from old, have from have-not, white from black.

In a situation of such immense complexity, almost any word is wrong. Caution so easily becomes special pleading. The disciplines of one generation are so easily declared irrelevant for another. Even so, at the risk of being misunderstood, I must say a word to this able and courageous generation of Negro youth.

First, there are still qualities that are basic to personal integrity and the power to maintain it. These qualities relate to one's conception of himself, his deeper faith in God and people, his attitude concerning work, and his willingness to give superior performance out of his own motivation. These are not old-fashioned virtues. They are as basic as health. Only the setting changes; the major qualities remain the same. When one finds that elusive quality that allowed my elementary school principal to bear himself with consummate dignity in a rigidly segregated world, he will have that which is basic in any age or time.

Second, there are qualities of social identity and support which pertain greatly to ourselves as Negroes and to white persons also. There is no way to escape this double reference in the present age. But one's maturity can be read in the accent which he places on a common humanity rather than on the variable of color as color.

For three and a half centuries race and culture have been gods in the American pantheon. With integration as a goal, many Negroes acted as if color did not matter at all. The disillusionment was to find that it mattered greatly in getting a job, in social activities, in housing, and in promotions. For many the result was a bitter conclusion: color is everything. Then they fell into an idolatry which is to be greatly deplored. White people are often seen as enemies. Negroes are often considered worthwhile because they are black. Whenever black power comes to mean this, it is as pernicious a doctrine as white supremacy ever was.

It may be that what I am struggling to say is that our basic self-identification should be as human beings. There is, after all, a life which rises above color, but we experience it so seldom as to doubt its existence. For life is too full of ordinary demands to be lived ideally all the time. And so it is proper for me to recognize and respond to that peculiar set of circumstances, based on color, which most Negro youths have had to share. I have obligations to the whole human race, but I feel a special obligation to help those who carry on their backs the accumulated deficit of slavery and segregation. It takes several generations to overcome a period of history so filled with handicaps and unnecessary difficulties. Even so, there has been notable progress.

The Negro student of today all too rarely enjoys the privilege of college and graduate school; too many are denied these opportunities because the circumstances of their lives are fraught with major difficulties and problems. Such a student will therefore wish to be known first of all as a man among men. He will aspire to the highest standards and meet them. But, if he has a sense of social obligation, he will want to do his part to erase some of the deficit which others like him must carry.

The time will probably never come again when discipline will be so strict and personality count for so much as it did in my early school years. Life is too full of other interesting possibilities. But there really is no effective substitute for a good teacher. The lessons of life have never been easy to learn. Yet the man for all seasons is one who has learned them well from one who knows them thoroughly and communicates them with dignity and pride.

Thrust For Identity

Note

Unlike the contributors in the other sections, who were asked to express their views on a subject of their own choosing, those in this section, "Thrust for Identity," were requested to deal specifically with a phase of the new militancy, such as Black Power, Black Awareness, or Black Identity. Among the four essayists represented here are two young men of promise: Nathaniel Landry, introduced by Carroll Harvey, Executive Director of Pride, Inc.; and Lloyd McNeill, introduced by Walter Hopps, Director of the Washington Gallery of Modern Art. The other two writers in the group, Julius W. Hobson and Benjamin H. Wright, are prominent persons of established reputation. Their biographical sketches are included.

Introducing NAT R. LANDRY

by Carroll Harvey

Nat Landry is a human dynamo in his late twenties who typifies the "new thrust" of the zestful, zealous, Black Pragmatist. He also typifies the "new thrust" of a structurally sound economic venture known as Pride, Inc. Organized to provide solutions to problems which have been created by the larger society and which fester within the lower economic black community of Washington, D.C., Pride assists the hard-core unemployed by utilizing their skills within the organization, demonstrating that many of the kinds of people Pride seeks to help—needy in-school teen-agers, school drop-outs, those with prison records, and those who have failed or de-faulted in one way or another according to society's standards—*want to* and *will* work.

Pride, offering a truly comprehensive program of social reform, is youth oriented and its total efforts are geared toward establishing a viable economic community for the have-nots. The program in-cludes Neighborhood Services (cleaning streets, alleys, and back yards in the blighted areas of the city), Landscaping and Garden-ing, Commercial Painting, an Automotive Service Center, and Building Maintenance Services.

Its expanding supportive services are projected to include a Continuing Education Department focusing on reading, mathe-matics, and communication skills; an Orientation Department stressing the cultural and social development of black people; a Health Services Department; a Legal Services Department; a Recreation Department; and Project Reach, devised to "reach" and teach impressionable youths about the dangers, pitfalls, and pernicious effects of narcotics.

With a current budget of approximately four million dollars, largely provided by the U.S. Department of Labor, the organization expects this year to provide part-time and full-time employment for approximately 1,500 ghetto youths.

Nat Landry has become one of the top young executives in the organization not only because of his collegiate and graduate training in financial matters, but also because of his firsthand knowledge of the people he serves. The product of an urban environment himself, he understands the problems of the streets. He has an unshakeable belief that given opportunity and direction, the most cynical and disillusioned of the young blacks in the city's ghettos can become useful and productive members of society.

This is Nat's stand, and this is the story he tells.

THE NEED FOR PRIDE

by Nat R. Landry

BLACK, American, a college graduate still in my twenties, I am very much dissatisfied with this country's double standard of living. Where have I come from? What have I learned? Where do I want to go? How do I plan to get there?

The turbulent events occurring in our cities have caused me to re-examine my goals in life and to reassess my responsibility to myself and to my people. Earlier in my brief professional career I worked in different capacities in various establishments, mainly for "big business" organizations on a "white-collar" level, often as the "first Negro" in the position I held, with my desk usually in a prominent place near the front door. For a while I felt that I was making a contribution, but I finally realized that I was really doing nothing in these capacities for the benefit of the masses of my underprivileged fellow blacks. It was then that I broke with the "establishment" and joined Pride, Inc., a black organization engaged in a self-help program for inner-city residents. It is about this program, and my experience in it, that I wish to talk.

Some of what I am about to say has already been said. But not much has been said about Pride from the perspective of the ghetto itself, for that is not the traditional thing to do. I, however, make no claims to being a man of tradition. Tradition, as it is known in the "establishment," was put aside as soon as I recognized that, as a black American, I too had a place in society, and if that place was to be obtained, I would have to go out, create it, and then take it. I have recently discovered others with the same goals and objectives, and collectively we are working to obtain them through the Pride program of self-help.

My association with Pride has given me insights into the authoritarian structure of the street and a better understanding of why those with whom we deal in our organization are frustrated and limited in their outlook on life. I have learned much about such things as self-hate, distrust, and the loser complex.

I have learned further, contrary to the general notion that street life in the ghetto is characterized by utter chaos, that there exists, in fact, a type of order in what some sociologists have classically described as "social disorganization." The deprived street youth, or "dudes" as they are known in our program, are pyramided in a barnyard "pecking order" of "top dudes" and their followers. A "dude" gets to the top by mastering the three "M's" of the street— mind, mouth, and muscle. He is the one who knows the ins and outs of all the various "hustles" and con games. He is articulate; yet, when logic or facts fail to convince, he does not hesitate to use the expertise of his fists or employ whatever other force may be necessary as the ultimate persuader. If he has "done time" in a reformatory or prison, that only enhances his status. In fact, most of them—unable to find work, dignity, and a place in the sun of society—have engaged in criminal acts of one kind or another for a variety of reasons.

It is in street gangs that "dudes" find the emotional comradeship, the leadership, and the warmth of human association often lacking in their homes. The authoritarian structure of the streets gives them a security that is otherwise wanting.

Eighty percent of our three hundred out-of-school workers and area supervisors are either high school dropouts and/or have multiple jail records. We at Pride believe that it is absolutely essential to build secure futures for those in our program, emphasizing the idea that they can have tomorrows *without* the prospect of prison— and *with* the prospect of dignity and security.

R——— is a typical example of what Pride has meant to the seemingly incorrigible. The eldest of seventeen children, he began a life of crime at the age of seven with numerous acts of pilfering. Now twenty-seven years of age, he has been charged with over one hundred housebreakings and has spent a major portion of his life in receiving homes, institutions, and jails, on charges ranging from petty thievery to armed robbery. Unable to obtain a job because of his record, he seemed consigned to a life of perpetual crime. About a year ago, however, he signed up with Pride and now, for the first time in his life, he experiences a sense of belonging, he feels that he can hold his head up high. As he expresses it, "I'm not going back to crime. I'm not thinking of doing any more wrong, because Pride has done for me what everybody else has failed to do, and that's to make me feel like a human being with a future."

R——'s rehabilitation has not been easy. The majority of the cases with which we deal are difficult ones, for the young men in our program consider themselves, for the most part, "losers" according to the system. Most of what they have witnessed in their environment has been defeat. They are angry with the white man in general and have little faith in the leaders of their own race. Society has projected for them only white successes and black failures and has bred in them a suspicion concerning the competence and motives of black people who try to lead them. No wonder then that black leaders and black institutions find it difficult to get underprivileged black people to believe in them or to follow them.

The glorification of "white," the denigration of "black," and the deliberate attempt to repress black consciousness and thwart efforts to achieve black solidarity have been to a large extent responsible for the problems of R—— and his counterparts in urban centers throughout the land.

The "white is right" attitude is not a twentieth-century phenomenon, but has existed since the first slaves were introduced to our shores. A totally new culture, designed by slave masters and slave traders, was forced upon the slaves to insure their servile status. At the heart of this culture was the glorification of white values and institutions on the one hand, and the damning of black values and black institutions on the other.

The destruction of African cultures and the deifying of "whiteness" and damning of "blackness" by the dominant society created in time a massive self-hate complex and a schizophrenia among American blacks which still exist in varying degrees.

Racial conflict as we know it today, with its increasingly disastrous results, will not be resolved until ingrained attitudes of white superiority and black inferiority have been totally eliminated.

Obviously there is no one solution to the problem; it must be attacked on many fronts. We have demonstrated on one front that what is needed is more economic institutions like Pride, Inc., for the young, black, hard-core unemployed. These are the people who are still basically unserved. These are the "losers" who need to feel that they are wanted, that they have a place in society, that they have a future to which they can look. They are the "untouchables" who must be given their place in the sun.

Introducing LLOYD McNEILL

by Walter Hopps

It seems almost impossible to adequately introduce Lloyd McNeill by using words. Lloyd McNeill is an artist, but his world of creation reaches out so far: in images in drawings, paintings, silkscreened graphics, assembled sculptural relief of wood and of metal, murals (two major examples to date and I dream of those to follow); in musical compositions (not widely known yet except as scores for educational films); in jazz performance (the flute is his basic instrument), working in groups as a key soloist or as the leader of his own group; in writing, his words as a poet; in spectacles, as Lloyd McNeill identifies his creations of largest scale in space and time, in which works in all media are brought together—his own as well as the selected works and creative activity of many other artists and musicians. Doing all these things, with strength and quiet ease, he interacts with an amazing range of people.

For Lloyd McNeill art does not exist merely for its own sake. He instinctively seeks to engage and involve both colleagues and a wide-open public. In this, neither his disciplined skills, sophistication in art, insights into contemporary life, nor identity as a Black American are compromised. While Lloyd McNeill has evolved a powerful, personal visual and musical language, the times and places and ways he uses his "artistic language" are chosen to allow the maximum sharing of experience and feeling.

Although Washington, D.C., is birthplace and home for Lloyd McNeill, he has traveled, studied, taught, performed his music, and exhibited his art both in this country and abroad—primarily in France, for which he has a special fondness. Already he has gained and given so much creative experience. Yet it is startling to realize that for Lloyd McNeill, himself, he has just begun.

MUSIC, ART, AND NEGRITUDE

by Lloyd McNeill

IT wasn't until I went to college in Atlanta, Georgia, that I began to realize the importance of thorough personal investigation for the purposes of ascertaining who I was and what my goals in life should be. Being immediately caught up in the wave of student sit-in demonstrations then sweeping the South, I had my eyes opened to the fact that a definition of my existence began with the brutal realization that in social, political, economic, and ethnic contexts, I was black. Black meaning being spat upon as I sat at lunch counters in "five-and-ten-cent" stores; black meaning watching as girls were kicked and beaten when their only defense was the nonviolent crouch position; black meaning watching my six-foot, four-inch roommate being pistol-whipped by a redneck cop!

Experiences such as these brought me face to face with the realization that I was sitting on the sidelines, not really living, missing out on "history in the making." Internally, I could not control the fires that burned as I physically, intellectually, and emotionally experienced the social injustices that were so starkly vivid in the South. I saw myself as a hypocrite as I participated in the usual nonviolent activities. Passive resistance seemed a waste of valuable energy. I wanted to strike out at the wall of ignorance which stood between black people and freedom, and I knew that I would never be able to give vent to my deeper emotions if I continued in my major field, zoology.

The switch to painting and music, two "loves" in my life which had fascinated me for years, was a natural one. Through these two media I felt that I would be able to express my blackness, my deep concern for my frustrated brothers, my intense yearning to make whatever talent I possessed a meaningful reflection of black consciousness. Many thought that my decision to pursue the creative fields of music and art was my way of seeking a "haven of refuge"

369

from more difficult courses of study. No one except my art instructor seemed to comprehend that my decision to change was an effort to better understand myself and to release creatively some of the energies which had been trapped within me.

To these pursuits, music and art, I have devoted all my time and energy, and in them I have found the answers to many of the problems that disturbed me. Of the two idioms, it is easier for the black American to express his feelings, his concerns, and his ideas in music than in art. The average black child grows up in an environment which lives and breathes the essence of "black music," with its complexity of rhythm and syncopation. The streets of an area like Harlem are alive from morning till night with its insistent and pulsating beat. Even for the black musician, musical experiences have been largely intra-racial, utilizing for the most part only music which was indisputably his own. Because of the discriminatory practices which have pervaded this country for years, the possibilities for participation in certain of the various types of musical organizations—with the resultant exposure to other types of musical forms—have been limited for the black musician. There is no question that the musical and sociological conditions normally affecting the maturation of the black musician differ drastically from those affecting the white musician. Conditions of strife and oppression— the hard and cruel facts of America for the black man—are the conditions which have contributed to the "blues," the "cry," and the "shout," to name but a few of the sub-forms in the jazz idiom.

To express one's black consciousness or black awareness by means of music is thus relatively easy. When the medium is art, however, the challenge is far more difficult. Because of the heritage of the black musician, it is often possible to identify the race of a musician by the mood and technique of his performance alone. The black musician gets the "message" across. This is not necessarily true where the black artist is concerned. A few years ago, when I was a student, I noticed that the imagery of my black classmates in art classes was largely "white" and quite removed from their personal lives. It was almost as if they were looking at the world through "white" eyes. Our training dealt conventionally with learning to paint still-life set-ups, portraits, and traditional landscapes. The results, for the most part, were bland and insignificant. Only recently have black artists, affected by the powerful social impact of black consciousness, begun to tell the truth about their own lives. Only recently have they begun to search themselves for subject matter related to their physical or metaphysical worlds and to express it in terms relevant to their black brothers and sisters. They have learned to be artistically honest, and this means utilization of symbols, colors, and forms drawn from their own personal lives. They are beginning to establish a new aesthetic: a black aesthetic. The black artist is now developing his skills as the black musician has done. Since the birth of jazz the black musician has played for the pure joy of playing. His interest in publishing his music, making records, or gaining recognition has been secondary.

As far as I am personally concerned, I have never felt any great attachment to the final products of my creative efforts. I remember that when I was still a student my friends would criticize me for leaving my paintings and materials out overnight or unguarded when I went to class or to lunch. Frankly, I didn't care if they were stolen or not, because I had long ago concluded that the creative process was more important than the product. When a piece is finished, it is of very little value to me except that it serves as an item for study and analysis. I find it difficult to hang my works in my living or working areas merely for decorative purposes. My paintings are to me but expressions of my identity.

But it is not enough for a black artist to express his identity. He must strive to capture and express the identity of his people—their essential and innate characteristics. To this end he must go into the streets and alleys of the ghettos and work with black faces, the black milieu, doing all he can to encourage, inspire, and develop a pride in self. This I have attempted to do, for I am in complete agreement with those whose aims are to institute changes, drastic as they may be, in order to create a society which understands the urgency of practicing a philosophy favoring the concept of equality among men. I do not walk blindly through life. In America, I am aware of my Negritude from the moment I awake in the morning to the time I fall asleep at night. Social, political, and economic realities do not allow me to forget.

JULIUS W. HOBSON

Julius W. Hobson, economist and Civil Rights activist, was born in Birmingham, Alabama, on May 29, 1922. After receiving his undergraduate degree from Tuskegee Institute in 1946, he did graduate work at Howard University and American University and subsequently served as an economist with the Library of Congress from 1950 to 1959. Since 1960 he has been employed as Social Science Analyst in the Social Security Administration.

Mr. Hobson has been deeply involved in community organizations and activities for many years. He served as President of the Woodridge Civic Association (1950–53), as Vice-President of the District of Columbia Federation of Civic Associations (1955–57), as a member of the Executive Committee of the D.C. Branch of the NAACP (1956–59), and as Chairman of the D.C. Chapter of CORE (1960–64). Following his expulsion from CORE at the Kansas City Convention in 1964 because of his views on Black Power and Socialism, he formed his own organization called ACT (Associated Community Teams): The Organization of the Militants, an activist-research group, the motto of which is "Research and Destroy."

In the nation's capital, Mr. Hobson has led successful campaigns to change the hiring and promotion policies of the Police Department and of various public utilities agencies, to eliminate job discrimination in private employment (department, furniture, hardware, and chain-food stores; bread companies; and automobile dealerships), to desegregate private schools and hospitals, and to bring about changes in housing laws. Over the years, he has organized and conducted demonstrations of various types and has been sentenced to jail on several occasions for his activities.

For his contributions in the broad area of Civil Rights, Julius W. Hobson has been honored by a number of groups in the District of Columbia. He has received a "Man of the Year" type of award from such organizations as the Federation of Civic Associations (1962 and 1967), the Capital Press Club (1963), CORE (1964), the Chamber of Commerce (1965), the Y.M.C.A. (1965), and Citizens for Better Education (1966). In 1968 the Howard University School of Law bestowed upon him its nationwide award for the most significant lay contribution in the field of law.

BLACK POWER

AND CAPITALISM

by Julius W. Hobson

PORTUGAL began the black slave trade at the opening of the sixteenth century, and the other "civilized nations" of Christian Europe engaged in this inhuman practice almost immediately thereafter. The first Englishman to realize that there was money to be made by seizing unsuspecting blacks in Africa and selling them as "raw material" to be worked to a quick death on plantations in the new world was John Hawkins. "Good Queen Bess" thought so much of the great work of this murderer and kidnapper that she knighted him after his second slave-trading expedition. Sir John promptly chose as his crest a black man in chains.

It was in 1619 that the first black slave was brought to the shores of America. From that date until the abolition of slavery, more than two hundred years later, thousands of black men, women, and children were taken by force from their homes in Africa and shipped to this country to be sold into bondage.

Conquest, piracy, plunder, and exploitation were the means that brought huge profits and a growing supply of cheap labor—black labor, or Black Power, on which the capitalistic system of this nation has been built. It is within the framework of this historical background that the contemporary Black Power struggle was born.

The American market has been flooded with books and articles on the Negro, the Civil Rights movement, and more recently, Black Power. Urbanologists, sociologists, psychologists, and representatives of other disciplines have poured millions of words into print on the meaning of freedom, the characteristics and viability of Negro leadership, the strategy of nonviolence as well as on the educational needs of black children, crime on ghetto streets, and even the proposal that intermarriage is the sole and final solution to America's racial sickness.

I make no attempt to explain the struggle for freedom from the point of view of any of these analysts. Their limited perspectives make their explanations as useless as the varied descriptions of the elephant given by the blind men of Hindustan who attempted to describe the beast after touching different parts of it.

I can attempt, however, to place the freedom struggle—the Civil Rights and Black Power movements—in proper historic perspective. The efforts of black Americans to secure the full freedom and rights which are their birthright have been undertaken within the impossible framework of capitalism. Whether the freedom struggle should head toward integration or black separatism, toward massive federal programs or private black entrepreneurism is a question to be answered. Can black people ever win the fight for freedom so long as they accept America's exploitive capitalism as the economic system within which they must wage their battle? Black leaders have not confronted this question. Those to whom the White House, Congress, and the white press turn as spokesmen have not dealt with the fundamental problems of the political and economic systems in which black Americans are trapped. They have raised a multitude of questions but have avoided the basic issue. Whether from a lack of understanding of our economic and political systems or from an unwillingness to challenge them, their silence is a betrayal of trust of the black people they purport to lead. The concern of our "so-called" leaders with such matters as integrated lunch counters or community control of schools neatly sidesteps the one major issue to which all others are satellite: under a capitalist system, can America *afford* to eliminate poverty and an exploited class of citizens? I believe not.

Racism in the United States was born of slavery, and it has been said that racism is a rationalization for economic exploitation. Economic in origin, racism soon evolved into the deeply rooted sociological and psychological institutions to which the freedom struggle has devoted itself to date. Hating the black man and regarding him as inferior is a deeply felt psychological need of many white Americans. In their efforts, for example, to recruit poor whites for the recent Poor People's Campaign in Washington, the Southern Christian Leadership Conference ran into a wall of resistance from poor white Appalachians and Southern farmers who refused to join the black-led campaign. If every black resident of Mississippi were to disappear from that state tomorrow, one would wonder what would happen to the entrenched power of Senators Eastland and Stennis, who would then have to address themselves to the deplorable poverty of their poor white constituents. These constituents, no longer preoccupied with looking down on black people, could be expected to run out of office men who had so long neglected their own needs.

Sociologists have often stated that black Americans measure themselves against white people and white standards by accepting their values and customs. But it is the psychological dependency of white Americans upon black people—as a constant stimulant to their feelings of superior status, as a constant measure of their self-respect and sense of worth—that needs discussion and exposure. The power and superior status of white Americans is thus relative, not absolute. This is true not only of the poor, unlettered white Mississippian but of white Americans in general. One has only to study the violent reactions of educated white liberals everywhere following Stokely Carmichael's cry of "Black Power" on the 1966 Meredith march through Mississippi. Since then, white Americans, faced with the loss of their most dependable psychological prop, the Negro, have reacted with fear, calling for repressive Congressional and police measures.

Two groups actually have been rudely awakened by the Black Power thrust: white liberals and middle-income blacks. Both have been exposed and affected.

Among the whites most seriously disturbed by the Black Power movement are the white liberals who proclaimed support for Civil Rights goals, who marched in Selma (but rarely in their own home towns) and who have dominated the board of directors of every major Civil Rights organization. These typical white liberals exhibit an astoundingly presumptuous attitude. They consider themselves experts on poor people in general and on black people in particular, and assume that they alone can provide leadership in the freedom struggle. Shouts of "Black Power" stunned these "white liberal" activists. Some understood and moved quickly to the task of working in the white community, the fountainhead of the problem; others shied away and whined about not being appreciated; still others fought back, struggling to hang onto the "We Shall Over-come" slogans and goals of a dying movement, bitter in their at-tacks on new black leadership, from Malcolm X to Stokely Car-michael.

Those who understood, the radical young whites who, in 1964, were maligned and murdered along with black workers of the Stu-dent Nonviolent Coordinating Committee (SNCC), are now or-ganizing the white poor of Appalachia and students on campuses across the nation. Some have joined the "hippie" world, itself a cry of outrage at the traditional way of life. Those who would not relinquish their claim to leadership of black people are gradually diminishing in power and importance, nudged out of the way by an increasingly militant and vocal black middle class.

The concept of accomplishment through liberal white leadership only has drastically changed. Even federal anti-poverty agencies find that they cannot function in black communities under white lead-ership. Church and social agencies, eager to pour money into urban programs, now find it necessary to hire not only black intermedi-aries but those affecting African hair styles and dress. Irrelevant as these are to the issue of economic exploitation, they nonetheless represent a massive and growing response by white liberal institu-tions to the demands of Black Power.

Traditionally the black middle class has been so white-oriented that it has fled in fear from organizing and directing its own destiny. Aping and coveting white American values, it has not recognized the historic tradition of other ethnic groups in America of solidify-ing, retaining, and celebrating their own ethnic origins and values. It has drawn no message from the Irish, who paint a great green strip down New York City's Fifth Avenue every St. Patrick's Day; it has even donned shamrocks to support the Irish. It has taken no note of the fact that Jewish organizations have not a single black board member or staff director; it has never questioned such ethnic single-mindedness. There are organizations of Catholics, Poles, Italians, Hungarians. None have been challenged by middle-class blacks any more than by white America; none have been charged with racism. In fact, all are accepted as a healthy stimulant to self-pride and self-identity, protective of the new immigrant in a strange, often hostile land, proud guardians of the diversified cultures to which America attributes her claims to greatness.

The greatest obstacle to the freedom struggle rests not with the die-hard segregationist whose hate and bias are paraded before the world. It rests rather with the liberal who firmly believes that he has all the answers, and with members of the black middle class who serve as mercenaries to a colonial master. These latter are the black lawyers, whose urgently needed skills are denied to the struggle in their desire for a special appointment, a judgeship, or the like; the upwardly mobile businessman, dependent on financial favors from white banks or other institutions; federal officials appointed to high posts as a cover for shameful employment records in hiring black people. These are the persons to whom white America can smugly point as examples of the improved lot of black Americans. These are the persons who divert national attention from the pitiful condition of the vast majority of America's twenty-two million black citizens.

The main question that has to be answered before the concept of "Black Power" can be defined is whether the Black Power movement is a reform movement designed to duplicate the existing system under black control or whether it is a revolutionary concept with the objective of replacing the present economic and political systems.

If Black Power advocates are concerned with the establishment of black capitalism, as most of their pronouncements indicate, then the definition of the concept becomes a simple one. It is the same as white power: ownership of the means of production, capital, control of money; and establishment of private businesses. In other words, Black Power theorists of the far right who believe in the separatist concept would establish an economic entity or island on the larger American continent of capitalism. They call for reform, not revolution, and their desire is to be at the "head table" and to have a "larger piece of the pie." This is hardly a humanitarian concept, hardly the road to human dignity for all men. This concept has nothing to do with freedom. It merely accepts, apes, and fosters the present undemocratic economic system with all of its inequities. The advocates of this kind of Black Power, though well meaning, manifest a complete unawareness of the nature of their political and economic surroundings, for given the same set of economic circumstances, a black slumlord will act exactly as a white slumlord acts.

If, on the other hand, the Black Power concept is a cry for a movement to the left, it will join the world revolutionary movement, multiracial and rich with resources outside the black camp which it needs and must utilize. The world struggle for freedom from exploitation is a struggle between those who have and those who have not. Any serious effort to redistribute the world's wealth carries within it the seeds of revolution.

If Black Power means moving to the left, it must move toward creating a world economy that produces for need rather than for profit. It must fight to create a system that, by its very nature, eliminates starvation. It must join the world struggle for a classless society that believes in ownership of the world's national resources by the peoples of the world. It must declare itself the mortal enemy of the exploitation of man by man and must view all men, regardless of color, as earth-born companions and fellow mortals. In short, it must join directly those forces which are making revolutions everywhere.

Black people in the United States are in urgent need of the psychological freedom which the new emphasis on black history, art, literature, and pride in black beauty nurture. Alexander Pope said:

> Know then thyself, presume not God to scan;
> The proper study of mankind is Man.

To make a contemporary application of his immortal lines, one might well say that the proper study of the black man in the United States is Black Man. This is a concept that fits well in the much-needed move to the left.

BENJAMIN H. WRIGHT

Benjamin H. Wright is Market Development Manager of Clairol, Inc. and has the responsibility of working with company management in programs relating to advertising, general marketing, and community relations activities that are particularly relevant in dealing with minority groups. Born on August 5, 1923, in Shreveport, Louisiana, he was reared in Cincinnati, Ohio. He received the B.B.A. degree from the University of Cincinnati School of Business Administration in 1950 and the M.A. degree from the Graduate School of Arts and Sciences of the same institution in 1951.

After serving for two years in Liberia as a political and economic reporting officer for the U.S. Department of State, he joined the Johnson Publishing Company in 1953, becoming Sales Promotion and Merchandising Manager in 1956. Ten years later he left the Company to assume his present position with Clairol, Inc. Among the professional organizations to which he belongs are the American Marketing Association, the Sales Promotion Executives Association, and the New York Chapter of the National Association of Market Developers, Inc., of which he is President.

In the area of human relations, Benjamin Wright has been quite active for a number of years. He is a member of the NAACP, administrative aide to the Continuation Committee of the National Conference on Black Power, committee chairman of the National Interracial Council for Business Opportunity, and a former vice-president of the Bergen County, N.J. Chapter of CORE. In addition, he was one of the organizers of the Conference on Black Power held in Newark, N.J., in July of 1967, and a participant in the September, 1968 Conference in Philadelphia, Pennsylvania.

THE CONSTRUCTIVE FORCE

OF BLACK POWER

by Benjamin H. Wright

WE live in a country where there is great regard for those who stand with a sense of dignity and power. Everyone respects power, and every man needs to be part of a recognized group in order to maintain his own self-respect and a wholesome self-image. People who are powerless find frustration their daily lot, and such is the fate of the black masses in a place which might be called Everywhere, U.S.A. This frustration has led, to a large extent, to the concept we know today as Black Power.

Black Power—or the empowerment of black people—may be the only way the latent gifts of black Americans can be developed for the good of all in our nation. It is in our country's self-interest that black people have both that deserved sense of worth and personhood characteristic of all self-sustaining people, and the opportunities and motivation to contribute equitably to their nation's vast potential.

There are some people—both black and white—who condemn the concept of Black Power as one that produces violence and separatism. Nothing could be further from the truth, for the empowerment of black people may be the only nonviolent way to bring our racially divided nation into a unified whole.

Many people believe that "integration" alone is the answer to such unity. I would like to examine this term for a moment. If "integration" means the right of all people to work at jobs for which they are qualified without segregation by race, if "integration" means the right to live in the neighborhood of one's choice and the right to participate fully in the educational process without segregation by race, then I support this concept. However, I prefer the term "desegregation" to describe these legitimate and undeniable rights already guaranteed by the Constitution. I choose this term because the word "integration" often—and needlessly—conjures up in some minds the feeling that one's total social life may be ordered by legislative fiat.

Desegregation must be an immediate goal. Work forces, schools, neighborhoods, churches, and other institutions must reflect what we can honestly call an open or "integrated" society. No decent American would deny this. Social integration, however, must be a matter of individual choice—it should never be a group objective. To pursue it is a goal in itself is demeaning to the pursuer and unfair to the pursued. Yet empowerment of black Americans with self-respect will make integration of this type attractive for some as a personal choice.

Black people do not have to mix intimately with white people to gain power for themselves and to help this nation. They do have to develop respect for themselves in our divided society if they are to advance and gain the type of power that is meaningful. Black Americans are still set apart in terms of housing, jobs, and social relationships. They do not enjoy the privilege extended to other Americans of "identifying" socially with the major culture.

After long years of proclaiming "one nation, under God, indivisible" we have millions of people psychologically enslaved and a nation which, based on the widespread unrest in our major cities, is as greatly divided under God today as it ever has been. There is a reluctance generally to talk about the biracial nature of our society, probably because such discussion seems to point up one of the great failures of this land.

Beginning with Virginia in 1661, all Southern states passed laws not only indenturing black men into permanent slavery, but also dehumanizing them in a classification of statutory chattel. In contrast to the situation in this country, black men who were slaves in South America were always considered human beings with souls and were able to attend church with all others, to work their way to freedom, and to marry whomever they chose. There, black men could and did become integrated into and amalgamated with the dominant culture.

Some young black people who are yearning for identity today and are seeking an explanation for their race's negative identity of the past, see in the failure of black people to be "black" the root of our racial difficulties. Hence, for them, there must be a glorification of "blackness." "Black is beautiful." "Black is glorious." "Black is best." Such expressions become pathways to "being." They are a means to fulfillment, and fulfillment must come, for only as it is achieved by black Americans can it come to the nation as a whole.

The costly "riots" of recent times are acts of bitterness and frustration born of a feeling of hopelessness and despair. They are acts of men who have neither a self-image of worth nor a sense of belonging. They are crimes of self-destruction as well as social and civic expressions of conditioned self-hate. These so-called riots and other forms of destruction, along with physical decay and the burdensome correlative dollar costs of police and fire protection, welfare, and the incalculable costs of human life, should declare clearly to us that change is overdue.

All sorts of reasons, such as the lack of housing, jobs, and education, have been given for the turmoil that America has experienced. But housing is not the basic issue, even though we must have a place to live. Jobs are not the basic issue, even though we must have work. Education is not the issue, for we have educated people who cannot now get jobs for which they are qualified. Even police brutality, which is certainly an irritant, is not the fundamental issue. The key issue—and only issue—is that people who are black are not unified and have not moved with power into the struggle inherent in any free enterprise or democratic system. This is necessary in business, in politics, in professions, in social and political organizations, and in all other areas of life, for power leads to respect, and respect engenders a sense of personal dignity.

Dialogue or communication—a two-way "give and take"—is essential to an understanding of the problems that confront us. White people need help, and so do black people. We all need the vision that comes from enlightenment and new insights. Commenting on this point, the Reverend Dr. Eugene Callander of the Greater New York Urban League once said, "The white man in America has not yet accepted either the depth of his own racial bias or the repressive character of the society he controls. The black man has not yet accepted either his own human worth or the immense potential for social change implicit in Negro militancy."

Two things are abundantly clear. One is that white America

must look at itself and understand its implication or involvement in the most denigrating, dehumanizing, and depraved acts committed by modern man against another group of men—acts which have become a seemingly permanent part of every facet of our business, cultural, civic, religious, and social lives; acts which have not only divided man against man but have deprived one group of men of so much of their sense of dignity and worth that they would engage in wanton destruction of the urban centers of our nation.

It is true that present-day white Americans did not create these conditions of gross inequity, but they must be brought to understand that they are part of a culture that has never moved in a determined and understanding way to compensate for injustices or to remove the even more devastating psychological chains that continue to enslave and penalize both black and white America. When white persons are enlightened and made aware of their culturally induced and advantageous position, they often can be the black man's greatest friends in their intellectual and emotional commitment to do everything possible to bring about equitable changes.

The other thing that must be accomplished before we can have any effective communication is to see that black people think for themselves. They must stop looking to white America for the answers to their problems. They must support authentic black community organizations that allow no subterfuge either by direct or covert means. They must engage in activities that will emancipate them from ignorance of their roots so they will know for sure that they are "somebody" and can stand with dignity and personhood in this world of power relationships.

The myths of racial inferiority so permeate the American political, economic, and social atmosphere that no one operating normally within the American system can escape reflecting a prejudicial psychology regarding black Americans. To remedy this, there has to be a conscious acknowledgment of the fact that blacks not only have been forced to be different, but also have facing them problems that are often at variance with the American norm. Realizing this would help us see that blacks should never be treated "just the same" as whites in the educational system, in the church, or in any other enabling enterprise when the problems they encounter differ greatly from those of other Americans.

If America has the will to make an intelligent attack upon the problems that confront our nation, there are several matters that must be understood.

We must understand that if black people, who now comprise over 50 percent of the population of our major cities, are not empowered by adequate training, a sense of worth, and the will and opportunity to achieve, all of us will be shackled with the spiraling and needless costs of welfare and police and fire protection, as well as with the costs of many other ameliorative government programs.

We must understand that every white American's current assets and opportunities have resulted, in part at least, from the withholding of opportunities from black Americans. Hence, no white American can claim immunity from the daily denial of the inherent birthright of black Americans. Unfortunately, the ultimate consequence, whether we like it or not, is that all white Americans are by cultural circumstances cast in the uncomfortable role of oppressor. Those who would be true friends must assist in providing compensatory programs for their black fellow Americans, for merely equal treatment programs will only perpetuate the status quo.

We must understand that power is never freely given, and that black people must move through their own solidarity to direct their destiny as other ethnic groups have done. Others can work in enabling ways, but black leadership must be the respected leadership in problem areas relating primarily to blacks.

We must understand that forbearance will be needed to overcome the agony, pain, and misunderstanding resulting from the changed relationships of power that must come if we are to achieve unity as a nation. On my job, and elsewhere, I know that I have sometimes caused white people pain—and have experienced pain myself—solely because of the dynamics involved in changed relationships. Black men and women are understandably resentful of patronizing attitudes and often are so mistrustful that they mistake genuine concern and good will for condescending largess. Adam Powell's type of full-fledged arrogance is needed by many black men at this stage as a compensatory defense for the hurts and misdeeds of the past and present. White America must understand this as black America moves to maturity.

Finally, we must understand that all yokes must be removed from the oppressed if the oppressor, too, is to become free. Segregation in all its forms must come to an end. Only when this is accomplished, only when white America rids itself of racial bias, only when black America achieves respect based on dignity and power will the crisis in American race relations come to an end.